College Grad Resumes to Land $75,000+ Jobs

By Wendy S. Enelow

College Grad Resumes to Land $75,000+ Jobs

WENDY S. ENELOW, CCM, MRW, JCTC, CPRW

IMPACT PUBLICATIONS
MANASSAS PARK, VA

College Grad Resumes to Land $75,000+ Jobs

ISBN: 1-57023-223-7

Library of Congress: 2004116429

Publisher: For information on Impact Publications, including current and forthcoming publications, authors, press kits, online bookstore, and submission requirements, visit our website: www.impactpublications.com

Sales/Distribution: All bookstore sales are handled through Impact's trade distributor: National Book Network, 15200 NBN Way, Blue Ridge Summit, PA 17214, Tel. 1-800-462-6420. All other sales and distribution inquiries should be directed to the publisher: Sales Department, IMPACT PUBLICATIONS, 9104 Manassas Drive, Suite N, Manassas Park, VA 20111-5211, Tel. 703-361-7300, Fax 703-335-9486, or email: info@impactpublications.com.

The Author: Wendy S. Enelow is a recognized leader in the executive job search, career coaching, and resume writing industries. For more than 20 years she has assisted thousands of job search candidates through successful career transitions. She is the founder and past president of the Career Masters Institute, an exclusive training and development association for career professionals worldwide. Author of nearly two dozen career books focusing on resumes, letters, interviews, and the career transition process, she has earned several distinguished professional credentials – Master Resume Writer (MRW), Credentialed Career Master (CCM), Job and Career Transition Coach (JCTC), and Certified Professional Resume Writer (CPRW). Wendy can be contacted at wendy@wendyenelow.com.

Contents

Introduction

Congratulations!

You've done it! I'm sure there were times over the past several years when you thought that you would never graduate, but finally the time has come (or almost come) and your journey is over. You can now look back with pride knowing that you've accomplished something for which you will be proud the rest of your life. Great job!

Unfortunately, now comes the hard part! With your degree in hand, it's time to start looking for a job, a career, an opportunity. It's what you've been preparing for virtually your whole life. Everything has been about getting yourself to the point where you are now, where you "take over." Your life is no longer your parents' responsibility or your school's responsibility. It's now yours – lock, stock, and barrel. What happens from here on out is largely up to you and the choices that you make. Decisions that you make about your career today can, and most likely will, impact the quality of your life for years and years to come.

One of the most critical steps in setting the stage for a successful career is the development of a powerful resume – a resume that positions you as a qualified candidate in your career of choice and gives you the competitive edge over other individuals vying for the same jobs. And, that's what this book is all about – how to write and design resumes that will get you noticed, not passed over.

We'll explore, in depth, resume writing strategies, tips, and techniques for all the different populations of graduating students:

- Traditional graduating students with four-year degrees (usually in their early 20s with some limited work experience)

- Graduate-level students earning master's or doctoral degrees (usually in their mid to late 20s with some solid professional, internship, research, and/or related experience)

- Graduating students already engaged in their careers (early 20s with lots of relevant work, internship, research, and/or volunteer experience)

- Non-traditional graduating students ("older" students who have returned to college to earn degrees to further their existing careers or propel themselves into new professions)

Most importantly, as you read this book, you'll quickly come to appreciate the fact that resume writing, just like the entire job search process, is all about sales. You have a product to sell – YOURSELF – and your challenge is to make the product (and its features and benefits) appealing to your buying audience – A PROSPECTIVE EMPLOYER. We'll talk a great deal about how best to merchandise your skills, qualifications, and experience, and how those merchandising strategies will vary based on your particular academic training, work experience, and objectives.

This book has it all - what type of resume to write, what format to use, how to word the content, and how to make your resume look great. Just follow the advice and guidelines to find the answers that are right for you and your career. Then, when you're finished, you will have created a powerful resume that will position you to win in today's competitive job search market.

Once again, congratulations on your graduation. Now, let's get down to work on your career!

CHAPTER 1

A Resume Is . . .

Introduction

To begin our discussion of resume writing, it's best to begin with a clear definition of what a resume is and what it is not.

A resume is a:

- **Sales and marketing document** written to sell you – the job seeker – into your next position or launch you into your next career.
- **Distinctive communication** that presents a clear and concise picture of who you are and the value you bring to an organization.
- **Dynamic document** that effectively communicates your professional skills, qualifications, knowledge, experience, and achievements.
- **Powerful tool** designed to sell the high points of your academic and/or professional career.
- **Visually attractive document** that communicates a sharp, professional image.

A resume is not a:

- **Biography of your entire life**, every job you've ever had, every course you've ever taken, and every activity you've ever participated in.
- **Dense document containing lengthy job descriptions** and long lists of duties and responsibilities.
- **Passive, low-energy, and narrative summary** of your life.

With that definition in mind, consider the one and only purpose of a resume – TO HELP YOU GET AN INTERVIEW. That's it. Your resume will NOT get you a job. Your only expectation should be that it will generate enough interest for a prospective employer to call and offer you the opportunity for an interview. Remember, **a resume is a sales and marketing document** designed to make you – the product – attractive to your buying audience.

Look at it this way. Suppose you're in a bookstore and a really attractive book cover catches your attention. What do you do? You pick up the book. Or maybe you're shopping in a department store one day and see a beautifully designed gift box that instantly makes you pick up the merchandise and look at the product more closely. These are merchandising strategies and techniques that, when done well, yield strong results (meaning that people will purchase the product).

Now, the same can be said about your resume. If you make the resume attractive, interesting, dynamic, and success-oriented, employers will want to know more about the product and, in turn, will call you for an interview. It's referred to as **career merchandising** or **talent merchandising** – the ability to write and design a resume that represents the job seeker as a well-qualified, competent, and success-bound candidate that would be a "wonderful buy" for a prospective purchaser (company).

To further explain, resume writing (in particular) and job search (in general) are all about communicating your success and achievements – what you have accomplished thus far in your career (either through your work experience or academic training) and how that indicates what you might accomplish in the future. Said another way, past performance is the best predictor of future performance, so be sure you include your past successes and track record of performance so prospective employers will appreciate what you've accomplished.

This concept – that past performance is the best predictor of future performance – is the foundation for the latest trend in job interviewing. Known as behavioral (or situational) interviewing, these techniques are now used by companies and recruiters to get a better understanding of what candidates have done in the past and how they would react to future situations. If you're not familiar with behavioral or situational interviewing, do an online search and spend a few minutes reading about these interviewing styles. Then, if you want more information, go to www.impactpublications.com to select an excellent book on interviewing. I can guarantee you will encounter both types of interviews, no matter your industry or profession!

Now, back to our discussion about using your resume to communicate your success and achievements. Today's difficult economic market has forced companies to look carefully at each new hire to evaluate whether or not that individual can bring value to their organization – value that can be measured in increased revenues, improved profits, cost savings, productivity improvements, efficiency gains, and more. No longer do companies hire "just to hire." Rather, they hire to fill a need and they demand measurable results. If an employee cannot add value – monetarily, intellectually, operationally, or organizationally – then there is no value in the company hiring or retaining that individual.

Therefore, your challenge is to write a resume that showcases your unique talents, skills, and qualifications, and how they will benefit the hiring company. It's the same challenge every job seeker faces, whether a recent college graduate, a highly skilled engineer, or a CEO. Your resume must, within the first few words, grab your reader and hold his attention by clearly articulating what you know, what you've done, and what you can do for that organization. If you are able to do that, you will have won the first half of the job search battle – you'll have gotten yourself in the door for an interview!

The 10 Critical Rules of Resume Writing

Resume writing is part art and part science, and perhaps that's what can make the process seem so difficult. In order to overcome some of the obstacles that many people face when writing their resumes, I've outlined the 10 critical rules of resume writing. These should provide you with some structure and order for what to do and how to do it. Read each rule carefully and then use them when writing your own resume.

Rule #1	There are no rules in resume writing!
Rule #2	Sell it to me; don't tell it to me!
Rule #3	Use the "big" and save the "little."
Rule #4	Write with the right words, language, and tone.
Rule #5	Write in the first person.
Rule #6	Use the "right" keywords.
Rule #7	Remain in the realm of reality.
Rule #8	One size does not fit all.
Rule #9	No need to tell your whole life story!
Rule #10	100% perfection is the standard.

Now, let's explore each of these rules in greater detail.

RULE #1: There are no rules in resume writing! One of the greatest challenges of resume writing is that there are no specific rules about what to write, how to write it, and how to visually present it. There are certain guidelines, of course – things like including your education credentials and your work experience. Beyond that, however, there are no formal rules or standards for how to write a resume, and this can make the process seem difficult and frustrating.

Don't be alarmed! As you read through this book and review all of the sample resumes, you'll be able to determine what type of resume is right for you, how to write it, how to format it, and how to prepare a powerful visual presentation that will showcase your skills, qualifications, and experience. I can't give any rules, but I can give you the direction, insight, and examples that you need in order to build your own winning resume.

RULE #2: Sell it to me, don't tell it to me! Earlier in this chapter, I discussed the concept that your resume is really a sales and marketing document. It is your calling card, your promotional copy, your personal advertisement. But it's not just enough to say that. Rather, your resume must be written in such a fashion that it does indeed sell, market, and promote your skills, qualifications, and experience.

The most effective way to achieve that is by using the "sell it to me, don't tell it to me" writing strategy. More simply put, you don't just want your resume to **tell** what you have done. Instead, you want your resume to **sell** what you have accomplished and the value you bring to a hiring organization.

So, how do you do that? The answer is simple ... you write powerful sentences which highlight your capabilities, skills, qualifications, and achievements. Here are a few examples of how effective this strategy can be:

Telling it: "Graduated from Clemson University in 2004."
Selling it: "Graduated from Clemson University in 2004 with a 3.98 grade point average and a commendation as one of the top five students in Clemson's graduating class."

Here's another example:

Telling it: "Worked as an intern in the Mayo Clinic's anatomical research laboratory."
Selling it: "Worked in cooperation with professional staff and Ph.D. students at the Mayo Clinic's anatomical research laboratory to plan and conduct a double-blind study investigating the effects of next-generation antibiotics on specific anatomical structures."

You can see for yourself what a significant difference in impact there is between each of the two sets of statements. Be sure that you "sell" yourself when writing your resume and don't simply "tell" the facts. Remember that each and every word in your resume should be written to communicate skill, knowledge, success, and achievement. If you can accomplish this, you will have created your own winning resume that is bound to open doors, generate interviews, and help you land a great professional opportunity.

RULE #3: Use the "big" and save the "little." When writing, constantly remind yourself that your resume should be written as a "teaser," with just enough information to entice someone to offer you an interview. If you don't hold back some information about yourself, there won't be anything left that's different, unique, and interesting to share during your job interviews.

To achieve this, the best strategy is the "big-to-little" technique where you share the "big" things in your resume to communicate the overall message of who you are and then save the "little" things (the specific projects, activities, achievements, etc.) for the interview. So, what does that mean? Here's a great example:

The "big" (for your resume) – "Honored as the 'Top Engineering Graduate of the Year'."

       The "little" (for your interview) – "I was selected as the 'Top Engineering Graduate of the Year' as a result of both my 3.95 GPA and my pioneering research into the design of alternative energy supplies for mobile hand-held radio systems."

Here's another example:

       The "big" – "Founded the first Hispanic sorority on the campus of the University of Maryland and built the organization to over 500 members."

       The "little" – "When I founded the first Hispanic sorority on the campus of the University of Maryland, I didn't realize what a huge task I had undertaken. Over the course of three years, I built the organization from the ground up with full responsibility for membership development, program design, fundraising, special events, and so much more. Today, we have more than 500 members and are one of the most active on-campus sororities."

You can see how effective this strategy can be in accomplishing two distinct benefits for you: First, it will help you craft a powerful resume and, second, your resume will become an effective tool for guiding the interview precisely where you want it to go so that you can share the highlights of your education and experience.

RULE #4: Write with the "right" words, language, and tone. The words that you select to include in your resume will set the tone and energy of the entire document. If you use words such as "responsible for" or "duties included," your resume becomes passive, repetitive, and not very exciting. But, when you use action verbs such as "designed," "developed," "facilitated," and "led," your resume comes to life and communicates energy, drive, enthusiasm, results, and success. Compare these two sentences:

       Without the "right" words: "Responsible for daily accounts payable and accounts receivable functions for the company."

       With the "right" words: "Planned, staffed, and directed daily accounts payable and accounts receivable for a $2 million company with 45 key accounts and hundreds of vendors nationwide."

You can easily see and feel the difference in tone. Sentence #1 simply states the facts of the job while sentence #2 much more effectively communicates the scope of the position and the magnitude of what that person was responsible for.

RULE #5: Write in the first person. Always write in the first person (dropping the "I's"); never, never in the third person. What does this mean? Here's an example:

       First person – "Orchestrated the start-up of the University's first on-campus food drive."

       Third person – "Sally Jones orchestrated the start-up of the University's first on-campus food drive."

Can you see the difference? The first example communicates "I did this." The second example communicates "Sally Jones, some other girl, did that," and it moves ownership away from you. Your resume must be a part of who you are and not a distant third-party voice.

RULE #6: Use the "right" keywords. It is essential that you use keywords specific to your professional goals and aspirations. If you're looking for a job in sales, write about your skills in customer service, public relations, communications, and product merchandising. If you're interested in an entry-level engineering position, write about your strong academic skills in mathematics, experiment design, fault analysis, and more. If your goal is a position in business management, talk about your experience and educational training in finance, organizational management, economics, marketing, and information technology.

Not only are keywords critical in communicating that you have the "right stuff" for the job, they are also the foundation for technology-based resume scanning. Right or wrong (we won't have a philosophical discussion here!), chances are that when you submit your resume, a computer will view it before human eyes ever see it. When the computer is scanning your resume, it's looking for specific words and phrases that the company has identified as key to the position (thus keywords). If those words are in your resume, you'll get passed along to the next step – hopefully a real person. If those words are not in your resume, that's it. The computer is not going to "read between the lines" and assume because you did one thing, you also have experience with the other thing. As such, using keywords specific to the job you are pursuing is critical in order to get you and your resume noticed.

RULE #7: Remain in the realm of reality. Nearly everyone you know pushes the envelope just a bit when writing their resume. Remember, it is a sales and marketing document. In fact, most employers will know that you've pushed your experience to the edge, so to speak, in order to make yourself appear as an extremely well-qualified candidate. And you know what? That's okay . . . okay as long as you remain in the realm of reality! Resume writing is a self-promoting activity and, as such, it's expected that you work hard to sell yourself. However, always remember that every single thing you write on your resume must be 100% accurate, truthful, and verifiable. Only push so far. If you go beyond reality, you will lose the opportunity.

RULE #8: One size does not fit all. Ever looked at someone else's resume and thought it was great? The wording was right on target and the visual presentation was really sharp. "Okay," you thought to yourself, "I'll just copy this resume when I write mine." Wouldn't that be so easy?

Unfortunately, resume writing is not that standardized, and it is often difficult to take one resume sample and simply put in your information and have it "work" for you. Resume writing is a much more customized process than that, where your goal is to highlight YOUR specific skills, qualifications, and achievements, which, in most instances, will be quite different from those of your friends and colleagues. You can certainly use resume samples (like the ones in this book and those of your friends, associates, mentors, and others), but you'll have to individualize the document to be sure that it's selling **you** and **your specific assets**.

RULE #9: No need to tell your whole life story! It is important to remember that resume writing is not the same as writing an autobiography. You want to look at everything about yourself – school, work, activities, internships, community service, honors and awards, memberships, athletics – anything at all. Then, critically evaluate each of those items to determine which are relevant to your current career goals and which are not. It's that simple ... only include what matters. (NOTE: Bear in mind that it is essential that you include your education and work experience whether related or not. All of the rest of the information is up to you.)

RULE #10: 100% perfection is the standard. Forbidden: typographical, spelling, punctuation, and grammatical errors. Your resume reflects of the quality of work that you will produce on a company's behalf, so be sure that it's perfect. Nothing less is acceptable!

Top 20 Resume Writing Mistakes to Avoid

In the preceding pages, I've outlined the 10 critical rules for resume writing that every job seeker should live by. Now, we're going to switch gears and focus on the top 20 resume writing mistakes that you must avoid.

All too often job seekers (graduating students as well as experienced professionals) submit resumes with serious writing errors, errors that I can almost guarantee will put you out of the running for a position. A prospective employer will think to himself, "If this is the quality of work that this individual produces, I certainly don't want them in my organization. I can't have the department sending out correspondence that is confusing and disorganized, and fraught with typographical, grammatical, and wording errors. My customers would be appalled!"

To be sure that this doesn't happen to you, avoid the following common errors:

1. Resume is unrelated to the position being filled.
2. Resume is too long or too short.
3. Resume is unattractive with a poorly designed format, small typestyle, and little white space, making it extremely difficult to read.
4. Resume is sloppy with handwritten corrections.
5. Resume has misspellings and poor grammar, is wordy and repetitive.
6. Resume has obvious punctuation errors.
7. Resume appearance is amateurish, gimmicky or too slick; in other words, it's over-produced.

8. Resume is too boastful, aggressive, and egocentric.

9. Resume repeatedly uses the word "I" and, therefore, the job seeker appears overly self-centered.

10. Resume includes information that seems suspicious and untruthful.

11. Resume lacks credibility and content and includes lots of fluff and canned resume language.

12. Resume is missing major categories such as Education or Experience.

13. Resume is difficult to interpret because of poor organization or lack of focus and, therefore, it is difficult to determine what the job seeker has done (or studied) and what he/she wants to do now.

14. Resume has no evidence of past accomplishments (work- or school-related) or a pattern of strong performance from which a prospective employer can predict future performance.

15. Resume uses jargon and abbreviations unknown to the reader.

16. Resume states a strange, unclear, or vague objective.

17. Resume includes distracting personal information that does not enhance the resume nor the individual's candidacy for the position.

18. Resume fails to include critical contact information (e.g., telephone number, email address, mailing address).

19. Resume does not clearly communicate, "This is the value I bring to your organization."

20. Resume looks and reads the same as everyone else's resume, giving you no edge over your competition.

Top 15 Resume Production and Distribution Mistakes to Avoid

Now that you've carefully reviewed your resume to be sure that you haven't committed any of the 20 critical resume writing mistakes, it's time to move on to the actual production and distribution of your resume. Again, this process is often fraught with very common errors that you can easily avoid if you pay close attention to detail. Here's what you should avoid:

1. Resume is poorly typed and poorly reproduced, making it difficult to read.

2. Resume is printed on odd-sized, poor-quality, or extremely thin or thick paper.

3. Resume is soiled with coffee stains, fingerprints, or ink marks.

4. Resume is sent to the wrong person or department.

5. Resume is mailed, faxed, or emailed to "To Whom It May Concern" or "Dear Sir." (Be smart ... call and get a name whenever possible!)

6. Resume is emailed, but the attachment (or pasted-in copy of the resume) is forgotten.

7. Resume is mailed in a tiny envelope that requires the resume to be unfolded and flattened several times.

8. Resume is mailed in an envelope that is double sealed with tape and virtually impossible to open.

9. Back of envelope includes a handwritten note stating that something is missing on the resume, that the phone number has changed, or some other important message.

10. Resume is accompanied by extraneous enclosures (e.g., recommendations, transcripts, samples of work) which were not requested.

11. Resume arrives without proper postage and the company has to pay!

12. Resume arrives too late for consideration.

13. Resume arrives without a cover letter.

14. Cover letter repeats exactly what's on the resume, does not command attention, and, therefore, does not entice the reader to action (calling you for an interview).

15. Cover letter is fraught with typographical, grammatical, wording, and/or punctuation errors.

Expert Resources

In order to give yourself a competitive job search advantage and be sure that you adhere to the 20 critical resume writing rules and avoid all of the production and distribution mistakes outlined above, it is often wise to consult a resume, career, or job search expert. These individuals can provide you with insights and expert guidance as you plan and manage your job search – today and in the many years to come. You have your choice of working with a professional resume writer, career coach, career counselor, outplacement consultant, recruiter, or others who deliver job search services and support to candidates just like yourself.

What's more, there are companies that will post your resume online, other companies that post position announcements online, and others that produce targeted email and print campaigns to send your resume to prospective employers that you select. There are reference checking companies, coaches who specialize in interview training, and publications galore on resume writing, job search, and career marketing.

The list of potential resources is virtually endless, from the resume writer down the street to the global outplacement consulting firm with offices on six out of seven continents. The emergence of all these firms has created a wealth of resources for job seekers, but it has also made the process much more difficult with so many choices. How do you determine exactly what help you need and from whom? And how do you find the right person?

That's easy! The 46 professionals who contributed their resumes to this book are all expert resume writers who work with job seekers worldwide to help them plan and manage successful search campaigns. What's more, each and every one of these writers, in addition to other career-related credentials they may have, has also attained one of the following five prestigious resume writing certifications:

MRW   **Master Resume Writer** (awarded by the Career Masters Institute – www.cminstitute.com)

CFRWC   **Certified Federal Resume Writer & Coach** (awarded by The Resume Place – www.resume-place.com)

CPRW   **Certified Professional Resume Writer** (awarded by the Professional Association of Resume Writers – www.parw.com)

NCRW   **Nationally Certified Resume Writer** (awarded by the National Resume Writers Association – www.nrwa.com)

CRW   **Certified Resume Writer** (awarded by the Professional Resume Writing & Research Association – www.prwra.com)

In addition, many of these experts also offer additional services such as career coaching, career counseling, Internet resume postings, direct mail campaigns, and more. You'll find complete contact information for each of the contributors in Appendix A. Feel free to contact them for information about their services, pricing, and specific experience. They can be a wonderful addition to your job search toolkit.

CHAPTER 2

The Structure and Strategy of Your Resume

Making the Best Choices

Before you can even begin to write your resume, you must decide the **resume style** and **presentation style** that are right for you. This chapter, which focuses on the structure and strategy of your resume, will help you make those decisions before you proceed to Chapter 3 – Writing Your Best Resume.

The **resume style** you select will be dictated by your educational qualifications, related experience (e.g., internships, co-op assignments, research projects, leadership activities), employment experience, and current career objectives. For many of you reading this book, your focus will be on your educational credentials and track record of academic performance. As a recent college graduate, chances are that your education is your #1 selling point to a prospective employer and the section that you want to be most dominant in your resume.

Beyond that, you will need to select a resume style that will allow you to highlight your educational credentials while also bringing attention to any other skills, qualifications, and experience that are noteworthy. You can select from one of the three basic resume styles:

- **Chronological**: heaviest focus on education and employment experience
- **Functional**: heaviest focus on education and specific skills and qualifications
- **Combination**: combined focus on education, skills, and employment experience

If you are the "traditional" graduating student (early 20s, recent degree, limited work experience), a chronological resume is definitely going to be the best selection for you. On the other hand, if you're a "non-traditional" graduating student (a bit older and using your degree to either further your existing career or propel yourself into another career track), then you'll want to carefully consider which of the three resume styles will work best in your particular situation. Further discussion on this topic will follow shortly.

The **presentation style** you select for your resume will be determined by the manner in which you are planning to use and distribute your resume. If you are going to be printing and mailing copies, you'll want to use a Printed Resume. If you plan to send your resumes via email, an Electronic Resume will be right for you. And if you want to combine the aesthetic qualities of the Printed Resume with the ease in transmission of the Electronic Resume, you may consider a Web Resume.

The following sections explore each type of resume style and presentation style. After reading these sections you should be able to quickly determine which style is right for you based on your current situation and career objectives.

The Three Types of Resume Styles

For as long as resumes have existed (particularly in their current state over the past 20 years), there has been an ongoing controversy about the use and effectiveness of a chronological resume versus a functional resume versus the more recent combination-style resume. To better understand the difference between each of them and to help you determine which is right for you, let's explore the pluses and minuses of all three.

THE CHRONOLOGICAL RESUME

Chronological resumes provide a step-by-step path through your career. Starting with your current or most recent position, chronological resumes are written backwards, allowing you to put the emphasis on your current and most recent experiences. When students use the chronological format, the education section is almost always included before the work experience section in order to draw particular attention to recent academic achievements and degrees. Chronological resumes are the resume style preferred by the vast majority of employers and recruiters. They are easy to read and understand, clearly communicating essential information about your education and work experience. Unless your particular situation is unusual, a chronological resume is generally your best career marketing tool. Wilson Gillespie's resume on the following page is an excellent example of a resume with a chronological format.

Wilson B. Gillespie

890 John Street • Rochester, New York 14623

E-mail: williebg@frontiernet.net

(585) 334-2297 (Home) / (716) 789-7012 (Cellular)

OBJECTIVE:

Entry-level opportunity that will lead to a career in Photojournalism and/or Documentary Photography. International travel both welcomed and desirable.

EDUCATION:

Bachelor of Science, Cinema & Photography   December 2004
(Concentration in Still Photography / Minor in Environmental Studies)
Rochester Institute of Technology, Rochester, New York
Dean's List / Eastman Filmmaking Award

Significant Courses:

- Photojournalism
- Advanced Studio Photography
- Contemporary Photography Issues
- Documentary Photography
- Digital Photography
- Color Photography

- Environmental History
- Environmental Anthropology
- Environmental Biology
- Advanced Sculpture
- Int'l. Film Aesthetics & Analysis
- Film Production

Semester at Sea - Institute for Shipboard Education   Spring 2000
University of Pennsylvania, Philadelphia, Pennsylvania
Circumnavigated the globe, visiting 10 countries as part of program encompassing classroom instruction in geography, religion, and other aspects of the local culture in each country. Destinations included Cuba, Brazil, South Africa, Kenya, India, Malaysia, Vietnam, China, and Japan. Traveled independently during 3-week period in People's Republic of China and was part of an exclusive group of American students allowed to visit Cuba.

WORK EXPERIENCE:

Photo Lab Technician, Inspirational Images, Rochester, New York   Feb. - Aug. 2003
Processed film and printed photos for consumers and commercial accounts.
- Developed color and black & white negatives, both 35mm and other formats.
- Scanned photos onto digital media (CD or disk); printed photos and prepared enlargements.

Sales Representative, Campus Custom Graphics, Philadelphia, Pennsylvania   Jan. - Feb. 2003
Visited college campuses in eastern US to market posters and other merchandise.
- Set up product displays in various campus venues.
- Managed inventory and maintained contact with headquarters office.
- Accounted for daily receipts and reported sales to corporate office.
- Produced above-average sales results for the markets serviced.

Delivery Driver, All Occasions Catering, Rochester, New York   Summer 2001
Made timely deliveries of perishable foods to various party and special-event locations.

SPECIAL SKILLS:

Mac / PC Literate; HTML, PhotoShop (5.0/5.5), PageMail, Color Film & Paper Scanners.
Certified SCUBA Diver.
Additional hands-on training and experience through Eastman Kodak Camera Club.

References & Portfolio Available Upon Request
Portfolio May Also Be Viewed At: **www.wilsongillespie.com**

THE FUNCTIONAL RESUME

Functional resumes focus on the skills and qualifications you offer to a prospective employer. It is this type of information that is brought to the forefront and highlighted (along with your educational credentials since you're a recent graduate), while your employment experience is only briefly mentioned at the end. Individuals who might consider a functional resume are students with a great deal of internship, co-op, or research experience that is directly related to their career objectives. The functional format will allow you to detail all the skills and competencies you have acquired through these experiences and position you as a qualified candidate and not "just" a graduating student.

Others who might consider this format are career changers, professionals returning to work after an extended absence, or individuals who have been in the job market for a lengthy period of time. Put succinctly, individuals choose this style when they want the emphasis of their resume to be on their professional qualifications and not their particular work history.

Functional resumes are much less frequently used. Many corporate human resource professionals and recruiters look at these resumes with less interest, believing that the candidate is hiding something or attempting to "change reality." Be extremely careful if you decide this is the right style for you (which it might very well be), and be sure to include your complete job history at the end of the resume. Allison Winland's resume on the following page is an excellent example of a resume with a functional format.

ALLISON M. WINLAND

5555 Madison Road, Unit 104-B   Cincinnati, Ohio 45208   (513) 555-1820   Awinland@mail.com

CUSTOMER SERVICE MANAGEMENT

Outgoing and conscientious professional seeks position in customer service management. Experience in ensuring customer satisfaction and handling complaints and problems, in addition to excellent organizational skills and organizational leadership focused on results. Just earned B.A. degree in Business Management.

Customer satisfaction	★ Ran own business that required customer interaction and resolution of any service problems encountered.
Leadership skills	★ Won the *Margaret Ryson Award for Best All-Around Member*.
	★ Awarded the *Outstanding Leadership Award* due to success in organizing, creating, and then improving the budgeting and administration process.
Training	★ Developed lesson plans and content for teen audience on a variety of subjects. Delivered 25% of the training sessions.
Budget development/ administration	★ Created, implemented, and improved strict budgeting process for non-profit organization.
Newsletter development	★ Wrote, solicited content, produced and distributed newsletter for organization on a monthly basis.
Sales skills	★ Received significant donations from business community for scholarship fund by soliciting local businesses and making targeted presentations.
Coaching skills	★ Improved teen program through coaching adult volunteers on performance and goal attainment.
Planning	★ Chosen to lead 3 project teams based on strength of planning timelines, motivating team members, and getting projects completed on time with high quality.
Data entry & computers	★ Performed data entry and checking. Proficient in Microsoft Word, Excel, PowerPoint, and several graphics programs.
Phone skills	★ Worked as receptionist and handled incoming calls for large office with many subcontractors. Completed administrative duties such as filing, faxing, and ordering credit reports.

EDUCATION

B.A. in Business, University of Cincinnati, Fall 2004
A.A. in Business Administration, University of Dayton, Spring 2000

EXPERIENCE

Cincinnati Junior Woman's Club: First Vice President
Party in a Package – Professional Party Planners: Co-Owner
Hyde Park United Methodist Church: Youth Director
IBW Mortgage Corporation: Mortgage Processor

THE COMBINATION-STYLE RESUME

The most recent trend in resume writing is to combine the structure of the chronological resume with the skills focus of the functional resume. By starting your resume with a Career Summary or Professional Skills Summary, you can begin with a heavy focus on your core skills and qualifications (functional approach) and then follow up with your educational credentials and work history (chronological approach). Many of the resumes in this book reflect this new Combination-Style Resume, which is well received by both recruiters and corporate human resource professionals.

Combination-style resumes give you the "best of both worlds" – an intense focus on your skills and qualifications combined with the strength of your academic experience and work history. These types of resumes are powerful marketing tools. Joseph Wellessey's resume on the following page is an excellent example of a resume with a combination-style format.

JOSEPH WELLESSEY

3901 Somerset Street ◆ Seattle, WA 98118 ◆ (206) 313-3253◆ eyeswell4509@yahoo.com

CAREER TARGET: OPTICIAN in a quality neighborhood clinic

Dean's List opticianry graduate with 2 years' industry experience, a strong work ethic, proven sales/customer service skills and an ability to calmly execute concurrent priorities. Earned top grades while working days in school dispensary and managing a neighborhood bistro at night. Service oriented: Take great pride in helping people see better. *Experienced in.*

- Insurance Billing
- Selling, Building & Fitting Glasses
- Problem Solving & Customer Care
- Servicing Special Needs Clients

- Selling Contact Lenses
- Inventory Ordering & Control
- Vendor Relations & Claims
- Retinal Imaging

- Client File Management
- Office Mate Practice Mgt. System
- Visual Field Testing
- Dispensary Operations & Lenses

EDUCATION & TRAINING

A.A.S., North Seattle Community College School Of Opticianry. GPA 3.79. Graduate June 2004
Coursework: Medical terminology; small business management; computer training; optical lab; contact lens technology; laboratory methods; dispensing; optical theory

Liscensure:
American Board of Opticians Certified (ABOC)
National Contact Lens Examiner (NCLE)
Washington State Boards. Sitting for State Board in December 2004

PROFESSIONAL EXPERIENCE

NEIGHBORHOOD VISION CLINIC, Seattle, WA   September 2003 - Present
Opticianry Intern ▪ 30 hours per week

Support Senior Optician/Owner in running 3-year-old neighborhood vision clinic. Assist doctor in processing patients through exams and testing. Provide front desk support: triage patients, schedule appointments, sell and fit glasses, handle all billing/insurance issues, and resolve problems as they arise. Sell, order and fit glasses, addressing patients' special needs and individual style preferences. Handle all dispensary issues. *Sample achievements include:*

- **Improved ability to fit glasses.** Trained by Optometrist to adjust and fit eyewear to optimize fit/patient satisfaction.
- **Learned to perform tests.** Aided Optometrist in glaucoma/retinal imaging/visual field testing workup screenings.
- **Built client load.** Provided outstanding sales and customer service, building referrals and goodwill that doubled patient load in 6 months (from 3-4 appointments per day to 6-8 appointments daily). Clinic is expanding staff.
- **Reorganized and cut inventory 25%.** Tracked turnover of style, eliminating slow-moving inventory. Got vendors to take back stock overages. Deepened inventory on items that sold quickly, improving ability to deliver items on time.
- **Eliminated lapsed insurance billings and aged accounts,** cleaning up 6-month backlog.
- **Improved marketing and reduced appointment no-shows.** Updated and optimized utilization of Office Mate computerized practice management system. Sent appointment reminders, contributing to doubling of patient load.

Other Experience:
N. SEATTLE COMMUNITY COLLEGE DISPENSARY ▪ Work 6 hours a week in the lab, cutting lenses ▪ 2002 – Present

FIVE SPOT ▪ BARTENDER/NIGHT MANAGER / SERVER ▪ Manage inventory, cash reconciling, and daily service operations for a 17-table, 15-seat bistro. Learned to handle all walks of the public and calmly multitask ▪ 2001- Present

POSITIVE ILLUSIONS, SALESPERSON ▪ Sold and fitted high-end eyewear ▪ Summer, 2003

The Three Types of Presentation Styles

No resume discussion is complete these days without a dual focus on both printed resumes and electronic resumes. Chances are you will be sending just as many resumes via email as you will on paper, if not more. Therefore, it is critical to understand the similarities and the differences in the visual presentation of the two. What's more, over the past several years, the Web Resume has appeared, a Web-based resume presentation that offers tremendous flexibility. You'll read about it further in this section.

THE TRADITIONAL PRINTED RESUME

The single most important thing to remember when you are preparing a printed resume is that you are writing a sales document. You have a product to sell – yourself – and it must be attractively packaged and presented. To compete against hundreds, if not thousands, of other qualified candidates, your resume must be sharp, distinctive, and dynamic in both its wording and its visual presentation.

Your resume should have an up-to-date style that is bold and attracts attention. This doesn't mean using an italic typeface, cute logos, or an outrageous paper color. Instead, be **conservatively distinctive**. Choose a sharp-looking typeface such as Bookman, Soutane, **Krone**, Garamond, or Fritz, or, if your font selection is limited, the more common Times Roman, CG Omega, or Arial typefaces. The samples in this book will further demonstrate how to create documents that are upscale while still remaining conservative and "to the point."

Paper color should be clean and conservative, preferably white, ivory, or light gray. You can even consider a bordered paper (e.g., light gray paper with small white border around the perimeter). It is only for "creative" professions (e.g., graphic arts, theater, media) where colored papers can be appropriate and are an important part of the packaging. In these situations, it is recommended that your resume be more design-like and stylish, thus demonstrating your own creative talents.

If possible, adhere to these formatting guidelines when preparing your printed resume:

- Do not expect readers to struggle through 10- to 15-line paragraphs. Substitute two or three shorter paragraphs, or use bullets to offset sentences and sections.
- Do not overdo bold, underlining, and italics. Excessive use defeats the purpose. If half of the type on the page is bold, nothing will stand out.
- Use nothing smaller than 10-point. If you want employers to read your resume, make sure they don't need a magnifying glass!
- Don't clutter your resume. Everything you have heard about "white space" is true. Let your document "breathe" so readers do not have to struggle through it.
- Use an excellent printer. Smudged, faint, heavy, or otherwise poor quality print will discourage red-eyed readers.

Refer to the next page for an excellent example of a printed resume for George Dukane.

GEORGE P. DUKANE

gpd24@yahoo.com
119 Old Stable Road   *   Alta Vista, VA 24592   *   Home Phone (434) 299-9802

SKILLS & EXPERIENCE:

- Basic skills in collecting blood, urine and feces from animals, and blood specimens from humans, in addition to performing red and white blood cell counts.
- Prepared specimens for laboratory analysis and testing. Prepared and stained slides for microscopic testing for specific disease pathogens.
- Observed veterinary surgical and autopsy procedures on both domestic and farm animals.
- Skilled in the use of laboratory equipment and instrumentation.

EDUCATION:

Zoology Major (2003 to Present)   SOUTHERN ILLINOIS UNIVERSITY – CARBONDALE
General Studies (2001 to 2003)   CENTRAL VIRGINIA COMMUNITY COLLEGE
High School Graduate (2001)   STATE OF VIRGINIA

RELATED VETERINARY EXPERIENCE:

Veterinary Assistant / Veterinary Phlebotomist – HO CLINIC, Ho, Ghana, West Africa
August 2001 to November 2001

Three-month international volunteer assignment in a Third World African nation. Lived in African compound and worked at local veterinary hospital that cared for both animals and people because of their relatively modern laboratory facilities. Acquired outstanding hands-on experience in phlebotomy, hematology, routine and emergency surgical procedures, field autopsies, and general animal health care.

Animal Care Assistant – PEAKS VIEW ANIMAL HOSPITAL, Alta Vista, VA
1999 to 2000

Worked weekends while in high school. Cared for domestic animals, cleaned kennel facilities, and provided routine hygiene. Coordinated animal drop-offs and pick-ups for the kennel.

OTHER EXPERIENCE:

Factory Worker – PARMALAT, INC., DuQuoin, IL
Spring Semester 2004

Fast-paced commercial bakery preparing products for shipment to Wal-Mart, Kmart, and other retail chains.

Commercial Nursery Laborer – JACOBON'S GREENHOUSE, Wasilla, AK
Summer 2003

Cared for, transported, and loaded trees, plants, and shrubs for one of the region's largest nurseries.

Catalog Sales Representative – J. CREW & COMPANY, Lynchburg, VA
September 2002 to December 2002

Received and processed incoming telephone orders from customers nationwide. Demonstrated excellent customer service, sales, order processing, and computer skills.

Cook & Server – THE REMINGTON GRILL, Lynchburg, VA
March 2002 to August 2002

Member of this restaurant's start-up crew managing its grand opening and then ongoing service operations.

THE ELECTRONIC RESUME

When discussing electronic resumes, take everything that is really important about preparing a visually pleasing printed resume and forget it! Electronic resumes are an entirely different creature with their own set of rules. They are "plain-Jane" resumes stripped to the bone to allow for ease in file transfer, email, and other technical applications. Professional resume writers, who work so hard to make each resume look distinctive and attractive, freak out, while engineers love how neat and clean these resumes are!

If possible, adhere to these formatting guidelines when preparing your electronic resume:

- Avoid bold print, underlining, italics, and other type enhancements. If you want to draw attention to a specific word, heading, or title, use CAPITALIZATION to make it stand out.

- Type all information starting on the left-hand side of the page. Do not center or justify any of the text, for it generally does not translate well electronically.

- Leave lots of white space just as you would with a printed resume. Ease in readability is a key factor in any type of communication.

- Length is not as critical a consideration with electronic resumes as it is with printed resumes. Therefore, instead of typing all your technical skills in a paragraph form, type them in a long list. Instead of putting your keywords in a double-column format, type them in a list. It is a much easier read for the human eye!

NOTE: Your electronic resume will automatically be presented in Courier typestyle. You have no control over this, for it is the automatic default.

See the next two pages for an electronic version of George Dukane's resume. Note that both this resume and George's printed resume on page 19 contain exactly the same words; only the presentation style is different.

GEORGE P. DUKANE

gpd24@yahoo.com
119 Old Stable Road
Alta Vista, VA 24503
434-299-9802

SKILLS & EXPERIENCE:

- Basic skills in collecting blood, urine and feces from animals, and blood specimens from humans, in addition to performing red and white blood cell counts.

- Prepared specimens for laboratory analysis and testing. Prepared and stained slides for microscopic testing for specific disease pathogens.

- Observed veterinary surgical and autopsy procedures on both domestic and farm animals.

- Skilled in the use of laboratory equipment and instrumentation.

EDUCATION:

Zoology Major (2003 to Present)
SOUTHERN ILLINOIS UNIVERSITY – CARBONDALE

General Studies (2001 to 2003)
CENTRAL VIRGINIA COMMUNITY COLLEGE

High School Graduate (2001)
STATE OF VIRGINIA

RELATED VETERINARY EXPERIENCE:

Veterinary Assistant / Veterinary Phlebotomist
HO CLINIC, Ho, Ghana, West Africa
August 2001 to November 2001

Three-month international volunteer assignment in a third-world African nation. Lived in African compound and worked at local veterinary hospital that cared for both animals and people because of their relatively modern laboratory facilities. Acquired outstanding hands-on experience in phlebotomy, hematology, routine and emergency surgical procedures, field autopsies and general animal health care.

Animal Care Assistant
PEAKS VIEW ANIMAL HOSPITAL, Alta Vista, VA
1999 to 2000

Worked weekends while in high school. Cared for domestic animals, cleaned kennel facilities, and provided routine hygiene. Coordinated animal drop-offs and pick-ups for the kennel.

OTHER EXPERIENCE:

Factory Worker - PARMALAT, INC., DuQuoin, IL
Spring Semester 2004

Fast-paced commercial bakery preparing products for shipment to Wal-Mart, Kmart and other retail chains.

Commercial Nursery Laborer - JACOBON'S GREENHOUSE, Wasilla, AK
Summer 2003

Cared for, transported and loaded trees, plants and shrubs for one of the region's largest nurseries.

Catalog Sales Representative - J. CREW & COMPANY, Lynchburg, VA
September 2002 to December 2002

Received and processed incoming telephone orders from customers nationwide. Demonstrated excellent customer service, sales, order processing and computer skills.

Cook & Server - THE REMINGTON GRILL, Lynchburg, VA
March 2002 to August 2002

Member of this restaurant's start-up crew managing its grand opening and then ongoing service operations.

THE EMERGING WEB RESUME

As one would expect, a new phenomenon is unfolding that allows you to merge the visual distinction of the printed resume with the ease of the electronic resume. The new Web resume is hosted on your own website where you can refer recruiters, colleagues, potential employers, and others. Rather than pasting your plain-looking electronic resume into an email message, include a link to your URL. With just one click, your printed resume instantly appears. It is easy and efficient, the visual presentation is sharp and classy, and resume writers around the world are breathing much easier!

With a Web resume, you also have the opportunity to include more information than you would with the traditional printed resume that you mail. You can have separate sections (separate Web pages) for internship and co-op experiences, research projects, volunteer contributions, leadership highlights, technology skills, and more. Everything is just a click away.

For those of you in technology industries, you can even go one step further and create a multimedia presentation of your Web-based resume. Never before have you been able to create a resume that actually demonstrates your technical expertise. Just think of the competitive advantage a Web resume can give your job search.

Unfortunately, in a printed book, it is not possible to visually represent the dynamic nature of a Web-based resume. To view samples, be sure to visit www.eresumes.com.

One final note about presentation style . . . it is quite likely that you will have at least two versions of your resume – printed and electronic. In today's employment market, chances are that you will have the need for both, allowing you to send your resume in the manner that is preferred by a particular company or recruiter. With that said, it is recommended that you prepare both versions simultaneously so you will have them available as necessary.

Web resumes are not yet the norm so you may not need one today. However, they are increasingly accepted and used, so don't be surprised if the opportunity for you to use a Web-based resume appears just around the corner.

CHAPTER 3

Writing Your Best Resume

Step-by-Step Process for Writing Your Best Resume

Writing your best resume would be an easy task if I could only give you a standard outline or template. All you would need to do is answer the questions, fill in the blanks, and your resume would be ready. Not much time, not much serious thought, and no tremendous effort. Life would be great!

Unfortunately, as you already know, that is not the case. Each resume must be custom-written to sell each candidate's individual talents, skills, qualifications, experience, educational credentials, professional achievements, technical proficiency, and more. Resumes are NOT standardized, they are NOT prescribed, and there is NO specific formula.

On the one hand, this gives you tremendous flexibility in what you choose to include and how you include it. In addition, this freedom allows you to be creative in the visual presentation of your resume, designing a document that is unique to you.

On the other hand, the fact that there are no rules for resume writing is what makes it such a difficult task. There is no single road map to follow, nor a one-size-fits-all strategy. Each resume is unique to each individual.

Further complicating the resume writing process is that fact that most people do not understand that a resume is a sales and marketing document. A resume is NOT a career biography and it is critical that you understand that distinction. Your resume must be written to SELL you into your next position; not to simply list what you have studied, where you have worked, what you did and when. Rather, your strategy must be to integrate your recent college degree and related academic experiences with your work history to create a resume that clearly states "This is who I am" and "This is the value I bring to your organization."

You must also realize that writing your resume is not a two- or three-hour task. Most likely, it will take days and days of thought, writing, editing, and hard work. Invest the time that is necessary to build a resume that really does sell you and what you've achieved – in school and at work. If you can do this, you will see a remarkable increase in the number of responses and interviews you'll get. The stronger your resume, the stronger your performance in the job market!

Now that we have established that resumes are individualized documents that can vary dramatically in their structure, format, tone, and presentation, it is also important to note that resumes do share certain common features: **Most will include Education and Experience sections.**

Beyond that, what you include will depend entirely on your own background and your current career objectives. Look at the following list of common sections often found on resumes and determine which are appropriate for you.

- Career Objective
- Professional Skills Summary
- Honors and Awards
- Athletic Achievement
- Personal Profile

- Technology Skills and Qualifications
- Internships and Co-Op Experiences
- Project Highlights
- Volunteer Experience
- Professional and Civic Affiliations

To help you better understand the structure and function of each resume section, a short but comprehensive discussion of each follows. Use the information below to help you determine (1) if you need to include a particular section in your resume, and (2) what style and format to use for that particular section.

OBJECTIVE

One of the greatest controversies in resume writing focuses on the use or omission of an Objective. Resume writers, recruiters, career coaches, and others discuss it all the time! To help you decide whether you need an Objective on your resume, ask yourself these three questions:

1. **Do you have a specific objective in mind?** A specific position? A specific industry? If so, you can include a focused Objective statement such as: "Seeking an entry-level position in the Pharmaceutical R&D industry" or "Customer Service Representative with a nationwide call-center operation." As you can see, each of these Objective statements clearly indicates the type of position the candidate is seeking along with his industry preference. *If you are this focused in your job search, do include an Objective.*

2. **Is your Objective constant?** Will your Objective stay the same for virtually all positions you apply for and all the resumes you submit? If so, include a focused Objective such as that outlined in #1 above. If not, do not include it. You do not want to have to edit your resume each and every time you send it, adjusting your Objective

to fit the position. It's a time-consuming process and stalls the flow of resumes out your door. *Only include an Objective on your resume if your career goals are focused and constant.*

3. **Is your Objective unclear?** Are you considering a number of opportunities? Are you pursuing a number of different positions? Are you interested in opportunities in many different industries? If your answer is yes, do not include an Objective statement, for it will be unfocused and vague. Consider an Objective such as: "Seeking a professional position where I can help a company achieve revenues and profits." Doesn't everyone want to help a company make money? These are useless words and add no value to your resume. They do not tell your reader "who" you are or "what" you are pursuing. *If you are unclear about your Objective, do not include it on your resume.*

Remember, every time you forward a resume you will also be sending a cover letter. If you do not include an Objective on your resume, be sure to state it clearly in each cover letter that you write. This allows you to customize your Objective to each specific situation and each company's needs.

If you choose to include an Objective, here are a few sample formats you can select from. Or look through the samples in this book for other formats and ideas.

PROFESSIONAL OBJECTIVE:

Challenging Sales and Marketing Position in the Pharmaceutical Industry.

CAREER OBJECTIVE:

Entry-level position in Network Design/Administration where I can apply my strong academic training and practical hands-on experience in systems design, development, and commercialization.

CAREER GOAL: MANAGEMENT TRAINEE - TRANSPORTATION & LOGISTICS

PROFESSIONAL SKILLS SUMMARY

Consider this. When you write an Objective, you are telling your reader what you want FROM them. When you start your resume with a Professional Skills Summary, you are telling your reader what you can do FOR them, what value you bring to their organization, what skills you have, and how well you have performed. In both, you are writing about the same kinds of things - same profession, same industry, same skills, same career goals. However, the Professional Skills Summary is a more upscale and harder-hitting strategy for catching your reader's attention and making an immediate connection. And isn't that the point of your resume? Your goal is to entice a prospective employer to (1) read your resume, (2) invite you for an interview, and (3) offer you a position.

To simplify this concept, compare these two examples:

Example #1:

PROFESSIONAL OBJECTIVE: Professional Position in Corporate Finance.

Example #2:

PROFESSIONAL SKILLS SUMMARY:

Recent college graduate with B.S. in Finance and two years' hand-on experience as a Financial Services Intern with American Express. Acquired excellent skills in:

- Financial Analysis and Reporting
- ROI, ROA, and ROE Analysis
- Financial Systems Software
- Software Installation and Support
- Contract Review
- Data Collection and Compilation
- Account Reconciliation
- Project Coordination

In both of these examples, is it clear that the individual is seeking a position in corporate finance? Yes! In essence, they both communicate the same overall message, just in dramatically different ways.

Now, ask yourself which is a stronger presentation and which better sells the candidate's qualifications. Obviously, the Professional Skills Summary is a more powerful presentation. It is more dynamic, more substantial, and clearly communicates the value and experience of the candidate.

Finally, ask yourself the following question: If you started your resume with a Professional Skills Summary as presented above, would you need an Objective that stated your goals? Probably not. The Career Profile paints a clear and concise picture of "who" you are. It is not necessary to include an Objective above the Career Profile which states, "I want a job as a such-and-such" when you have already indicated "who" you are.

In addition, there may be instances when you are not 100% focused on one specific Objective and want to be open to a number of different opportunities in different industries. This is precisely the reason why you would not include an Objective and why a Professional Skills Summary would work so well. The Summary allows you to present a number of different, but generally related, qualifications; in turn, you can position yourself for a number of different opportunities. Be advised, however, that a well-targeted cover letter is essential in this situation. Your letter must highlight your **specific** qualifications as they relate to that **specific** position.

One critical reminder for all recent college graduates: The skills, experiences, and competencies that you include in your Professional Skills Summary should be a combination of knowledge you have attained through your education and your work experience. It is perfectly acceptable to include a skill such as "public relations" even if your only experience with that was a class you took in college. Remember, you're only saying that these are skills that you have; you're not proclaiming to be an expert!

Although I have referred to this section as the Professional Skills Summary, there are a number of different headings that you can use. Select the one from the list below that you're most comfortable with and which best describes that content within that section.

- Skills Summary
- Professional Skills Profile
- Qualifications Summary
- Professional Achievements
- Value Offered
- Qualifications Profile

- Technology Qualifications
- Summary of Qualifications
- Career Highlights
- Career Achievements
- Experience Summary
- Career Summary

When writing this section of your resume, consider these two strategies used by professional resume writers worldwide. I guarantee they will make it easier for you to write and faster.

1. **Resume writing is a condensation process.** When you write your resume, you are, in essence, taking your career and consolidating it into one or two pages. Then, to write your Professional Skills Summary, take those one or two pages and condense them into one or two inches at the top of your resume. You will then have your Professional Skills Summary.

2. **The Professional Skills Summary is the LAST resume section you should write.** How can you write the Summary if you haven't written the text and determined what information you want to include in your Summary, how, and where? You can't! Write the rest of your resume and save the Summary for last. You will find that the words will come much more easily.

Here are three great examples of different styles and formats for your Professional Skills Summary:

Emphasis on a Skills-Based Format

BANKING MANAGEMENT

Dependable, outgoing, and conscientious professional with B.A. seeks entry-level position in bank management. Experience in ensuring customer satisfaction and handling complaints and problems. Excellent organization and planning skills. Previous bank teller experience in a busy branch.

Administration	☆ Chosen as lead teller for busy branch and assisted bank management with daily operations
	☆ Reorganized office filing system, updated accounts receivable, and processed collections
Customer satisfaction	☆ Worked as customer service representative in retail store taking custom orders and ensuring delivery on a tight timetable
Dependable	☆ Worked overtime and unscheduled hours to make sure all holiday orders were filled on time in busy retail store
Managing the public, resolving unpleasant situations	☆ As lead teller, resolved many customer complaints and issues
	☆ Coordinated many public fund raisers and committees
Organization, planning, and multi-tasking skills	☆ As President of an organization, ran a 33-board member group with multiple projects
Computer skills	☆ Proficient in Microsoft Word and bank teller systems

Emphasis on an Achievement-Based Format

LEGAL ASSISTANT

Energetic new graduate with substantial experience in property management. Core strengths in solving problems, negotiating conflicts, and motivating others toward goals.

ACHIEVEMENTS

- **Implemented professional property management practices**; generated 5-10 new leases per month and closed 2-3 new tenants per month.
- **Secured the lease on a client who had been targeted for several years** by building a proactive relationship and remaining in constant communication.
- **Saved $600 annually** in mailing costs by transitioning to e-based communications for rent notification.
- **Financed 100% of college expenses** through full- and part-time employment.

Emphasis on a Headline Format

INFORMATION TECHNOLOGY PROFESSIONAL
Technical Support * Equipment Sales/Purchasing * Customer Service
Troubleshooting * Programming * Database Administration

There are countless other formats that you can use for your Professional Skills Summary. See the samples in Chapters 4-9 of this book for ideas on how to write and design the most powerful Summary for your own resume.

EDUCATION

For most recent college graduates, the Education section is the foundation for their resumes and where the greatest emphasis will be put. It is what I refer to as the **key selling point** in the resume - the most important component around which everything else centers. If you are a traditional graduating student, you have devoted the past four or more years to your academic career and now it's time to market that career to prospective employers.

Most "typical" graduating student resumes begin with a Professional Skills Summary or Objective, which is then immediately followed by Education – in one of the following formats:

Emphasis on the College/University

HARVARD UNIVERSITY, Cambridge, MA
Bachelor of Business Administration, Marketing Concentration, May 2004
Summa Cum Laude Graduate – 3.95 GPA

Emphasis on Degree and Academic Performance

Bachelor of Music / Emphasis in Music Education, 2004
University of Southern California, Los Angeles, CA

- Dean's List, Cum Laude Graduate
- Treasurer, Delta Omicron Music Honor Fraternity
- Semester Abroad – Vienna Symphony – Vienna, Austria (Spring 2003)

Emphasis on Degree, Coursework, and Professional Certifications

Bachelor of Science in Behavioral Science and Health, 2004
University of Utah, Provo, UT

Highlights of Coursework:

- Human Anatomy and Physiology
- Microbiology and Biology
- Organic Chemistry
- Psychometric Drug Therapies
- Social Theory and Research
- Case Planning and Management
- Behavioral Intervention
- Abnormal Psychology

Professional Licensure and Certification:

- National Pharmacy Technician Board Certified
- State of Texas Pharmacy Technician License

Emphasis on "Complete" Academic Career:

Bachelor of Arts in Communications, Western Michigan University, 2004
Dual Minors in Writing and Journalism

Academic Honors and Awards:
— Magna Cum Laude Graduate
— Overall GPA – 3.5; Major GPA – 3.8
— Elks 2003 Scholarship Recipient

Notable Coursework:

— Interpersonal Communications
— Business Communications
— Intercultural Communications
— Video Production

— Public/Professional Writing
— Public Speaking
— Creative Writing
— Structure of English Language

Internship Experience:
— **Programming/Production Intern** – WTKD Channel 8 – Kalamazoo, MI (Spring 2004)
— **Production Intern** – Charter Communications – Kalamazoo, MI (Spring 2003)
— **Intern** – WKLD Radio 1200 – Lansing, MI (Spring 2002)

Total of 12 months experience in radio and television programming, production, scheduling, and directing. Experience in idea generation and script writing. On-air personality for local sporting events.

Note that there are certain situations where Education is not a graduating student's key selling point. This would include professionals who are currently employed and have returned to school to earn degrees and advance their careers. In this situation, it may be that your current work experience is your greatest selling point and your academic career supports that. If so, Education would follow Professional Employment on your resume.

Or perhaps you are a "typical" graduating student and academics are important, but your most significant selling point is your internship experience. In this situation, your resume might begin with a Professional Skills Summary, followed by Internship Experience and then Education.

You will have to determine, based on your particular background and qualifications, the proper positioning of information on your resume. In essence, you want to rank order the information on your resume, placing the most important information closer to the top and the least important information at the bottom.

INTERNSHIPS AND CO-OP EXPERIENCES

For many college graduates, internships and co-ops (whether paid or volunteer) have provided a wealth of skills, experiences, and qualifications that they can now proudly display on their resumes. If you do have substantial internship or co-op experience to highlight, you can either position it directly after the Professional Skills Summary on your resume or right after Education. In either position, it should be thoroughly explained and documented to substantiate what you've learned and, in turn, the value you now bring to the market. By focusing on these experiences you are clearly communicating to a prospective employer that you're not "just" a graduating student. Rather, you're a graduating student with real-world professional skills and experiences!

Here are two great formats you can use. The first is more traditional, yet extremely well presented; the second is more innovative and really draws attention to the value of the internship.

INTERNSHIP EXPERIENCE:
Engineering Technician   Summer 2004
Department of Defense, Engineering and Construction Division,
Fort Detrick, MD

Coordinated various civil and mechanical design projects. Developed technical, teamwork, and communication skills. Took initiative in assuming staff support functions to lighten workload. Earned a Certificate of Achievement from the Department of the Army for performance.

> **Civil Design Projects:** Independently drafted designs for an office room, a security gate installation, and wall sections added to improve security. Met with key internal customers and contacted outside vendors to define project requirements and specifications. Drafted designs with AutoCAD; made modifications to meet final approval of customers and Chief Engineer.

> **Mechanical Design Project:** Assisted mechanical engineering contractor with testing and modifying HVAC system to improve air flow for better climate control of computer lab.

> **Staff Support:** Took over task of organizing CAD files and database for division secretary. Reworked CAD drawings for division engineers to fill gap left by retiring draftsman.

PROFESSIONAL INTERNSHIP:

The Subject: Case Studies in Enterprise-Wide Systems

The "Company": Maryland Health

The Project: Team project to act as "Business Analysts" implementing SAP Enterprise Buyer Professional 3.0 (EBP)—a Web-based procurement solution to be used throughout all state hospitals.

Personally selected by academic supervisors to contribute to a 13-week team project to support Maryland Health's e-Procurement *Proof of Concept* pilot project. Working from a framework of existing issues, produced costing and process models encompassing proof-of-concept, business process reengineering recommendations, expected functionality, feasibility of technology for long-term expandability, and forecasted investment returns.

Using ARIS Toolset 5.0, mapped business processes and gathered data via a series of interviews with cost center general managers, supervisors, and key employees. As appointed Communications and Time Manager for the team, presented meeting minutes outlining issues delegated, discussed, and resolved.

- Volunteered to preside over performance measurement issues. Conducted research and produced recommendations that compared the value of implementing or not implementing EBP functionality.
- Added value by introducing idea to interview vendors for feedback on an EBP implementation. Project managers were delighted with positive responses from Johnson & Johnson and Pfizer.
- Presented formal e-procurement solution findings before audiences of 30-plus attendees on two separate occasions.
- Estimated and "sold" the benefits of a new e-procurement solution citing cost savings of 35%.

PROJECT HIGHLIGHTS

For many graduating students their key selling point is their project experience, projects usually completed in association with their college or university or as part of their internship program. Regardless of how or where this experience has been gained, it is a wonderful and substantial addition to any college graduate's resume. What's more, projects are easy to highlight on a resume and are best presented in the following format:

ACADEMIC PROJECT HIGHLIGHTS

Recent examples of academic projects, challenges, and team work that support career goals:

Music Technology

Solo project to produce a 24-track maximum, 5-minute recording. Secured services of popular local bands—Five Flavored and Fergus Recliner, to donate time to the project. Project challenges included band members with limited availability, excess noise on the night of recording due to a music festival, and a faulty analog-to-digital converter.

- Overcame external noise leakage and faulty equipment, by altering layout recording plan to four microphones, no drum effects, and two tracks for keyboard. Fine-tuned gates and expanders to eliminate ambient sound from the festival.
- Awarded a distinction for efforts. As evaluated by lecturer, "This is a very slick recording. Well done. The documentation is great, and the data sessions well organized. The project is of a high standard."

Media Arts—Sound Project

Independently recorded and mixed original music composition by local band, and augmented presentation with a re-mixed compilation of previous recordings presented as a sound biography. Achieved distinction result and top-of-the-class status for the subject.

Live Content

Produced 10 minutes of material focusing on MIDI in a live context using self-designed patches and networks, real-time digital signal processing, and sound reinforcement. One hour prior to performance, requested equipment had been incorrectly supplied, monitor connections were incompatible, and MIDI Controller Driver had been deleted. Quickly sourced correct monitors, installed back-up drivers on computer, and identified and resolved mixer issues affecting the PA system.

Or, if you'd like to summarize your project highlights in a more traditional format, consider the following which was included as a sub-heading in this graduate's Education section:

Related Projects:

Portfolio Management and Derivatives – Organized equity, options, and bond portfolios, calculated holding period returns and beta/standard deviations, computed required and initial rates of return, and evaluated/assessed equity and bond market indexes.

Comparative Financial Study – Researched, contrasted, and presented a literary review of Merrill Lynch and Lehman Brothers; compared principal activities, examined business models, analyzed differences in overseas activities, and evaluated size, market cap, profitability, and other performance measures.

ATHLETIC PERFORMANCE AND ACHIEVEMENT

Just as with internship and research experience, a record of athletic achievement is a great entry into a professional career. Companies like to hire people who are athletic, competitive, energetic, and more. A record of athletics - whether school-based or community-based – represents you well before potential employers. This information can be presented in a quick and easy format such as:

Competitive Athletic Career:

Certified Wrestling Trainer and Coach
2004 Minnesota State All-Around Wrestling Champion
Wrestling Judge, Minnesota State Level

Competed in state and nationwide competitions for more than 10 years; State Medalist 3 years; All-American 3 years; Scholar Athlete.

VOLUNTEER EXPERIENCE

Volunteering speaks so much of an individual's character and commitment, and is a wonderful addition to anyone's resume, whether a recent college graduate or a seasoned business executive. In fact, for some college graduates, your volunteer experience may be the most important selling point on your resume, particularly if that experience is directly related to your professional career goals and/or demonstrates outstanding leadership skills. Here's an example:

VOLUNTEER AND LEADERSHIP EXPERIENCE:

—CHAIRPERSON – PUBLIC RELATIONS COMMITTEE – STUDENT GOVERNMENT ASSOCIATION (2004)
Coordinated a volunteer staff of three responsible for public relations, media affairs, and other promotional programs in support of all SGA programs and events. Consulted with on-campus, local, and regional media representatives.

—CHAIRPERSON – SPECIAL EVENTS COMMITTEE – STUDENT GOVERNMENT ASSOCIATION (2003)
Planned, organized, and promoted the annual SGA fundraising event hosting more than 2,000 students, parents, and alumni. Event raised nearly $500,000 to support SGA development, programs, outreach, and educational initiatives.

—VOLUNTEER – HABITAT FOR HUMANITY, UNITED WAY, UCP OF MARYLAND (2000 TO PRESENT)
Active in a diversity of volunteer and community outreach programs since the age of 17. Contributed through field construction, door-to-door fundraising, event planning, and volunteer recruitment.

EMPLOYMENT EXPERIENCE - FOR TRADITIONAL GRADUATING STUDENTS

For many traditional graduating students, the employment section on a resume may be the least important. If you're one of these students, you've probably had several jobs – part-time and summer jobs – maybe in restaurants, retail stores, or construction. In fact, you probably acquired some good skills in these positions and you'll want to highlight them on your resume.

However, for most graduating students, employment is not their key selling point. Rather, the focus of most graduating student resumes will be on education, internship and co-op experiences, volunteer activities, research projects, athletic achievement, and more. The Employment Experience section will be brief and generally at the end of the resume.

Here are a few strategies and formats for listing your work experience:

EXPERIENCE HIGHLIGHTS:

RENEE LOUIS USA, INC. – New York, NY   Spring/Summer 2004
Sales Team Assistant

Part-time position while completing Fashion Degree at FIT. Provided marketing, customer service, and account management support for this international, high-fashion design house in NYC. Key retailers included Bergdorf Goodman, Neiman Marcus, and Jacobson's. Assisted with trunk shows and sample sales, coordinating licensee communications and training new account executives.

RANDOLPH SIMON – Albuquerque, NM   Summer 2003
Sales Associate
Exclusive retail sales establishment catering to high-end shoppers. Offered personalized shopping services, maintained own client book, designed merchandise displays, and coordinated in-store events.

THE GAP – Albuquerque, NM   Summers 2001 & 2002
Sales Associate
High-volume, fast-paced sales and customer service position.

WORK EXPERIENCE:

Graduate Assistant, Doctor of Veterinary Science Program
Department of Infectious Diseases
University of Texas, Austin, TX
January 2003 to May 2004

Office Assistant / Secretary
Phillips & Barberry Medical Clinic, Austin, TX (Summer 2003)
Walter M. Jones, M.D., Destin, TX (Summer 2002)
Lawrence Medical Clinic, Destin, TX (Summer 2001)

Resident Assistant
University of Texas, Austin, TX
August 2001 to May 2002

EMPLOYMENT HISTORY:

PENNINGTON GREEN * Ely, MN	**Manager**	Summer 2004
RED LOBSTER * Duluth, MN	**Waiter**	Summers 2001-2003
OUTBACK * Duluth, MN	**Server**	2000-2001

EMPLOYMENT EXPERIENCE - FOR "NON-TRADITIONAL" GRADUATING STUDENTS

If you fit into this category of graduating student, ignore what I wrote in the section above about employment and use this section as your guideline instead.

If you're NOT the typical 23-year-old college graduate, but rather a professional already engaged in your career - and earning your degree to advance your career - then your resume may look quite different than that of the traditional young graduate. In fact, chances are that the employment section of your resume may be the most important and where you can really sell your qualifications, achievements, and track record of performance.

When writing your Professional Experience, your challenge is to briefly, yet completely, describe your employment history with emphasis on four key items:

1. **The company.** Is it a manufacturer, distributor, worldwide technology leader, or multi-site service organization? What are the company's annual revenues? How many locations? How many employees? Give a brief summary of the company and its operations, customers, products, markets, or technologies as they relate to your current objectives and ONLY as they relate. If your current employer is a technology company and you are looking to remain in the technology industry, briefly highlight who the company is because it is relevant to your current career objectives. If, however, you currently work for a plastics manufacturer and your goal is a position with a technology manufacturer, do not mention what your current employer does. Rather, refer to them as a $29-million production operation. In essence, "leave" the industry behind if it is not related to your current objectives.

2. **The challenge.** Is this a start-up venture, turnaround, or high-growth company? Were you hired to lead a new initiative? Were the company's costs out of control? Were there organizational weaknesses? If there were any particular challenges associated with the company and/or your position, be sure to clearly state them. As an example, a great introduction under a job description for a sales representative would be, *"Recruited by Sales Director to launch the company's introduction into the San Diego consumer marketplace."*

3. **Your accountability.** Include your major areas of responsibility (e.g., functions, departments, organizations, personnel, budgets, revenue and profit objectives, facilities, operations). In just a few sentences you want to communicate the depth and range of your overall responsibilities.

4. **Your achievements.** Herein lies the heart and soul of your resume. Not only do you want to "tell" your reader what you were responsible for, you want to "sell" how well you performed and the value you delivered to each company. Did you reduce costs? Design new products? Implement new technologies? Better train staff? Improve efficiency and productivity? Reduce liability and risk exposure? Penetrate new markets? Streamline operations? Eliminate redundant operations? Negotiate big deals? Raise money? The list of potential achievements goes on and on.

To begin writing your position descriptions, start with a brief introductory paragraph highlighting information about the company, your challenges, and your overall responsibilities. Then follow with a bulleted listing of your achievements, contributions, and project highlights. In essence, you are telling your reader, *"This is what I did and this is how well I did it."* The concept is simple; the impact, significant.

Here's an example of a position description for a Logistics Manager:

Logistics Manager   1998 to Present
SIMMONS MANUFACTURING, Dayton, Ohio

Directed the planning, staffing, budgeting, and operations of a 6-site logistics, warehousing and distribution operation for $200-million automotive products manufacturer. Scope of responsibility was diverse and included purchasing, vendor management, materials handling, inventory control, distribution planning, and delivery operations. Led a team of 55 employees through six direct supervisors. Managed a $25-million annual operating budget and $5 million per year in capital improvements.

- Introduced continuous improvement and quality management programs throughout the organization and at all 12 operating locations. Results included a 35% increase in daily production yields, 22% reduction in waste, and 52% improvement in customer satisfaction/retention.
- Spearheaded cost reduction initiatives that reduced labor expense 18% and overtime 34%.
- Renegotiated vendor contracts and saved $4.5 million in first year.
- Sourced and implemented $2.2 million in IT improvements to improve workflow.

Prospective employers who read that description can sense the scope (range, size, and diversity) of the individual's experience as well as get a clear understanding of his specific accomplishments and successes.

Follow the same format all the way through your resume for each and every job description you write, becoming briefer and briefer as you get further back in time. Do not focus on the day-to-day responsibilities of your older positions, but, rather, emphasize your achievements, notable companies you worked for, new products and technologies you helped design or launch, your international experience, or any other distinguishing characteristics of your career.

TECHNOLOGY SKILLS AND QUALIFICATIONS

Fifteen years ago, Technology Qualifications were virtually never seen on a resume, except for people working directly in the technology industry as programmers, database administrators, and the like. Today, that has totally changed. Technology is a part of every professional's life and must be addressed on your resume. How you address it will depend largely on your current career goals - whether you're seeking a position in technology or not.

If your goal is a hands-on technology position, it is critical that you include a detailed listing of your technology skills, competencies, and qualifications. Here's a great example:

TECHNOLOGY SKILLS AND QUALIFICATIONS:

Applications:	Microsoft Office Suite; MS Project
Databases:	MS Access
Platforms:	Windows 2000/NT/95/98/ME/XP
Multimedia:	Media Player; Quick Time; Real Player
Networks:	Cisco VPN Altiga, Cisco Wireless Aironet; Net Store; TTIL 5.0
Email:	Lotus Notes; Eudora; Netscape Mail

If, on the other hand, you're not looking for a technology position, a brief mention of your technology skills is sufficient. Try something like:

> Proficient with Microsoft Office Suite (Word, Access, Excel, PowerPoint), Adobe Illustrator, QuarkExpress, and Dreamweaver. Internet research savvy.

You can include the above statement as part of your Professional Skills Summary or include it in a separate section titled "Technology Skills and Qualifications."

HONORS AND AWARDS

An excellent addition to any resume is a listing of honors, awards, and commendations, earned either through academic, athletic, or work-related achievements. This information can be included at the top of your resume in your Professional Skills Summary, noted under Education or Experience (where appropriate), or listed in a separate section such as:

HONORS AND AWARDS:
- 2004 Graduating Student of the Year – Philosophy Department – Andover College
- 2004 Presidential Award Nominee – Andover College
- 2004 Summa Cum Laude Graduate – Andover College
- 2003 Recipient, Kellogg Scholarship for Academic Achievement
- 2001 Winner – Vincent Beach Athletic Achievement Award (Soccer)

PROFESSIONAL AND CIVIC AFFILIATIONS

Membership in professional or community-based organizations demonstrates that you are a participant and a contributor. As such, it's great information to include on your resume. Again, as with many of the sections above, you can either include that information in your Professional Skills Summary (best strategy if the membership is notable) or include it in a separate section (best if you have several to mention). Consider this format:

PROFESSIONAL AND CIVIC AFFILIATIONS:

Member	American Management Association (Student Chapter)
Member	American Marketing Association (Student Chapter)
Member	Oak Ridge Volunteer Development Foundation
Volunteer	Youth For Action Committee – United Way

PERSONAL PROFILE

You may have already heard vastly differing comments on whether or not to include personal information your resume. Here are my recommendations:

- **DO NOT** include personal information such as birth date, marital status, health, number of children, and the like.
- **DO NOT** include the fact that you enjoy sports, camping, reading, and water polo. None of that is relevant to your job search, particularly early on when you are simply trying to get your foot in the door for an interview.
- **DO** include personal information if it is required by the employer.
- **DO** include personal information if important to clarify your citizenship or residency status.
- **DO** include personal information that is unique. I've worked with job seekers who were past Olympians, raced as competitive triathletes, trekked through obscure regions worldwide, and much more. This is great information to include on your resume because it's unique and employers will remember you. Use whatever you have to get in the door!

If including personal information is appropriate in your situation, consider the following format:

PERSONAL PROFILE:

    US Citizen since 1994 (native of Greece)
    Fluent in English, Greek, Italian, and Spanish
    Competitive Triathlete and Skier

CONSOLIDATING THE EXTRAS

A great strategy for consolidating all of the "extra" categories at the end of your resume (e.g., Affiliations, Publications, Public Speaking, Foreign Languages, Personal Information) is to integrate them into one consolidated section called Professional Profile. You will want to consider this if you have little bits of information to include in many different categories and/or you are having trouble comfortably fitting your resume onto one or two pages. Here's an example:

PROFESSIONAL PROFILE:

Awards:	Academic Achievement Award – Union College – 2004
	Public Speaking Award – Marketing Dept – Union College – 2003
	John Young Award – Boulder Crew Team – 2001, 2002
Memberships:	Society for Human Resource Management (SHRM)
	National Career Development Association (NCDA)
	Association of Career Professionals (ACP)
Languages:	Fluent in Spanish, French, and German.
PC Software:	Microsoft Word, Access, Excel, Lotus, PageMaker, WordPerfect

The Resume Writing Process

Everything in life has a process and resume writing is no different. If you use the following structured outline, you will find that the task of writing and producing your resume is efficient, faster, and much easier.

1. **Open a file in your computer** and select a typestyle that (1) you like and (2) is easy to read. Type your name, address, email, and phone numbers (home and cellular).

2. **Type in all the major headings** you will be using (e.g., Professional Skills Summary, Education, Internship Experience, Work Experience, Personal Profile).

3. **Fill in the basic information** for all of the sections that you are using except Work Experience and Summary. Don't worry about formatting, exact wording, or anything else. Just get the correct information into each of the sections.

4. **Carefully review all of the information in each section and edit** as necessary to improve the wording and flow, enhance the visual presentation and ensure that you have not omitted any information.

5. **Write your job descriptions - from past to present.** If you're a traditional graduating student, this will be quick and easy – a brief listing of your past jobs with "just the facts." If you're a more experienced graduate with lots of experience, then follow these directions: Start with the very first position you ever held and work forward. The older jobs are easy to write. They're short and to the point, and should include only highlights of your most significant responsibilities and achievements. Then, as you work forward, each position requires a bit more text and a bit more thought. Before you know it, you will be writing your current (or most recent) job description. It will take the longest to write, but once it is finished, your resume will be 90% complete.

6. **Write your Professional Skills Summary.** This is the trickiest part of resume writing and can be the most difficult. At this point, you may want to re-read the preceding section in this chapter on writing career summaries. Be sure to highlight your most notable skills, qualifications, and achievements as they relate to your current

objectives and create a section that prominently communicates, "This is who I am and this is the value I bring to your organization."

7. **Add bold, italics, underlining, and other type enhancements** to draw visual attention to notable information. This should include your name at the top of the resume, major headings, job titles, and significant achievements. You may also insert lines and/or boxes to offset key information. But be careful. Overuse of type enhancements will instantly devalue the visual presentation and cloud a prospective employer's initial reaction. If you highlight too much, the resume appears cluttered and nothing stands out, clearly defeating your purpose.

   HINT: Using bold print to highlight numbers (e.g., sales growth, profit improvement) and percentages (e.g., cost savings, productivity gains) is a great strategy. Someone picks up your resume and those numbers instantly pop out and grab their attention. You can use this same strategy to highlight other key information; just be careful not to overdo it.

8. **Carefully review the visual presentation.** How does it look? If your resume is two pages, does it break well between pages? Is it easy to read? Does it look professional? Even more important, does it convey the "right" message about who you are? At this point, you may need to adjust your spacing, change to a different typestyle, or make other minor adjustments to enhance the visual presentation.

9. **Proofread your resume a minimum of three times.** Then have one or two other people proofread it. It must be perfect for nothing less is acceptable. Remember, people are meeting a piece of paper, not you. It must project professionalism, peak performance, and perfection.

Getting Started

The hardest part of any project is getting started and writing your resume is no different. To help you overcome writer's block and other barriers impeding your progress, and to ensure that you get off to a strong start, look closely at the samples throughout this book to get ideas for resume format, design, wording, and presentation. Then, refer to Appendix B, where you'll find three great resources to help you develop and write the content of your resume:

- Action Verbs
- High-Impact Phrases
- Personality Descriptors

With all these great resources in hand, you have the tools that you need to write and design a powerful resume that is guaranteed to open doors, get interviews, and help you nail a great career opportunity!

CHAPTER 4

Best Resumes for "Traditional" College Graduates

Overview

Do you consider yourself a "traditional" college graduate? Here's how I define what's traditional:

- You have just earned your degree (or are about to).
- You have some work experience but it's largely unrelated to your current career objective.
- You may have completed a professional internship or volunteer experience.
- You may have been actively involved in collegiate and recreational sports.
- You are relatively young (most likely, in your early to mid 20s).

If you meet the above criteria, or any combination thereof, then this chapter is for you. In it, you'll find 25 examples of great resumes, all written for "traditional" college graduates. They're great because:

- The resume writing strategies competitively position these graduates to land well-paying, upwardly mobile career opportunities.
- The words and language communicate that each graduate is uniquely qualified for his/her chosen career track.
- The resume formats and designs are sharp and distinctive, and get these graduates noticed, not passed over.
- The graphics, when used, convey a message of professionalism and competitive distinction.

Look closely at how these resumes are written, formatted, and visually presented, and you'll understand why they were so successful for these graduates. Then, use them as samples around which you can build your own winning resume to help you land a great career opportunity.

Index of Resumes Featured in This Chapter

Strategy: Emphasis on professional work experience while earning bachelor's degree and strong GPA

Resume: Jennifer L. Beeman, page 56
Writer: Jan Melnik, MRW, CCM, CPRW
Objective: General business position within the financial services industry
Strategy: Equal emphasis on strength of education, including volunteerism and leadership activities, along with excellent summary of related internship experience

Resume: Christopher Cooke, page 57
Writer: Darlene Dassy, BBA, CRW
Objective: Entry-level management trainee position with a major bank or financial institution
Strategy: Outstanding format that emphasizes strength of education and clearly highlights volunteer, leadership, fundraising, speaking and other unique experiences and qualifications

Resume: Erin L. Donofrio, page 58
Writer: Dayna Feist, CPRW, JCTC, CEIP
Objective: Position in the health and fitness industry, either in rehabilitation or personal training
Strategy: Excellent professional summary demonstrating strengths in both rehab and personal training, along with strong education section and excellent work history (internship, volunteer and paid combined into one section for most impact)

Resume: Staci L. Hayward, page 59
Writer: Ellie Vargo, CPRW, CFRWC
Objective: Position in corporate human resources
Strategy: Equal blend of emphasis on skills, educational qualifications and related work experience

Resume: Abygael Alexander, pages 60-61
Writer: Jennifer Rushton, CRW
Objective: Position in the field of journalism
Strategy: Unique format clearly demonstrating writing/research, leadership and teamwork skills, along with an excellent summary that really "beefs up" work experience section

Resume: Jeremy Davidson, page 62
Writer: Louise Garver, MA, CPRW, JCTC, CMP, CEIP, MCDP
Objective: Position in the marine business with emphasis on investment/financial analysis and market research

Strategy: "Traditional" young professional resume with equal emphasis on skills summary, education and experience (paid and internship)

Resume: Chris Rodriguez, page 63
Writer: Louise Kursmark, MRW, CPRW, CEIP, JCTC, CCM
Objective: Professional position in marketing, advertising, PR or promotions
Strategy: High-impact visual presentation demonstrates creativity and ability to capture a reader's attention; supported with excellent highlights of education, experience and the specific value offered to the employer

Resume: Carole A. Mehrman, page 64
Writer: Ellie Vargo, CPRW, CFRWC
Objective: Career opportunity in marketing and merchandising
Strategy: Clean, concise and easy-to-read presentation of skills along with highlights of academic career, professional experience and wonderful volunteer contributions

Resume: Edward V. Holt, page 65
Writer: Dayna Feist, CPRW, JCTC, CEIP
Objective: Entry-level professional opportunity in the highly competitive fields of public relations and advertising
Strategy: Keyword-rich resume with stylish presentation, good portrayal of skills and strong education section

Resume: Jessica Devlin, page 66
Writer: Susan Guarneri, CPRW, NCCC, LPC, CCMC, CEIP, MS, CCM
Objective: Opportunity for career position in the field of mental health
Strategy: Entire first half of resume is devoted to mental health education, skills, courses and experiences to immediately catch the reader's attention and clearly demonstrate candidate's qualifications

Resume: Sean T. Dillon, page 67
Writer: Igor Shpudejko, MBA, CPRW, JCTC
Objective: Field sales position in the pharmaceutical industry
Strategy: Focus on four key qualifiers - strong science background, sales-related skills, excellent work ethic and personal poise/confidence (from modeling)

Resume: Eden Morland, page 68
Writer: Louise Garver, MA, CPRW, JCTC, CMP, CEIP, MCDP
Objective: Position as a Physician's Assistant
Strategy: Excellent presentation of skills and hands-on experience that is sharp, succinct and easy to read

Resume: Francine Bley, page 69
Writer: Lorie Lebert, CPRW, IJCTC, CCMC

Objective: Position in public health or social/human services
Strategy: Excellent example of typical graduating student format with strong visual presentation and just the right amount of information

Resume: Jason B. Daniels, page 70
Writer: Marilyn McAdams, CPRW
Objective: Entry-level assignment in the public relations industry
Strategy: Emphasis on related coursework and internship, and use of writing, sports and music background to demonstrate well-rounded talents

Resume: Diane Starr, page 71
Writer: MeLisa Rogers, CPRW, MSHRD
Objective: Career opportunity utilizing sociology/psychology training and experience
Strategy: Communicate strength of volunteer contributions, excellent skills developed while financing her college education, and a message of energy and enthusiasm

Resume: Mark Foster, page 72
Writer: Christy Donner, ACCC, CPRW
Objective: Any one of a number of professional positions in the information technology industry
Strategy: Equal emphasis on academic achievements and practical internship experience

Resume: Paul Stevens, page 73
Writer: Louise Fletcher, CPRW
Objective: Position in the competitive world of video-game programming
Strategy: Highlight successful game development experience (both paid and unpaid) to distinguish from other candidates, and surround with academic achievements and strong technical competencies

Resume: Carter Rand, pages 74-75
Writer: Myriam-Rose Kohn, CPRW, CEIP, JCTC, CCM, CCMC
Objective: Position as a TV/Video Editor
Strategy: Leverage industry reputation of mentors and real-world professional experience to position as a more-than-qualified graduating student

MELISSA H. GILBERT

1538 Amyjudge Avenue   978-282-5555
Gloucester, Massachusetts 01930   mhg@hotmail.com

SKILLS SUMMARY

Customer Service • Data Entry • Purchasing • Research • Statistical Analysis

► Productive team member; equally effective leading or collaborating. Self-motivated to work unsupervised. Work well with people from diverse backgrounds and cultures and all professional levels. Strong communication, interpersonal, and presentation skills.

► Detail-oriented, committed to quality, diligent, enthusiastic, and flexible to changing priorities. Dependable follow-through. Plan and prioritize work; analyze and research information. Prepare required documentation and report data in an accurate manner.

► Exemplary organizational/troubleshooting skills. Methodically evaluate a situation and identify problems; participate in process to resolve problems. Thrive on challenges; demonstrate out-of-box thinking. Maintain composure under pressure. Learn new skills rapidly.

► Proficient computer skills on Windows platform include: MS Word, PowerPoint, Publisher; ClarisWorks; proprietary database programs; ArcView (GIS technology); email communication and Internet research. Foreign language knowledge: French, Spanish.

EDUCATION

B.A., 2004, Lowell State College – Lowell, Massachusetts
Major: Geography–Global Studies, GPA 3.94   *Minor:* Economics, GPA 3.94   *Overall:* GPA 3.78
Coursework included:
- ✓ Economic, Cultural, and Political Geography
- ✓ Geographical Perspectives on Environment
- ✓ Geographical Research Methods
- ✓ World Regional Geography
- ✓ Intro to GIS
- ✓ Statistics I, II
- ✓ Micro and Macro Economics
- ✓ Quantitative Economics
- ✓ Environmental Law and Policy
- ✓ Resource Management

EMPLOYMENT

Carried full-time courseload while working part-time to fund studies.

Gloucester Public Library – Gloucester, Massachusetts   2000 – Present
LIBRARY TECHNICIAN

- Competently work unsupervised in Children's Room in public library with annual circulation of 100,000+. Library is part of automated Minuteman System, a consortium of 32 member libraries. Assist patrons with reference questions, data entry to locate information, and Internet research.

- Learned new database system, rolled out system-wide, to enhance inventory tracking, speed requests from other member libraries, and manage membership information. Discovered "shortcuts" to access information and trained co-workers to boost productivity and save time.

- Performed tasks of Children's Librarian during her extended medical leave in summer 2000. Created daily task list for coworkers, presented 2 weekly children's programs, led 3 monthly book club meetings, and resolved customer inquiries.

- Present orientation tours of children's library to new hires and volunteers. Assign project tasks (e.g., planning and creating displays, researching topics, shelving books) to 2–10 junior volunteers and supervise their work.

- Edit and proofread flyers and schedules publicizing children's programs as well as press releases. Create program sign-up sheets and organize in notebook for ready access and retrieval. Write "question of the week" to entice children to improve their library research skills.

- Select titles and place online orders for DVDs and videos to add to Children's Room collection. Base selections on patron requests, reviews of material in catalogs and online, appropriateness of content for ages infant–12, knowledge of supply and demand of current inventory, goals for collection development, and cost of materials. Consistently remain within budget allocation.

ANDREW J. SYKES

7323 East 3rd Avenue
Albany, New York 12204
(518) 555-1372
sykes7323@yahoo.com

BUSINESS MANAGEMENT
Hospitality / Retail / Food Services

Professional Profile

Profit-oriented business graduate with hands-on experience that demonstrates accountability, initiative, and superior interpersonal skills. Team member with a commitment to supporting and promoting company goals and standards. Strengths include attention to detail, skilled leadership, and proven productivity.

Core Skills

Profit / Loss Oversight ... Customer Satisfaction ... Time Management ... Staff Training / Supervision ... Marketing ... Community Outreach ... Operation Start-up ... Quality Control ... Business Administration

Summary
- Worked closely with staff, providing training, motivation, support, and supervision for up to 50 employees to improve morale and increase retention.
- Oversaw the full range of business operations, including scheduling personnel to maximize coverage, supervising purchasing to take advantage of discounts, and managing financial activities, resulting in close adherence to budgets.
- Provided excellent customer service and demonstrated the ability to put people at ease, address their needs, and resolve their problems in a polite, professional, and prompt manner.
- Assisted in a variety of marketing projects designed to increase sales, promote awareness of services, and introduce products and programs.
- Utilized computer skills in Microsoft Word, Access, and Excel to enhance efficiency and accuracy.

Education

State University of New York at Albany, New York
Bachelor of Science Degree – Business Studies   2004

Curriculum included:

Business Accounting	*Business Communications*	*Managerial Accounting*
Principles of Marketing	*Principles of Microeconomics*	*Principles of Macroeconomics*
Business Law	*Business Strategies*	*Human Resource Management*
Corporate Finance	*Principles of Management*	*Statistics for Economics*

Nassau Community College, Garden City, New York
Associate in Arts Degree – Liberal Arts   2000

Professional development training:
   Media Play Bestseller Program
   Holiday Inn University
   Red Lobster Management Training

Continued...

Experience

<u>Media Play</u> Albany, New York   2002-2004
Assistant Manager / Intern
Developed marketing activities and coordinated bookseller events. Assisted in hiring, training, scheduling, and supervision of part-time staff. Developed advertising and community outreach programs. Assisted in the installation of new software system. Supervised opening and closing procedures. Reconciled daily cash receipts and generated sales and productivity reports.
  ➢ *Created TV spots and print ads to increase customer base and sales volume.*
  ➢ *Supervised 10 associates and ensured smooth and profitable operations.*

<u>Holiday Inn</u> Albany, New York   2000-2002
Acting Banquet Manager
Oversaw all banquet financial and operational activities for $2.5 million property. Developed monthly and yearly forecasts and created annual profit / loss statements. Created print advertising for hotel and restaurant. Dealt with customer questions. Trained and supervised up to 30-member staff.
  ➢ *Recovered failing Banquet Department. Decreased costs and increased sales within the first six months.*
  ➢ *Increased bookings by 25% by promoting consumer-incentive programs and special occasion packages.*
  ➢ *Implemented waste log to identify and reduce waste and loss, improve bottom line, and ensure appropriate inventory levels.*

<u>Red Lobster Division, General Mills</u> Garden City, New York   1998-2000
Assistant Manager

References

Credentials and Portfolio furnished upon request.

Tomas Perez

333 South Temple Goliad, Texas 77963   361-645-5291   tperez@msn.com

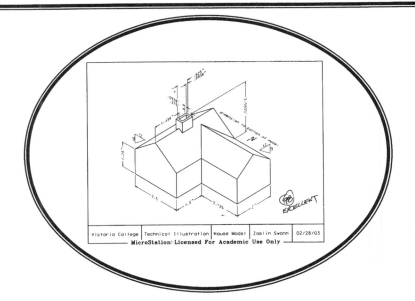

Victoria College | Technical Illustration | House Model | Zaelin Swonn | 02/28/03
MicroStation: Licensed For Academic Use Only

Sidebar

NEW GRADUATE

Drafting Technology

ASSOCIATE
of
APPLIED SCIENCE

May 2004

Coastal Bend College
Beeville, Texas

Financed 100% of education through scholarships and part-time employment.

Scholarships:
- Beeville College Community Partnership
- Beeville College Endowment Fund

SELECTED COURSEWORK

- Microcomputer Applications
- Basic Computer-Aided Drafting
- Advanced Machine Design
- Architectural Drafting
- Electrical Drafting
- Mechanical Drafting
- Machine Drafting
- Concrete Drafting
- Pipe Drafting

Drafting / Technology Background:

Technical Illustration

Isometrics / Obliques / Exploded Isometrics

CAD – Micro station V-8

One-Four Point Perspectives

Microsoft Office: Excel, Word, PowerPoint

Main content

ENTRY LEVEL DRAFTSMAN

ready to bring a high level of commitment and dedication to a reputable architectural firm. A creative, imaginative and independent work ethic will contribute to the achievement of the goals and objectives of the organization. Recognized in illustrating minute detail in difficult assignments and the creation of new designs.

PROVEN ABILITIES

- Drawing, reading and interpreting architectural drawings
- Performing independent and complex design analysis
- Identifying the names of drawing types
- Producing detail sheets and assembly drawings
- Generating electrical and mechanical drawings
- Reading and understanding schematics / drawings
- Calculate loads for equilibrium
- Writing Excel formulas

ACHIEVEMENTS

- ***Graduated cum laude*** – Ranked in the top 15% of class of 1,000 students.
- ***Received recognition*** in Calculus BC - Advanced Placement Test.
- ***Completed and received credit for 3 college-level courses*** while attending high school: Calculus I, Calculus II, College Algebra.
- ***Achieved an excellent rating*** for the most difficult assignment in Technical Illustration.

EMPLOYMENT EXPERIENCE
(While Attending School)

Pizza Hut – Beeville, Texas   **Delivery Person**   June 2003–July 2004
Order Taker at Counter; Delivered 5 – 10 orders per day; customer service.

YMCA – Beeville, Texas   **After - School Counselor**   Aug 2002–May 2003
Mentored students in homework assignments; conducted games and activities; prepared and served snacks and lunches.

Summer 2002 - Summer 2000
Multiple entry-level positions as a fast-food cashier and YMCA gym monitor.

Katherine A. Willemsen

Editing ~ Writing ~ Copyediting ~ Copywriting
Proofreading ~ Research ~ Word Processing

Well-read English major looking for an entry-level position using top-notch grammar, syntax, and editing skills. Thorough, meticulous, and organized, with ability to maintain good working relationships or work autonomously as needed. Strong aptitude for learning new concepts and applications.

Technical Skills

Computer Skills: PC / Macintosh Systems; Microsoft Office (Word, Excel, Access); WordPerfect. Quick learner with unfamiliar computer programs.

Reference Skills: Oxford English Dictionary; MLA Handbook for Writers of Research Papers; MLA Bibliography, Expanded Academic; and Internet research including AddAll, Book Search & Price Comparison, and Amazon.

Work Experience

ROD LIBRARY, NORTHWEST MISSOURI STATE UNIVERSITY, Maryville, MO
2002–2004

Student Assistant– Worked as part of a three-person team in Collection Management and Special Services department. Fielded telephone inquiries, answered patrons' questions, and managed other clerical duties. Provided maintenance for computers and typewriters.

- Learned duties of two positions (Special Collections and Art and Music) simultaneously during summer months.
- Trained, supervised, and mentored new employee to absorb duties of two positions and assume future training duties.
- Sorted, summarized, edited, and coordinated archival newspapers as part of three-year project. Entered information into database using key words.
- Oversaw entire Art and Music department as an unsupervised specialist. Organized, collected, and reshelved books, compact discs, and LPs. Researched information including music scores and reference materials.
- Designed artistic window display for Art and Music department. Received numerous compliments for creativity of entertaining "Elvis" theme.

ACTION RECRUITERS, MARYVILLE, MO
2000–2003

Executive Assistant– Managed office duties for information technology (IT) recruiting firm. Worked alone without supervision and entered up to 10 incoming resumes into computer on a daily basis. Selected key words from resumes to organize and retrieve from database quickly and accurately.

---

828 Wildriver Drive
Maryville, MO 64468
(319) 555-7911
katewill@hotmail.com

Education

Bachelor of Arts
English

Northwest Missouri
State University
Maryville, MO

May 2004

Relevant Coursework:

Theory and Practice of Writing

Critical Writing about Literature

Structure of English

Personal Essay

Film Theory and Criticism

Financed 100% of education while attending class full time.

KATRINA D. BAIRD

6803 CEDAR LANE ◆ ISLAND POND, VT 05846
(802) 854-7858 (H) ◆ kbaird@earthlink.net

PROFESSIONAL PROFILE

BOOK EDITOR with keen desire to maintain journalistic integrity while allowing the readership to have a context to evaluate literary choices. Versatile, energetic individual with a strong educational background in creative writing and literary criticism. Compulsive reader with a desire to maintain reading as a part of daily life. Highly driven, with the ability to meet deadlines and prioritize tasks. Precise writer, with a clear understanding that brevity is critical in journalistic writing. Computer savvy, with proficiencies in Microsoft Office in PC and MAC environments.

EDUCATION

BENNINGTON COLLEGE, Bennington, VT
BACHELOR OF ARTS – CREATIVE WRITING, December 2004
GPA: 3.86   MINOR: ENVIRONMENTAL STUDIES

HONORS

- Dean's List – nine semesters
- Awarded Most Poetic Poem – Poetry Contest, Bennington College
- Eckerd Special Talent Scholarship for Poetry, six consecutive semesters
- Newberry Award for Creativity – Poetry
- Who's Who in American Junior Colleges
- Departmental Distinction for English
- Crabtree Award for Biological Sciences, two years
- Honors Society

PROFESSIONAL EXPERIENCE

HANK'S ELECTRONICS, Bennington, VT   1995 – July 2004
Largest amusement distributor in Vermont with annual gross revenue of $1.2 million with 257 vending accounts.
GENERAL MANAGER (2001-2004)
ROUTE MANAGER / TECHNICIAN (1995 – 2001)
- **As General Manager,** prepared family business for sale, including completing inventory for five warehouses, public relations, and conflict resolution.
- Supervised ten employees, including five route service technicians.
- Assured that customer service remained priority by responding quickly to service calls and resolving conflicts with customers in an amiable manner.
- Reviewed and efficiently organized backlogged paperwork.
- **As Route Manager,** coordinated calendar scheduling, route collection, accounting, minor electronic repairs, as well as conflict resolution.
- Instituted CD filing system for inventory rotating stock of 5,000 CDs.

52

PROFESSIONAL EXPERIENCE *continued*

FUND PUBLIC INTEREST RESEARCH, Tampa, FL   May – September 2001
INTERNSHIP – FUNDRAISING SPECIALIST

- ◆ Directed Blue Ribbon Campaign, assuring that staff members understood goals and objectives of the program as well as being educated with an understanding of the facets of each individual campaign.
- ◆ Directly canvassed through door-to-door methods for various environmentally focused groups.

ADDITIONAL WORK EXPERIENCE

T&E VENTURES, Gilman, VT   August 2002 – April 2004
BARTENDER

ACTIVITIES

- ◆ President / Vice President, 10% Society
- ◆ Volunteer, Tampa Bay Watch
- ◆ Volunteer, Equality Vermont
- ◆ Volunteer, Human Rights Campaign
- ◆ Student Senator & SGA Multicultural Delegate
- ◆ Ambassador, Bennington College
- ◆ Treasurer, Biology Club

SALLY WALDON

3333 Broadway   **New York, NY 10027**   **(212) 777-1111**   **sw8@columbia.edu**

SUMMARY
Recent **Columbia University graduate** with diverse experience in market research, sales, software testing, customer service, text editing and layout design. Proven ability to compile and analyze data and make recommendations that positively impact business initiatives. Detail-oriented, team player with practical experience as a leader and organizer.

EDUCATION
B.S., Industrial Engineering Operations Research, Columbia University, New York, NY, **2004**
Relevant Coursework included Design and Management of Production and Service Systems, Industrial Information and Planning Systems, Computers in Engineering and Applied Science, Accounting and Finance, Production Inventory Planning and Control
Summer Study Abroad, Reid Hall, Columbia University, Paris, France, **2002**

EXPERIENCE
Testing 123, New York, NY   **9/03-Present**
*Selected for **New Markets Intern** position for this leading provider of standardized test-preparation tools. Researched and marketed the firm's CPA exam product.*
- Conducted market research on CPA requirements in all 50 states via cold calling, internet searches, and relationship building with professional associations.
- Edited current versions of four of firm's CPA Exam Review Books. Made recommendations that enhanced readability, design format, and layout.
- Partnered with marketing team on an advertising initiative to promote online CPA exam review course. Edited content of product marketing brochure distributed to colleges and universities.

LLL Consulting, New York, NY   **7/03-8/03**
*Recruited as an **Information Technology and Consulting Intern** for this London-based provider of human resource products and services. Managed quality assurance and data assimilation for the Peoplesource HR software product.*
- Tested approximately 30 mock profiles for company's new HR database product.
- Reduced system discrepancies by 25% by identifying and correcting software inconsistencies.
- Improved data integrity by authoring and editing 50 job descriptions.

University Boxes, New York, NY   **2/03-6/03**
*Joined company as an **Assistant Campus Manager** for this national provider of student shipping and storage services. Developed and managed advertising campaign for 6,000 students.*
- Captured 800 new customers in a four-month period. Generated approximately $200,000 in sales and oversaw service implementation and registration logistics.

Senator John Smith, Albany, NY   **Summer 2001**
Liaison between Senator Smith and his constituents. Fielded inquiries and requests; researched and coordinated responses from various agencies. Represented the senator at local events.

PROFESSIONAL AFFILIATIONS
The Society of Women Engineers
President, Columbia Chapter, **2003-2004**   *Community Service Representative***, 2002-2003**
Selected for President post by student body. Represented 250-member Columbia chapter at association board meetings and served as link between professional section of SWE and Columbia chapter.
- Organized conference to introduce 15 high-school girls to engineering. Secured six professors for presentation.

COMPUTER SKILLS
Microsoft Word, Access, Excel, PowerPoint, Photoshop, C programming, SQL, HTML, Internet Explorer

NORMAN STANLEY

5522 Ficus Lane #819
Los Angeles, California 90049

(310) 389-2983
nstanley@email.com

FINANCIAL SALES / PORTFOLIO MANAGEMENT
Expertise in Research / Analysis / Client Relations / Financial Planning

RECENT GRADUATE with demonstrated leadership strengths and proven ability to manage multiple responsibilities in a fast-paced environment with critical deadlines... Worked throughout college to partially self-finance education... Well organized with attention to detail... Works well independently as well as collaboratively in a team setting... Proven ability to "think outside the box" in identifying problems and implementing innovative and resourceful solutions.

——*Areas of Strength*——

Sales & Market Research & Analysis • Competitive Intelligence • Strategic Planning • Project Management
Budget Management • Team Building & Leadership • E-commerce • Website Maintenance

EDUCATION

UNIVERSITY OF SOUTHERN CALIFORNIA, Los Angeles, CA; 2004
Bachelor of Science in Business Economics; Minor in Accounting
GPA: 3.8

Activities: Treasurer—Alpha Beta Gamma Fraternity... President—Student Accounting Society... Vice President—Business-Economics Society

PROFESSIONAL EXPERIENCE

PORTER WARNER, INC., Century City, CA • Jan. 2003 to May 2004—*Concurrent with Studies*
Portfolio Manager / Finance Assistant to Senior Portfolio Managers
Set up and managed client accounts to ensure compliance with established policies and procedures. Collaborated with other financial institutions to facilitate money and account transfers. Conducted in-depth research utilizing Internet, Bloomberg, and direct corporate contact, etc.
- Implemented and maintained detailed database to accurately track clients and prospects.
- Streamlined client communication process.
- Collaborated with support staff to maintain account compliance and reduce missing documents.

INTERNAL REVENUE SERVICE, Los Angeles, CA • 2002, 2003, 2004 (*Tax Seasons*)
Volunteer Income Tax Assistance (V.I.T.A.)
Prepared income tax returns for low-income families and students; provided step-by-step instruction to guide taxpayers in filling out future returns.

ZEMAN & YOUNG, C.P.A.'s, INC., Los Angeles, CA • Oct. 2001 to Jan. 2003 (*Concurrent with Studies*)
Junior Accountant
Prepared individual and corporate income tax returns; audited company records to identify fraud; investigated, compiled, and summarized data to support records for IRS audit.
- Maintained client books through financial statement preparation.
- Prepared investment proposal for start-up company.

Previous Experience: Camp Counselor (Summers 1999 and 2000)

Computer Skills—Microsoft Word, Excel, PowerPoint, Access, Outlook, Peachtree, QuickBooks, Turbo Tax

Foreign Languages—Proficient in oral and written Spanish, including business terminology

Community Activities—Little League Coach, Big Brothers

Jennifer L. Beeman

Connecticut College, Box 34
New London, CT 06320

71 Forest Road
Glastonbury, CT 06433

College 860.444.2838 • Residence 860.333.1286 • jlbee83@aol.com

Qualifications Profile

Highly motivated finance major with strong customer-service orientation and background including brokerage/investment exposure. Track record reflects leadership qualities, initiative-taking, and a tenacious, results-driven approach. Adept in quickly learning new skills. Collaborative team player. Exceptional work ethic. Commitment to exceeding performance expectations. PC skills: Microsoft Word, Excel, and PowerPoint; Goldmine; Internet.

Education

CONNECTICUT COLLEGE • New London, CT

- **Bachelor of Science Degree, Finance** (May 2004)
    - Dual Minors: Economics / Accounting — Dean's List Standing; GPA: 3.86
    - International Education Program • Florence, Italy (Spring 2003)
- Connecticut College Finance Club; Elected Secretary ... Instrumental in successful founding of club with membership of 50–60; coordinated alumni presentations, bookkeeping, and administration.
- Connecticut College Accounting Club; Connecticut College Marketing Club
- Volunteer, New London Salvation Army Soup Kitchen and Relay for Life Cancer Society

Professional and Employment Experience

MERRILL LYNCH • Stamford, CT   9/03–05/04
Intern

- One of 6 undergraduates selected by Merrill Lynch; independently conducted research using data-mining strategies and demographics to identify clusters of prospective investors.
- Executed prospective client mailings and contributed to successful identification and recruitment of qualified candidates. Acquired broad exposure to investment and financial brokerage.

ADVICEONE LLC FINANCIAL • Glastonbury, CT   7/03–9/03
Client-Relations Liaison / Intern

- Directly supported Marketing Department; first-line representative with clients and prospects.
- Honed persuasive marketing skills and elicited business from current clients and prospective investors.
- Professionally coordinated special events and workshops attended by up to 40 clients.

SBC SOUTHERN NEW ENGLAND TELEPHONE COMPANY • New Haven, CT   5/02–8/02
Customer Service Representative (CSR)

- Monitored call-handling activities of approximately 25 CSRs, ensuring timely and professional closure of all calls. Acted in supervisory capacity, motivating CSRs, troubleshooting, and flagging calls. Exceeded goals.

CONNECTICUT COLLEGE • New London, CT   9/02–5/04
Tutor / Campus Information Center (on-campus, part-time employment)

- As an **Accounting Tutor** for students with learning disabilities, provided coaching and assistance with note-taking. Represented Connecticut College as an **On-Campus Guide;** professionally handled telephone inquiries.

CHRISTOPHER COOKE

123 South Oliver St. ▪ Elm Creek, PA 19990
267-555-1212 ▪ ccatelm@yahoo.com

FINANCIAL SERVICES PROFESSIONAL

Enthusiastic and versatile young professional seeking to secure entry-level position in financial/investment industry. Known as an ambitious, conscientious, loyal, and ethical individual who goes "above and beyond" to achieve personal and professional goals/objectives. Core areas of experience include:

- Demonstrated analytical, problem solving, customer service, team building, and administrative skills.
- Proven ability to investigate, research, and verify factual information with minimal supervision.
- Commanding presence with volunteer experience in leadership, fundraising, and motivational speaking.

Interact and work effectively with management and customers at diverse levels. Demonstrate strong communication and interpersonal skills within varying work environments. Computer literate with proficiency in Word, PowerPoint, Excel, and Access. Broad knowledge of conducting Internet research and utilizing proprietary database programs.

EDUCATION

B.S.—Cum Laude, Business Administration
DeKalb College (May 2004)
Obtained dual cum laude distinction in Honors Program at School of Business

Relevant Coursework:
- Financial & Operations Management
- Quantitative Business Methods
- Business Statistics
- Managerial & Financial Accounting
- Strategic Management & Decision Making
- Macro and Micro Economics

Honors Thesis Project: "The Evolving Corporate Payout Policy: Stock Dividend Versus Stock Reinvestment"

LEADERSHIP

Vice President of Sigma Nu Fraternity – second in command for 50 members. Directed training program for new candidates of national chapter. Effectively utilized management, leadership, and team-building skills to facilitate smooth operations and execute administrative tasks designated to individual members (2002).

FUNDRAISING

Developed and implemented fundraising event initiatives as Fundraising Chair of Sigma Nu Fraternity. Raised over $1,000 to cover on-going fraternity expenses (2001).

SPEAKING

Educated student groups regarding campus life issues, i.e. hazing/alcohol use. Integral part of peer education team nominated to present on-going motivational speeches to groups of 30-50 students per session (2001).

EMPLOYMENT

Assistant Manager	Ace Café, Ambler, PA	2003–2004
Assistant Manager	Breeze Grille, Ocean City, NJ	2003–2003
Waiter/Server	Three Chimney Inn, Durham, NH	2002
	The Eagle Grill at Lake Tahoe, NV	2001
Assistant Manager	Tague Lumber, Inc., Phoenixville, PA	1999–2000

OTHER ACTIVITIES

Mentored third-grade student as community service in Seacoast Reads Programs (2000).

Traveled Europe for four months and gained invaluable first-hand knowledge about European cultures through participation in London Study Abroad Program (2002).

ERIN L. DONOFRIO

Before May 16, 2004:
23 Henderson Street
Wilmington, NC 28401
(910) 555-6570

eldono@uncw.edu

After May 16, 2004:
265 Charlotte Street
Asheville, NC 28801
(828) 254-7893

*Adaptable, motivated college graduate with strong work ethic seeks challenge and opportunity in
Health & Fitness career in private, corporate, or rehabilitative environment.*

- Fitness Evaluation & Assessment
- Exercise Prescription
- Cardiac Rehabilitation
- Record Management
- Patient Services
- Patient / Client Education

- Use of medical and fitness machines: telemetry heart rate monitor, EKG, stationary bicycle, free weights, tread mills, elliptical trainers, Nautilus / Keiser / Cybex equipment.
- Evaluation and testing: % body fat, blood pressure, flexibility screening, strength and endurance testing, stress testing.
- Gregarious, with multicultural experience and good communications skills; focused listener. Goal-oriented, well organized; excellent management of time and priorities. Multi-tasking rapport builder.
- Familiar with medical terminology. PC proficient—Internet, Microsoft (Word, Excel, PowerPoint).

B.S., Exercise & Sport Science, May 2004
University of North Carolina-Wilmington

Relevant Coursework:

- Exercise Psychology & Physiology
- Exercise Prescriptions for Special Populations
- Motor Learning
- Biomechanics
- Anatomy
- Research & Evaluation
- Motor Development
- Health Management

Hall University, Hall, England, Spring 2002
- Overseas exposure to different cultures through International Student Association. Learned
rapid adaptability to new environments, global perspectives, independence, and self reliance.
- Traveled extensively in Europe (well-traveled domestically as well).

Certifications & Continuing Professional Training:
AFAA Personal Training Certification . . . CPR Certified, Adult and Child . . . First Aid / Red Cross Certified . . .
Cardiac Rehabilitation . . . NC Alliance for Health, Physical Education, Recreation & Dance Conference
(assisted with set-up of seminars and aide to presenters for this 2004 3-day event)
Gymnast (8 years)

Internship • Willamand Regional Medical Center, Wilmington, NC   Spring 2004
300 hours in 238-bed full-service regional hospital
- As member of professional health team, participated in patient orientations and staff meetings. Monitored and assessed cardiac exercise program; modified exercises as needed for pain relief. As-needed office work and medical records filing.
- Ability to "connect" with patients ensured success in teaching motivational techniques.

Occupational Therapy Volunteer • Memorial Hospital, Wilmington, NC   Fall 2003
- Assessed/observed OT and rehab treatments (40 hours) to better understand scope of rehabilitative choices.

Personal Training / Corporate Fitness • Personal Fitness Inc., Wilmington, NC   January 2004 - Present
*Private, in-house corporate fitness facility providing one-on-one assistance, serving 300-500 employees of several tenant
health care, administrative support, and financial services corporations (including American Express).*
- Perform initial client evaluation / testing; assist in design of personal exercise programs; train clients in proper use of exercise tools. Initiated use of medicine balls in weight training program, allowing client to diversify into more precise exercise movements for specific muscle groups, lowering injury rate in certain sports. Outstanding rapport with clients.

Sales Representative • Bass Outlet, Manasquan, NJ   1998- 2000
- Member of sales team responsible for this retail clothing outlet store earning company's 1994 Highest Grossing Sales Award.

Staci L. Hayward

11330 Meadowbrook Drive • Parma Heights, OH 44130 • 440.555.8479

Profile

Focused, energetic Human Resources Candidate with exceptional maturity, interpersonal and leadership skills, and good judgment.

- Confident and poised; adept at building strong client relationships.
- Skilled communicator with extensive public speaking and presentation experience.
- Flexible and adaptable; comfortable with change.
- Extensively computer literate.
- Eager for responsibility; accountable independently or as part of a team.

Education

B. S., Psychology, *cum laude,* Kent State University, Kent, OH, May 2004

Honors and Activities

- GPA 3.5, honors program.
- Recognized as "KSU Woman of the Year," for leadership, academic achievement, extracurricular involvement, communication skills and poise, 2003.
- Selected to participate in Emerging Leaders Program.
- Chosen as Presidential Ambassador/Assistant to University President and Student Ambassador welcoming prospective students and their parents on campus visits.
- Achieved Phi Eta Sigma freshman honor society, Psi Chi psychology honor society and Rho Lambda honorary (for Greek leadership).
- Recognized with Order of Omega for character and Greek leadership.
- Voted "Senior of the Year," Alpha Chi Omega Sorority: served as Vice President and Rush Chairman.

Experience

HARRIS PARTNERSHIP, Shaker Heights, OH   Summer 2003

Executive Recruiter/Internship
Managed customer accounts for retained search firm. Reviewed clients' detailed staffing requirements and evaluated their corporate cultures to determine complementary personality types. Searched applicant database to assess potential matches. Advertised available positions; screened and interviewed applicants. Assessed qualifications and made hiring recommendations. Counseled selected applicants and advised on career leveraging strategies.

A.G. EDWARDS, Cleveland, OH   Summers 2001-2002

Branch Recruiter
Screened resumes and conducted initial telephone interviews to evaluate applicants against outlined criteria for positions in Canada and the U.S. Prepared hiring reports and performed confidential human resources functions.

- Participated in hiring decisions for branch office administrative personnel.
- Developed competitive compensation plan to bring personnel to market standard.

AMERICAN AIRLINES, St. Louis, MO   Summer 2000

Marketing Intern
Performed market research and competitive analyses; created customer databases for promotional campaigns. Organized and participated in major client events.

ABYGAEL ALEXANDER

98 Ben Franklin Drive, Cherry Hill, New Jersey 07896
Home: (555) 312-8989 ▪ aalex@hotmail.com ▪ Mobile: (555) 606-2839

CAREER FOCUS – JOURNALISM & RESEARCH

Recent university graduate with a solid academic foundation and a demonstrated track record of achieving goals in a team environment. Long standing interest and desire to succeed in reporting and research.

- ☑ Well-reasoned, possessing solid research skills, progressive text development, and comprehensive results meeting deadlines.

- ☑ Ability to compose and synopsize, produce plausible and innovative interpretation, and provide written and oral commentary.

- ☑ Strong communication, interaction, and relationship-building skills acquired through experience in customer-service positions.

EDUCATION

Bachelor of Arts (Political Science & History)   2002 to 2004
UNIVERSITY OF NEW YORK – *New York, NY*

- **Course includes:** Introduction to Politics, Introduction to International Relations, Rural Policy & Politics, Bureaucracy Power & Politics, Security & Strategic Studies, Europe in the Modern Era, Development & Change, Strategy: Paths to Peace & Security, Ends of Empire, The Great War 1914-19, Pathways from the Periphery, World at War 1939 – 45, American Sixties, Italian.

Selected Achievements:

LEADERSHIP

- ☑ Elected as Vice President for the University – **Increased sponsorship** within the university and **secured allocation of funds and resources for events** by establishing and maintaining relationships with outside businesses.

- ☑ Sports Representative and Secretary for Interhall Sports Committee – **Coordinated cutting-edge, innovative social, cultural, and sporting events** designed to create exciting opportunities for students.

TEAMWORK

- ☑ Instrumental in organizing all merchandising for sporting, cultural, and other university events, **working collaboratively with the sport representatives** to ensure all events ran smoothly.

- ☑ Member of the NYU Boat Club, as part of the sub-elite squad. **Worked together with team members** to win the AIF Peace Regatta and earn a place at the local regattas.

- ☑ **Represented NYU** at the Eastern University Games in water polo and hockey and at the American University Games in rowing.

WRITING/RESEARCH

- ☑ Acknowledged **for strong writing, interpretation, and proofreading skills**, assisting fellow students in editing grammatical and composition errors.

- ☑ **Received Distinction** for research projects and essays on "Introduction to Politics" and "Bureaucracy Power and Politics."

60

PROFESSIONAL EXPERIENCE

These positions provided the opportunity to improve professional skill set while working with a wide cross-section of individuals. The knowledge and experience gained have proven invaluable, such as:

➢ Maintaining a calm and reassuring demeanour under high-pressure situations.

➢ Providing exceptional customer service, and maintaining a positive attitude when interacting with all customers, co-workers, and professional staff.

➢ Training junior staff in policies and procedures to ensure compliance with established preparation and sanitation practices, in addition to communicating a customer-service focus.

COMMONWEALTH CLUB – *Manhattan, NY* - **Silver Service Waitress**	2003 to Present
COLLIN BAY HOTEL – *Manhattan, NY* - **Waitress**	2002
FLORIADE FLOWER FESTIVAL – *New Jersey, NY* - **Waitress**	2001
THE OLD VIC CAFE – *Manhattan, NY* - **Waitress**	1999 to 2000

These positions provided the opportunity to improve horse management skills with leading horse studs and riding centers in Australia, Denmark, and Ireland. The knowledge and experience gained include:

➢ Teaching beginner to advanced riders in the various styles of horse riding.

➢ Preparing young horses for competition utilizing various horse management skills.

➢ Preparing yearlings for sales, while monitoring the spelling of racehorses and the upkeep of mares.

MONGERANG RIDE CENTRE – *Denmark* – **Working Pupil**	2001
LIAM & JANE BRACKEN – *Ireland* – **Working Pupil**	2001
CHITTERING GULLY STUD – *Australia* - **Yearling Preparation**	2000
THE OLD VIC CAFÉ – *Australia* - **Waitress**	1999 to 2000

COMMUNITY ORGANIZATIONS

Member, Youth Challenge America (youth aid organization)	Current
Member, Youth Interact (a body that gives youth a political voice in New Jersey)	Current

CERTIFICATES

First Aid Certificate

Bronze Medallion Lifesaving Certificate

Responsible Service of Alcohol Certificate

Workplace Discrimination & Harassment – Legal Compliance Certificate

JEREMY DAVIDSON

Email: jden45@aol.com   56 Larabee Street • Medford, MA 02122   (617) 825-7575

PROFILE

Marine Business ... Investment/Financial Analysis ... Market Research

Talented professional with a solid academic foundation and cross-functional training in **business and marine management**. Demonstrated analytical, research, quantitative, and problem-solving skills. Excellent communications, detail/follow-through, and organizational skills; excel in fast-paced, demanding environments. Customer-service and team-oriented. Recognized for productivity and dependability. Advanced computer skills; adept in quickly learning new technology and applications. Fluent in Italian and conversant in Spanish.

Computer Capabilities – Operating Systems: Windows 00/98/NT. **Applications:** Microsoft Word, Excel, Access, PowerPoint, FrontPage, Photoshop, Dreamweaver, Lotus Notes, C-PAS, financial applications. **Programming:** Knowledge of JavaScript, HTML, Visual Basic, website design/maintenance.

EDUCATION

BOSTON UNIVERSITY, Boston, MA, May 2004
Bachelor of Science in **Marine Business** with minor in **Resource Economics**
- Graduated magna cum laude, GPA: 3.9
- Financed college tuition and expenses through employment.

Relevant courses: Personal Finance Applications, Shipping & Port Management, Marine Resource Management, Human Use & Management, Economics of Resource Management, Economics & Politics, International Trade in Economics.

Activities: One of only 4 students chosen out of 230 applicants by the Alumni Relations Council to attend the Leadership Academy Training Program, a week-long seminar held at Purdue University.

EXPERIENCE

Intern in Market Research – PETERSON TECHNOLOGIES, Providence, RI (1/04–5/04)

Acquired market research experience and contributed to business development efforts at one of the nation's top 15 Internet technology consulting firms. Researched and generated sales lead contacts, as well as company and industry data. Updated and maintained an extensive client database. *Accomplishments:*
- Established more than 2,000 new client leads, boosting sales during the summer months.
- Co-authored training manual for new interns using both print and multimedia applications.

Administrative Support – MONROVIA ENTERPRISES, Boston, MA (9/00–5/03)

Initially hired as part of work-study program and quickly offered salaried position based on diverse qualifications. Performed general office assignments in alumni research that included data entry and updating key donor files. Created several new databases that streamlined and enhanced information access.

Dock Manager – NEWPORT MARINA, Newport, RI (9/99–9/00)

Promoted within first month of employment to co-manage dock area, seafood market, and lobster pound at one of the busiest marinas on the eastern seaboard serving recreational and commercial fishing fleets. Key role in managing major fishing tournaments with nationwide competitors. Liaison between commercial fisherman and area fish brokers. *Accomplishments:*
- Achieved record sales, resulting in one of the most financially successful years to date.
- Instilled teamwork; supervised and trained 8 employees in all aspects of marina operations.
- Initiated conversion to a computerized accounting system (QuickBooks), increasing efficiency.

Additional: Established seasonal landscaping service and grew business to 50 accounts with 50% repeat/referral clientele based on consistent service quality and excellent customer relations (6/97–9/99).

Chris Rodriguez

c-rod@hotmail.com • 206-870-2904
7529 53rd Avenue SW, Seattle, WA 98136

Career Focus	**Marketing/Advertising/Public Relations/Promotions**

Value Offered

- ☑ **Initiator and Leader:** On own initiative, planned, promoted, and drew large crowds to entertainment events in Seattle's competitive young-adult market.

- ☑ **Experienced Marketer/Promoter:** In demand as marketing representative for national agencies, using guerrilla marketing techniques to boost product awareness and acceptance in target populations.

- ☑ **Effective Communicator:** Successful in direct marketing and sales roles as well as in business communications, contract negotiations, and public speaking.

- ☑ **Attuned to Trends** in the volatile youth market (music, entertainment, fashion, consumer goods).

Education

UNIVERSITY OF WASHINGTON, Seattle, WA   **BS in Music Industry,** May 2004—GPA 3.6

Degree encompasses music fundamentals and extensive business coursework (Management, Accounting, Economics, Retailing, Entrepreneurship, Music Industry, Artist Management).

Honors

☑ Dean's List • National Society of Collegiate Scholars • Golden Key International Honour Society

Experience

EVENT MANAGER/PROMOTER   **C-Rod Productions, Seattle, WA,** 2002–Present

Launched company and independently plan, promote, and manage entertainment events that are well attended and consistently profitable.

Management & Marketing

- ☑ Found/secured venues and performers; wrote and negotiated contracts; managed event budgets; coordinated all details of safe, successful events that attracted hundreds of paying customers.
- ☑ Developed marketing and advertising plans, designed and distributed flyers, and secured free coverage in multiple media (newspapers, radio, web).

Event Highlights

- ☑ Drew 400 guests to an electronic music/hip-hop show at a popular downtown club.
- ☑ Promoted 10 shows per year for established production companies, drawing 200–300 per show.
- ☑ Planned, secured sponsors, and marketed a casino cruise event that attracted 175 guests.

PROMOTIONAL MARKETER   **US Concepts, ADD, other national agencies,** 2001–Present

Build consumer awareness and market acceptance for youth-oriented products including mobile phones, movies, TV shows, clothing, food, fragrances, and alcoholic beverages. Use guerrilla marketing techniques to build product visibility and status in sought-after demographic. Compile and submit marketing reports to agencies, documenting activities and results.

Highlights

- ☑ Demonstrated/promoted T-Mobile phones, Nokia N-Gage, and Verizon's Get It Now technology.
- ☑ Persuaded customers to participate in activities for beverage promotions.
- ☑ Promoted the movies Swimfan (Twentieth Century Fox), Win a Date with Tad Hamilton (DreamWorks), and Better Luck Tomorrow (MTV).
- ☑ Modeled for Goldwell, The Gap, J. Crew, and the cover of *Young Seattle* magazine.

ASSISTANT MANAGER/PROMOTIONS ASSISTANT   **Club Wa, Seattle, WA,** 2002

Maintained entertaining, comfortable atmosphere to attract guests to campus club. Supervised staff, dealt with contracts and bookings, coordinated events, created reports, and handled cash.

Highlights

- ☑ Planned, promoted, and managed entertainment event that drew 3rd-largest sales in club history.
- ☑ Leveraged connections at local record label to secure name entertainers.

SALES ASSOCIATE   **Nordstrom's, City Beat, J. Crew,** 2 years part-time/seasonal

Skills
Interests

MS Word, Excel, Works • Internet research • Networking • Reading music • Deejaying

Discovering new musical styles • Supporting/promoting underground music • Writing • Traveling

63

Carole A. Mehrman

11423 Evangelista Drive, #203 • Los Angeles, CA 90024

310.555.7870 • monarch21@aol.com

Career Interest in Marketing/Merchandising/Business Analysis/Planning

PROFILE

Outgoing, responsible, and energetic with proven initiative, interpersonal skills, and leadership.

- Detail oriented, organized, highly motivated, and productive.
- Expert in managing time and priorities for deadline project completion.
- Computer-literate, proficient writer.
- Effective independently or in a collaborative team environment.
- Flexible and adaptable.
- Fluent in written and spoken French.

EDUCATION

B. A., French, specialization in Business Administration, May 2004
University of Southern California, Los Angeles, CA

- GPA: 3.56
- Studied abroad in France, Summer 2003.

Honors

- Achieved Golden Key National Honor Society, Order of Omega Greek Honor Society, Alpha Lambda Delta and Phi Eta Sigma Scholastic Honor Societies.
- Named to National Dean's List.
- Voted "Most Outstanding Collegiate Member," Kappa Delta Sorority, 2003.

Activities

- Student Alumni Association: Sponsorship Director, 2003-2004; Events Director, 2002-2003; Marketing Director, 2001-2002.
- Kappa Delta Sorority: Chapter Treasurer, 2002-2004; Assistant Treasurer, 2001-2002; Chapter Executive Board, 2000-2004; Standards Board, 2001-2004.
- French Department: volunteer tutor, 2000-2004.

EXPERIENCE

Marketing Intern
INTERNATIONAL ASSOCIATION, Los Angeles, CA   Summer 2002

Assisted Executive Director in promotional, marketing, and hospitality activities. Participated in registering new students for ESL (English as a Second Language) classes. Responded to telephone inquiries and updated informational database. Composed internal correspondence and recorded staff meeting minutes. Worked with teachers in classrooms; facilitated role plays and interaction.

Tax Preparation Assistant
HOWARD L. KENNEY CPA, Los Angeles, CA   2001 Tax Season

Organized client documents to facilitate tax preparation.

COMMUNITY SERVICE

Hollygrove Orphanage, 2001-2003
Santa Monica Homeless Shelter, 2001-2002
Project Angel Food, 2001-2002

Carl Bean AIDS Hospice, 2001-2002
Fundraising for National Committee to Prevent Child Abuse, 2001-present

EDWARD V. HOLT

PO Box 1417707 • Asheville, NC 28801 • 828/555-6663 • evh22@hotmail.com

---

. . . Seeking Integrated Marketing Communications Career . . .

Training & Experience In . . .

■ Advertising   ■ Public Relations   ■ Marketing

Creation & Strategic Planning of Complete Advertising Campaigns . . . Market Research . . . Graphic Design
Public Relations Plan Development . . . Public Relations Crisis Management . . . Writing for Media
Presentations and Public Speaking . . . Consumer Behavior . . . Selling

- Primary research experience includes conducting surveys on buyer behavior and opinion polls to test advertising ideas.
- Secondary research experience in the interpretation of demographics (SMRB), advertising rates (SRDS), histories and statistics on a variety of individual businesses.
- Computer friendly: Email, WordPerfect, Aldus PageMaker, MacWrite, MacDraw, PowerPoint, Microsoft Picture Publisher, Microsoft Publisher, Microsoft Works.
- Creative; critical thinker; adaptive team player with good problem-solving abilities; persuasive.

Related Coursework:

- PR Management
- Advertising Management
- Principles of Marketing

- Media Sales
- Nonverbal, Interpersonal & Mass Communications
- Theory & Practice of Persuasion

- Broadcast Production
- Electronic Publishing
- Print Newswriting, Journalism

B.S., Advertising & Public Relations (double major), with **Minor in Marketing,** December 2004
MOUNTAIN STATE UNIVERSITY, ASHEVILLE, NC

- Dean's List ~ Awarded Harold R. Candler Memorial Scholarship for Outstanding Leadership, 2003
- Executive positions in Alpha Tau Omega —
coordinated special events and planned/executed formation of intramural athletic teams.
- Varsity Football (all-conference)

Graduate, Ledford Senior High School, Thomasville, NC, 2000
- Who's Who Among High School Students
- Active in student government and school organizations
- Varsity football, baseball, soccer (all-conference)

HIGHLIGHTS OF EXPERIENCE

Assistant Sales Manager • American Sports Store, Greensboro, NC • 1999 - 2004
Daily operations; acting general manager in absence of owner. Directly responsible for indoor/outdoor advertising, accounting, customer relations, opening/closing, screen printing, ordering and receiving merchandise, and strategic product placement.
- Directed move into new store location and handled grand opening of new store.

Production Manager • Colorwise Painters, Greensboro, NC • 2002
Directed crew of 5 house painters for company based in Chicago, IL. Accountable for meeting deadlines, payroll, and collections. Collaborated closely with customers on needs determination and discrepancies. Handled all advertising for district (Greensboro, NC).
- Grossed 3rd highest sales out of 85 crews nationwide in first year.
- Beat deadline on every job.
- Earned gross income of $52,000 in 3 months.

Sales Associate • A&E Outfitters, Statesville, NC • 2001 - 2002
- Exceeded ever-higher personal sales goals *every* month.

Waiter/Cook • Al's Seafood Restaurant, Asheville, NC • 2000-2001
- Tips averaged 7% above other staff; doubled sales of specials within 3 weeks of hire; set 2 daily sales records.

Referee & Coach • Lynchfield Soccer Association, Lynchfield, NC • 1998 - 2000
Taught teamwork, the value of team play, benefits of competition, and self-esteem and determination to youngsters ages 6-16. Settled parental complaints.

Jessica Devlin

64 Walnut Creek Drive, Yardley, PA 19089
(215) 919-5555 Home · (215) 919-8888 Mobile · jessdev@home.com

OBJECTIVE: Entry-level Mental Health Counseling position, such as Residential Counselor, Mental Health Counselor, Mental Health Associate, Clinical Case Manager, or Partial Care Counselor.

EDUCATION:

Bachelor of Science, Liberal Studies, Double Minor: Psychology / Professional Education   May 2004
Rutgers University, New Brunswick, NJ

Relevant Courses:

Introductory Psychology	Mental Illness	Developmental Psychology	Transcultural Health
Introductory Sociology	Psychodrama I	Educational Psychology	Theory of Personality
Physiological Psychology	Loss and Grieving	Sociology of the Family	Abnormal Psychology
Essential Helping Relations	Social Psychology	Field Experience I & II	Intro. Criminal Justice

MENTAL HEALTH INTERNSHIP:

Mental Health & Guardianship Advocacy, Public Defender's Office, Trenton, NJ   2002 – 2003

- Interned for 3 programs in mental health field within Public Defender's Office: Mental Health Unit (Mercer County Field Office), Guardianship Advocacy Unit, and Special Hearings Unit (Megan's Law).

- Interviewed individuals at in-patient public and private facilities, such as Hagadom State Hospital (specializing in geriatric psychiatric care), Trenton Psychiatric Hospital (adolescent and adults), as well as the Carrier Foundation (children and adolescents) for Mental Health and Guardianship Advocacy programs.

- Assisted attorneys in Megan's Law legal cases by interviewing defendants for upcoming hearings, documenting and evaluating statements, and preparing materials for the court.

- Performed follow-up case management, interviewing clients to complete cases assigned, and submitted timely documentation and reports. Ensured confidentiality of all records and communications.

EMPLOYMENT:

Substitute Teacher, Hamilton Regional School District, Hamilton, NJ   2004 – present

- Teach all subjects as substitute teacher for elementary and secondary schools, following lesson plans detailed by classroom teachers, as well as maintaining positive class atmosphere and discipline.

Hostess / Cocktail Waitress, Rusty Scupper, Princeton, NJ   2003 – present

- Coordinate seating, efficiently and promptly, for popular downtown restaurant with seating for 550 indoors and outdoors. Seat 200 customers per 8-hour shift, while serving 1000 bar customers per 5-hour shift.

- Efficiently seat and serve group parties and banquets, such as four 2002 holiday parties (75 customers each) in one day. Received recognition for top-notch customer service and positive attitude under stress.

- Entrusted with $450 bankroll at beginning of each shift. Maintain 99+% "count out" (cash reconciliation) accuracy for monies collected and disbursed daily.

- Chosen by management to promote upcoming shows and events via on-site and off-site marketing pieces and public relations appearances.

Administrative Assistant, Claims Administration, Public Defender's Office, Trenton, NJ   Summer 2001

- Maintained orderly and productive environment in busy office with 6 attorneys. Effectively answered and transferred incoming phone calls on 8 lines, and scheduled 50-60 appointments daily for all attorneys.

- Word-processed, edited, and revised large volume of homeowners' claims and legal settlement documents weekly (20 – 25 documents, each 75 – 80 pages in length). Consistently completed assignments with short turnaround time (within 24 hours). Received live dictation and composed/sent correspondence and memos.

COMPUTER SKILLS:

Windows 98, MS Office 2000 – Word, Excel, Access, PowerPoint, MS Outlook, PhotoShop, Internet Explorer

Sean T. Dillon

457 Glenview Road
Ramsey, NJ 07430

(201) 932 -3289 (C)
seandil30@hotmail.com

PHARMACEUTICAL SALES

PROFILE: Enterprising, self-directed, recent college graduate with strong interpersonal and organizational skills. Experience in teaching, catering, event planning, modeling, working with doctors, and waiting on restaurant patrons. Financed 40% of education by working part-time. Computer proficient.

STRENGTHS
- **Organizing** and **managing** catering staff for special events.
- **Calling on** modeling agencies for jobs and **cold calling** on wineries to **sell** catering services.
- **Qualifying, servicing,** and **interacting** with restaurant patrons.
- **Teaching** children and teachers about science and basic science principles.

EDUCATION
- **BS in Zoology,** University of California Los Angeles, 05/03
- **AA in Liberal Studies,** Pasadena City College, 12/01
- **Key Coursework:** Organic Chemistry, General Chemistry, Molecular Genetics, Calculus, Statistics, Psychology, and Complete Biology Series

INTERNSHIPS & DIRECTED STUDIES
- **EEMB 117:** Internship in Biological Sciences - 4 units, slide restoration and classification. Organized and restored thousands of biology slides.
- **EEMB 149:** Directed Studies - 4 units, "Kids in Nature." Taught 4th-6th graders about cellular biology and conducted workshops to instruct teachers on basic science skills. Selected by Botany professor because of strong <u>teaching</u> and <u>interpersonal</u> skills.

EMPLOYMENT HISTORY

<u>FRIDAY'S</u>	Ramsey, NJ	05/03 - Present

Waiter. Work 5 shifts per week.

<u>DAWN ROBERTS CATERING</u>	Santa Barbara, CA	12/99 - 12/02

Kitchen Manager
Catering business. Part-time position. Oversaw 2-3 prep cooks. Responsible for preparation of all food. Purchased food and trained new cooks. Made cold calls on wineries to promote business.
- Planned, organized, and catered Annual Benefit dinner for Santa Barbara Opera. Served a 5-course dinner to over 300 people.
- Promoted from prep cook to kitchen manager within one year.

<u>SANTA BARBARA CITY HOSPITAL, ER</u>	Santa Barbara, CA	12/99 - 12/01

E.M.T. Volunteer
Assisted doctors and nurses with basic medical procedures. Learned various ER medications.

<u>SANTA BARBARA CITY COLLEGE</u>	Santa Barbara, CA	12/99 - 12/01

E.M.T. Volunteer
Assessed and treated illnesses and injuries on school camping trips. Donated over 1,400 hours.

<u>CONTRACT MODELING WORK</u>	New York, NY	1996 - 1997

Model for Men's Clothes and TV Commercials
While in high school, contracted by modeling agencies like Wilhelmina, SKY and SEM&M. Featured in AT&T national TV advertisement and GAP advertisement.

EDEN MORLAND, PA-C
PHYSICIAN ASSISTANT
e-mail: emorland34@aol.com

67 Walden Road
Somers, TX 78734
(512) 263-6643

OBJECTIVE	**Physician Assistant – Acute Care**
	Experienced in acute care, urgent care, and primary care environments, providing high-quality professional care to a wide range of patients. Recognized by physicians/supervisors for maturity, dependability, and clinical capabilities. Successful in quickly building rapport and gaining patients' trust/confidence. Member of the Student Association of the American Academy of Physician Assistants.

CLINICAL SKILLS & PROCEDURES

- Completing patient histories; providing patient education and intervention.
- Performing and dictating complete and focused physical examinations, which include pelvic exams, pre-surgical exams and newborn physical exams.
- Development of diagnoses (including differential), assessments and treatment plans; comfortable in discussing diagnoses with patients.
- Skilled in performing various procedures: venipuncture, IV therapy, Foley catheter and NG tube insertions, ABGs, and suturing/stapling and removal.
- Assisting in surgical procedures such as inguinal and umbilical hernia repairs with mesh, laproscopic and open cholecystectomies, laproscopic appendectomies, valve repairs, coronary artery bypass grafts, complete and simple mastectomies, and surgical incision of lipomas and exploratory laparotomies. Preparation of SOAP notes.
- Pre- and post-operative management, fluid and electrolyte management and direct wound care experience.
- Interpretation of x-rays, CT scans and MRIs.
- Certified in Advanced Cardiac Life Support (ACLS).

EDUCATION & TRAINING

B.S., Physician Assistant Program, SOUTHLAND COLLEGE, Austin, TX   May 2004
Passed PANCE exam, April 2004

Clinical Rotations:

Medical training and experience in the Physician Assistant program acquired through 12 clinical rotations in various medical settings (2001-2004):

Supervisors' Evaluation Comments:

"Excellent in obtaining histories and putting patients at ease."

"History and physical exam presentations are top rate."

"A dedicated professional with exceptional general medical knowledge."

PETERSON MEMORIAL HOSPITAL, Austin, TX
- Pediatrics Department, including Neonatal Intensive Care Unit
- General, OB/GYN, & Cardiac Surgery
- Internal Medicine

CULVER HOSPITAL, Austin, TX
- Emergency Medicine

MALVERN PSYCHIATRIC ASSOCIATES, Austin, TX
- Psychiatry

PARKER & ASSOCIATES OB/GYN, Austin, TX
- OB/GYN – Private Practice
- Elective – OB/GYN

WEST ASSOCIATES, Austin, TX
- Ambulatory Medicine (urgent and primary care)
- Preceptorship – Ambulatory Medicine

MONROE HOSPITAL, Austin, TX
- Elective – Medical/Psychiatric
- Preceptorship – Medical

RESEARCH PROJECT

PETERSON MEMORIAL HOSPITAL, Austin, TX (1999-2000)
Research Assistant – Emergency Research Education Department
- Recruited patients, drew blood samples, started IVs, and maintained daily documentation as assistant to Dr. Smythe in the Nuclear Medicine Lab.

Francine Bley FrancineBley@hotmail.com

1455 Hiawatha Circle • Columbus, OH 43215 • 614.380.6101

Career focus: **Public Health**
Specialty in Cultural Awareness / Diverse Populations

Profile: Dedicated self-starter with experience working in both community and corporate situations. Highly motivated in advancing a professional career through professional work and personal growth. Outstanding ability to research, organize, deliver information, and communicate on all levels. Positive track record of responsibility and reliability.

Education: *OHIO STATE UNIVERSITY;* Columbus, OH
Bachelor of Arts Degree in Anthropology (3.72 GPA in major) • 2004
Specialization in Bioethics, Humanities, Society (3.5 GPA overall)

Coursework:

- Ethical Issues in Health Care
- Sociology of Health Care Systems
- Environmental & Organismal Biology
- Culture, Health & Illness
- Diseases in Society
- Native American Religions
- Alternative Medicine
- Osteopathic Medicine
- Physiology

Computer: Microsoft Word, Excel, PowerPoint; SOSS (State Of the State Survey) database; email, Internet research

Experience: *PUBLIC HEALTH CENTER;* Anchorage, AK
Intern • 2003
- Helped with diverse projects for native Alaskan public health center, as the only non-native personnel.
- Assisted in the creation of the native Alaskan website; researched census data, verified information, and provided input on design applications.
- Organized and built a census library database used for workers and the public.

LITTLE ONES FIRST CARE; Centerville, OH
Caregiver/Teacher • 2000-02
- Direct hands-on involvement with children from newborn to 4-year-olds; provided a safe, nurturing, and supportive environment.
- Helped with group play and art; taught life skills.

WASHINGTON ELEMENTARY SCHOOL / BIRCH RUN ELEMENTARY SCHOOL; Como, OH
Teacher Aide / Tutor • 2000-2001
- Assisted the teacher in coursework, one-on-one instruction, and group activities.
- After-school tutor for Math, Science, and General Studies (grades 3-5).

COLUMBUS COMMUNITY SCHOOL; Columbus, OH
Teacher Aide • 2000
- Assisted with mentally and physically challenged children.

CENTURY 21; Centerville, OH
Receptionist • 1999
- Performed office support in customer service/relations, administrative processes, and logistics management. Entered customer information in the corporate database.

Other: Published on anthropology website for the American Anthropological Association

Member of Ohio State University's Anthropology Club • 2001-04

JASON B. DANIELS

5165 Dryer Boulevard. Unit B2, Memphis, Tennessee 38126

901-959-5543   jbd24@aol.com

Entry-Level Public Relations

EDUCATION

SAINT LOUIS UNIVERSITY, Missouri
Bachelor of Arts in Communications
Summer 2004

Related Studies

Public Speaking	Journalism
Communication Research	Communication Theory
Public Relations Practices and Principles	Rhetoric Analysis
Intercultural Communication	International PR

Activities

Marketing Internship—Sheldon Music Hall & Ballroom, St. Louis, Mo., 2004
Writer—concert reviews for University News
Intramural sports

Private study—piano, 1987 – 2001

WORK EXPERIENCE

1999 – Present	Brad Newbie Band	
St. Louis	Founder of band and perform as keyboard player, rhythm guitarist and backup singer as well as songwriter. Retained for events and special occasions throughout the St. Louis area.	

2000 – 2001	Café Grand	
St. Louis	Performed as captain for waiters in dining room of service-oriented restaurant. Greeted and interacted with guests to assure excellent service. Assisted with valet functions.	

2000	Brake Landscaping	
St. Louis	Operated heavy equipment, developed and maintained landscapes, applied fertilizer, installed plantings, and repaired foundation problems.	

1998	Tennessee Diagnostic Specialists	
Memphis	Assisted administration in various clerical areas including filing, mail prep, and laboratory deliveries.	

Diane Starr

145 May Street Ft. Lauderdale, Florida 33309   954-308-6742 or 954-308-4152   dianestarr@hotmail.com

Enthusiastic new graduate with a
Bachelor of Science degree in Sociology / Psychology
brings a mature and solid background of organizational and analytical skills to the job market.

Excellent Customer Service   Highly Efficient
Excellent Communications Skills   Dependable / Reliable / Flexible
Multi-task Oriented   Project Focused
Exceptional Organizational Ability   Results Oriented

EDUCATION

Bachelor of Science – Sociology/Psychology   Florida State University – 2002

ACHIEVEMENTS

➢ *Awarded the highly recognized status as Order of Omega Honor Society* as a result of achieving a 3.0 GPA as a student at Florida State University.
➢ *Committee Coordinator of the Juvenile Diabetes Foundation* 5K-walk fundraiser and serve the organization as an active contributor.
➢ *Managed a statistical research project* with a focus on the analysis of social effects of individual behavior as it relates to certain factors affecting their likelihood to be concerned with health-related issues in today's society.
➢ *Managed 100% of college career* through occupational research, course selection, and financial management through part-time employment.

EMPLOYMENT EXPERIENCE

Ft. Lauderdale Independent School District – Ft. Lauderdale, Florida   August 2002 – present
Substitute Teacher – Grades K-5
- Manage classroom activities.
- Provide substitute teaching services with minimal disruption to daily curriculum.
- Implement creative activities to ensure assigned learning goals are met.

Exclusively Day Spa – Ft. Lauderdale, Florida   January 2002 – July 2002
Administrative Assistant
- Managed and directed telecommunications and personally handled visitors to the spa.
- Managed and completed clerical tasks such as filing, reporting, data entry, and document processing.
- Administered customer service for both internal and external customers.

VANCO, Inc – Ft. Lauderdale, Florida
Receptionist
- Managed and directed telecommunications, visitors, and vendors of the company.
- Administered customer service for both internal and external customers.

PROFESSIONAL ORGANIZATIONS AND TRAINING

Memberships in the following affiliations:
- Order of Omega Honor Society
- Pre-Law Society
- Sociology Club

Proficient in: MS Excel, MS Word, Keyboarding, Medical Terminology, and General Office Equipment

71

MARK FOSTER

500 Claremont Avenue • Independence, Missouri 64052 • mfost@aol.com • 816.222.5511

QUALIFICATIONS PROFILE

Quality-driven **IT Professional** with formal education and proven expertise in systems engineering, networks, databases, advanced technical support, and technical training.

- Well-rounded expertise in computer systems, programming, and networking, with experience and advanced-level skill with Microsoft Office applications.
- Proven troubleshooting and research skills for developing successful solutions to problems as well as ability to write effective documentation of technical procedures.
- Strong interpersonal skills and self-motivated. Quick to adapt to new applications and technologies.

EDUCATION

Bachelor of Science Degree (2004) ◆ **Major in Information Systems, Minor in Management**
UNIVERSITY OF MISSOURI, Kansas City, Missouri

- Winner of the Kemper Award for Highest Academic Standing of all Information Systems Majors – earned four-year academic scholarship.
- Graduated Cum Laude – 3.53 GPA

TECHNICAL BACKGROUND

Platforms:	Windows
Tools:	Microsoft Office (Word, Excel, PowerPoint, Access, Outlook) – Expert Level
Languages:	FoxPro 2.5, 2.6, and 6.0.
Databases:	Oracle, SQL, MS Access, MS FoxPro

PROFESSIONAL EXPERIENCE

H & R BLOCK, Kansas City, Missouri   7/2003 – 9/2003
Intern – Technology Division

Assisted in and maintained training programs for the use of Microsoft Office and Outlook. Trained employees on proper email usage. Documented tax record status, and tracked and reported transfer data for the department manager's daily use. Gained understanding of business rules for computer usage, and assisted in the development of databases for intra-office use. Assisted in database training.

- Increased department productivity by assisting in the organization of data for Office applications. Resulted in managers having quicker access to information and allowed them to make better decisions.
- Trained 35 employees one-on-one over a ten-day period on the use of a new email system and how to use Outlook to maximize their time, while saving space on the company email server.
- Became excellent liaison between system administrators and employees within the department for various technical issues, leading to relatively quick solutions and minimal downtime.
- Maintained high degree of accuracy with preparing and distributing data for tax management reports.

APPLEBEE'S BAR AND GRILL, Kansas City, Missouri   2000 – 2004
Waiter

72

PAUL STEVENS

video game programming ▫ scripting ▫ quality assurance

"I am passionate about building a career in video games because I know that my problem-solving skills and creativity will allow me to add real value. I simply won't give up when faced with a problem."

professional profile

□▒■

Talented recent graduate with a passion for video games and the video-game industry. Strong work ethic and a proven ability to meet tight deadlines. Blends innate leadership ability, attention to detail and creative approach to problem-solving to consistently deliver results. **Exceptionally quick learner, driven to succeed.**

education

B.S., Computer Science (Minor in Business Management), April 2004, University of Toronto

- Invited by faculty to apply for prestigious graduate scholarship ▪ Co-wrote XML research paper which is scheduled for publication ▪ Led multiple project teams ▪ Received two academic excellence scholarships

game development experience

- **Built complex, open-ended module for *Neverwinter Nights.*** Put in over 75 hours of design, coding, and testing to incorporate many variables and a challenging chess-based puzzle.

- **Developed a large, nontraditional, single-player campaign for *Warcraft III*** which incorporates terrain-editing, trigger-scripting, and camera manipulations.

- **Designed a story-driven, four-level module for *Unreal Tournament*** and utilized complex patrolling algorithms to add a stealth/espionage element to the game.

- **Created self-study program to enhance game-programming skills.** Currently developing expertise in DirectX.

- **Avid gamer since the age of ten.** Own PC, Xbox, GameCube, PS2, and Game Boy Advanced. Play games of all genres with a particular passion for RPG, action/adventure, and real-time strategy.

technical skills

Languages:	C/C++, HTML, Python, Java, VB Script, XML, currently studying DirectX
Compilers & Tools:	Microsoft Visual C++, Microsoft Visual Basic, Borland, Gcc
QA:	Black Box (functional) and White Box (structural) Testing
General:	GUI Design & Programming, Program Architecture Design, TCP/IP Networking, Relational Database Design, Database Administration

work history

SELF-EMPLOYED – COMPUTER REPAIRS   2002 – PRESENT
Solve a wide array of hardware and software problems for clients while studying full-time. Offer an average turnaround time of only 24 hours due to extensive knowledge of both hardware and software.

IT SUPPORT - SUMMER POSITIONS WHILE IN UNIVERSITY (Juno, Davco Welding, and Rice & Davenport)
Deployed/configured workstations. Diagnosed network, hardware, and software problems. Provided follow-up to ensure problems did not reoccur.

- Built test servers and assisted in corporate migration to new machines for the Juno Corporation.
- Solved technical issues inherent in file-sharing at Rice & Davenport by implementing an FTP system.
- Facilitated Davco Welding's transition from paper-based invoicing / costing to a computerized process.

4832 Bayview Avenue, #45, Toronto, Ontario, M4G 3A6 / 416-555-5555 / paul.stevens@net.ca

CARTER RAND
carterrand@aol.com

TV/VIDEO EDITOR

PROFILE
Innovative, hands-on editor, writer, producer. Active sports involvement (dirt biking, surfing, skateboarding, wakeboarding) and music scene participant (punk rock, most recent rock & roll, reggae, folk music) lead to unique combination of sports and music savvy to fuse appealing sounds with images in extreme sports. Aptitude to produce quality work with limited resources; frequently go above and beyond the call of duty in creativity and commitment. Studied with mentors **Stan Kellam** and **Randy Wells.**

Able to work under pressure in fast-paced, time-sensitive environments. Establish and build positive, solid relationships with clients and all levels of management. Outstanding listening and interpersonal skills: good communicator with writers, talent, crew, production, and post-production techs. Professional and articulate; meticulous, detail-oriented, well organized; good natured, quick learner. **Strong work ethic.**

Extensive travel; understanding of multicultural diversity. Basic conversational Spanish.

EQUIPMENT

Premiere   Final Cut Pro
After Effects   Avid Express
Media 100   Avid 9000

Experience with digitization and basic effects on *Inferno* editing system. In-depth knowledge of DV, Mini DV, Beta SP, ¾ tape, patch routing, any type of dubs.

Computer skills: MS Word, Excel, PowerPoint; Mac-based programs; PC proficient.

PROFESSIONAL EXPERIENCE

CAMERAMAN, SET P.A.   *Yoga Flava,* yoga fitness video.
                                 Common Sense, band, live DVD shoot.

WRITER, PRODUCER, EDITOR   *Cooperfish Surfboards,* surf video.
                                 Featured on *Fuel,* Fox Sports Net;
                                 currently selling in stores.

CAMERAMAN, EDITOR   *Action Girl Sports,* television pilot for
                                 Fox Sports Net.

SET P.A., ASSISTANT EDITOR   *Jakey Moves,* Serial P.O.P. music
                                 video.

EDITOR   Comedy demo reel for comedian Mike
                                 Batayeh.

ASSOCIATE PRODUCER   2002
Citrus Group - Hollywood, CA

Promoted from intern to head of sales **within three months.** Frequented clubs
to approach smaller bands to shoot and edit music videos. Negotiated their
contracts with record labels and followed up with clients.

Produced two music videos and edited first cuts. Logged tapes and made dubs.
Interacted daily with editors, directors, and producers. Handled all office
administration for producers.

NON-RELATED EXPERIENCE

OPERATIONS MANAGER   2001 - Present
Designosaur - Santa Clarita, CA

Developed process to reproduce fossils set in rock. Trained staff of 4 in this
process. Designed website in collaboration with webmaster. Conceived layout for
personal month-long art exhibit held at California Lutheran University.

BELLHOP   Summers 1999, 2000
Hyatt Hotel - Valencia, CA

Trained in space efficiency. Provided guest services to hotel patrons and solved
various guest problems.

Award: Thinking Outside The Box.

LABORER / BRICK LAYER   1996 - Present
The Masonry Place - Granada Hills, CA   (Concurrently)

Read blueprints, mix cement, and weld. Learned to keep everything level. Assist
on an as needed basis.

EDUCATION
Bachelor of Arts, Communications (2004) with emphasis on **Electronic
Media;** minor: Fine Art.
California Lutheran University, Thousand Oaks, CA

CONTACT INFORMATION
1631 Kelton Lane — Los Angeles, California 90064
Residence: 310-488-5577 Cellular: 818-767-3069

CHAPTER 5

Best Resumes to Highlight Internship, Research, and Related Career Experiences

Overview

If you've been fortunate enough during your academic career to have had the opportunity to participate in an internship program, research project, freelance assignment, or other activity directly related to your career objectives, then you're one of the fortunate graduates! It's great to be able to highlight truly relevant skills, experiences, and contributions on your resume, and it definitely gives you a strong and sustainable advantage over other recent graduates.

What's most important to you when writing your resume is that these experiences become the focal point of your resume – both in terms of content and visual presentation. This is basically a two-step process:

- You want your reader's eye to be drawn immediately to those sections in your resume where that information is presented. You can achieve this using a wide range of resume formats, styles, graphics, lines, and more. The samples in this chapter and throughout this book should give you lots of ideas for how to design your own resume and be sure that your most critical information is prominently displayed.

- Once you've captured your reader's eye with a strong visual presentation, you want to be sure that the content is well-written and keyword-rich, that your achievements and skills are clearly communicated, and that your reader can get a real grasp of what you did and how well you did it.

If you are able to achieve the above, you will have instantly positioned yourself as "part of the industry" or "part of the profession" and not "just" a graduating student looking for his/her first-ever professional opportunity. Obviously, this gives you a remarkably competitive edge within the employment market. How great for a company to be able to hire a young and talented new professional who already brings a good blend of experience into their organization!

Index of Resumes Featured in This Chapter

Objective: Professional IT position with the company that this candidate is currently interning with

Strategy: Emphasis on recent college graduation, strong technology toolkit and practical experience gained directly with the company to which graduate is applying

Resume: Juan Gonzalez, page 89
Writer: Janet Beckstrom, CPRW
Objective: Entry-level business management or management trainee position with a well-established company in the food, beverage, or consumer products industries
Strategy: Primary emphasis on strong work-related experience (internship and paid) supported by excellent summary of qualifications

Resume: Laura L. Petersen, page 90
Writer: Arnold G. Boldt, CPRW, JCTC
Objective: Position as an Elementary School Teacher
Strategy: Eye-catching format and design filled with strong academic performance and excellent student-teaching experiences clearly highlighted on the resume

Resume: Marcus Blackmarr, page 91
Writer: Gayle Howard, CCM, CPRW, CERW, CRW
Objective: Position in the building and construction industry
Strategy: Highlight professional achievements with award and affiliations at top of resume, followed by keyword-rich summary and two strong industry internships

Resume: Susan J. Davenport, page 92
Writer: Louise Fletcher, CPRW
Objective: Entry-level position in any capacity within the entertainment industry
Strategy: Solid presentation of entertainment-related internship experience and notable academic achievements, complemented by three wonderful testimonials

Resume: Jane Rualana, page 93
Writer: Alice Hanson, CPRW
Objective: Research position at the Bali Primate Research Center
Strategy: Majority of resume devoted to her field research experience in the US and abroad with a nice presentation of educational qualifications

Resume: Belinda A. Lincoln, page 94
Writer: Arnold G. Boldt, CPRW, JCTC
Objective: Position in the field of botany and/or environment sciences
Strategy: Heavy emphasis on three unique internship experiences, combined with a

thorough presentation of academic studies; minimal mention of unrelated work experience

Resume: Josie Vargas, page 95
Writer: Lorie Lebert, CPRW, IJCTC, CCMC
Objective: Position in critical care / emergency care nursing
Strategy: Strong introduction following by concise and easy-to-read summation of clinical training, supported by her achievements and experience in sports and fitness

Resume: Carla Saaks, pages 96-97
Writer: Myriam-Rose Kohn, CPRW, CEIP, JCTC, CCM, CCMC
Objective: Position marketing biomedical products and technologies
Strategy: Detailed presentation of graduate's science and business skills and experiences presented in a comprehensive review of educational background, work experience, and research/internship opportunities

DAVID BRADLEY
Video Game Programmer
1978 Ninth Avenue East, #12, Seattle, WA 98102 / 206-555-5555 / jcrowser@juno.net

Math wizard with over 5 years experience programming in C++ and a proven ability to meet tight development deadlines. Creative, tenacious approach to problem-solving has resulted in a reputation for "always finding a way."

"I am self-motivated, hard-working, and once I am given an opportunity, I always succeed. I promise to put in as many hours and as much sweat as necessary to become the best coder on your team."

Education

Bachelors of Science in Real Time Interactive Simulation (Minor in Mathematics)
DigiPen Institute of Technology, April 2004

Technical Skills

Languages... C/C++(5 years), Winsock (UDP/TCP 3 years), DirectX, DirectInput, Direct3D, DirectDraw, OpenGL, Windows API, Assembly (x86, Motorola, Game Boy Color), JavaScript, ASP, SQL, PHP
Tools.... Visual Studio (6.0/.net), Concurrent Versions System, Photoshop, Discreet 3D Studio Max.
Math/Graphics.... Algorithm/Numerical Analysis, Physics, Linear Algebra, Curves and Surfaces, Hidden Surface Removal, Inverse Kinematics, Skeletal Animation, Ray Tracing, Software rendering

Game Development Projects

Designer and Programmer: *The Deep* – real-time strategy game. Designed game, created technical specifications, and developed AI. The game was highlighted in Game Power magazine, Vol. 176 (p.25).

Producer and Senior Programmer: *Awaken* - vertical-scrolling 3D space shooter. Designed and developed enemy AI, core game code, and networking. Led team of six on this senior-year project which was awarded the "Best Game in Class" award for 2003.

Project Manager and Developer: *Starburst* - 3D space combat simulator. Created the direct input wrapper, designed and programmed the menu system, and enabled networking. Managed schedule and team of five.

Work Experience

DIGIPEN INSTITUTE OF TECHNOLOGY - TEACHING ASSISTANT   2003 – 2004

Lectured on object-oriented programming and designing data-driven applications. Scheduled and graded assignments and led class discussions.

HART CROWSER, INC., SEATTLE WA - INFORMATION TECHNOLOGIES (IT) INTERN 1999 – 2001

Maintained corporate network and provided on-call assistance for IT issues and problem-solving. Assisted with corporate conversion from Novell to NT.

Affiliations

Active Member, International Game Developers Association (IGDA)

Mark C. Hesse

1234 Frederick Street ➢ Wheaton, MD 20915   301.791.0794 ➢ mchesse@vt.edu

Entry-level Mechanical Engineer ➢ Design or Product Development

QUALIFICATIONS

➢ Recent college graduate with proven technical and analytical abilities.
➢ Engineering In Training (EIT) Exam Qualified.
➢ Hands-on design and mechanical engineering internship experience in a government setting.
➢ Self-initiative and ability to independently plan, develop, and complete projects efficiently.
➢ Persistence and discipline in testing, troubleshooting, and solving challenging problems.
➢ Windows 98/2000, AutoCAD R14/2002, MATLAB, Word, Excel, PowerPoint, C ++, MPLAB

EDUCATION & ACADEMIC EXPERIENCE

Bachelor of Science, Mechanical Engineering   December 2004
Virginia Polytechnic Institute and State University   Blacksburg, VA

Internship Experience

Engineering Technician   Summer 2004
Department of Defense, Engineering and Construction Division   Fort Detrick, MD
Worked on various civil and mechanical design projects. Developed technical, teamwork, and communication skills. Took initiative in assuming staff support functions to lighten workload. Earned a Certificate of Achievement from the Department of the Army for performance.

➢ **Civil Design Projects:** Independently drafted designs for an office room, a security gate installation, and wall sections added to improve security. Met with key internal customers and contacted outside vendors to define project requirements and specifications. Drafted designs with AutoCAD; made modifications to meet final approval of customers and Chief Engineer.

➢ **Mechanical Design Project:** Assisted mechanical engineering contractor with testing and modifying HVAC system to improve air flow for better climate control of a computer lab.

➢ **Staff Support:** Took over task of organizing CAD files and database for division secretary. Reworked CAD drawings for division engineers to fill gap left by retiring draftsman.

Senior Project: Proportional Fuel Injector Design   Aug 2003 – May 2004

Participated in a team project to design an active combustion control system for the gas turbine industry. Key contributor to Design Fabrication Group, responsible for successfully fabricating a piston bracket and designing a new throttling valve. Researched scaling effects to implement on existing operational system. Prepared memos, reports, and a PowerPoint presentation of accomplishments.

Mechanical Design Labs   Aug – Dec 2003

Participated in five-person team lab assignments to conduct performance testing, statistical and error analyses, and troubleshooting of various mechanical systems (a jet engine, residential air conditioner, hydraulic gate, and duct fan). Presented findings and corrective recommendations via PowerPoint presentations to students and faculty.

Educational Outreach Initiative   Aug – Dec 2002

Participated in an education and career awareness program for elementary and middle school students to rouse interest in engineering and physics as a future career path. Conducted physics experiments and educational presentations for student groups.

WORK EXPERIENCE

Held part-time jobs while carrying 15 + credits per semester and worked full-time during summers. **First National Bank**: processing back statements and telephone customer service; **Wal-Mart:** stocking frozen foods; **Back Street Pizza:** making deliveries.

Greg Vincent

8 Chappell Place
Rocklin, CA 95677

Mobile: (916) 818-6545
Residence: (916) 922-7876
Email: gv@one.net

Sound Engineer ~ Graduate

"This is a very slick recording. Well done"—Lecturer, UWS

A **passion for technical excellence**, an intense commitment to deliver to deadline, and the vision to inject creativity into everyday tasks are performance characteristics that have underscored work ethic throughout university studies and hands-on freelance assignments in sound engineering. Acknowledged by lecturers and clients as a meticulous trouble-shooter, rapid-paced learner, and independent thinker. Dedicated to enriching and maintaining the integrity of musical compositions of all genres, optimizing sound quality, capitalizing on equipment capabilities, and making a high-impact "behind-the-scenes" contribution.

Value Offered

- Sound Engineering
- Mixing and Synthesis
- Advanced MIDI Application
- Digital and Analogue Editing
- Time Management

- Microphone Technique
- Video Editing
- Script Writing
- Real-time Digital Signal Processing

- Sound Reinforcement
- Control Surface
- Analog Mixing Desk
- Instrument, Voice & Foley Recordings

Technology Snapshot: ProTools, Cubase, Logic, Cool Edit, DSP, Final Cut Pro, Premiere, Reason, Logic Control, Control 24, 02R, analogue desks.

Education

Bachelor of Arts Communication
University of California, May 2004

Academic Highlights

Recent examples of academic projects, challenges, and team work that support career goals

Music Technology
Solo project to produce a 24-track maximum, 5-minute recording. Secured services of popular local bands—*Five Flavored* and *Fergus Recliner*--to donate time to the project. Project challenges included band members with limited availability, excess noise on the night of recording due to a music festival, and a faulty analog-to-digital converter.

- Overcame external noise leakage and faulty equipment, by altering layout recording plan to four microphones, no drum effects, and two tracks for keyboard. Fine-tuned gates and expanders to eliminate ambient sound from the festival.
- Awarded a *distinction* for efforts. As evaluated by lecturer, *"This is a very slick recording. Well done. The documentation is great, and the data sessions well organized. The project is of a high standard."*

Media Arts—Sound Project
Independently recorded and mixed original music composition by local band, and augmented presentation with a re-mixed compilation of previous recordings presented as a sound biography. Achieved *distinction* result and top-of-the-class status for the subject.

Live Content
Produced 10 minutes of material focusing on MIDI in a live context using self-designed patches and networks, real-time digital signal processing, and sound reinforcement. One hour prior to performance, requested equipment had been incorrectly supplied, monitor connections were incompatible, and MIDI Controller Driver had been deleted. Quickly sourced correct monitors, installed back-up drivers on computer, and identified and resolved mixer issues affecting the PA system.

Special Freelance Projects

Tapestries of Melody
Recorded and arranged a CD of 8 classical Indian, Irish, folk, and improvised musical compositions featuring 10 instruments and several solo vocals. Produced a brief, biographical music showcase, interspersed with audio commentary by the group's founder edited from 40 minutes of discussion to 4 minutes of highlights.

- Promotional tool was an outstanding success, scoring job offers for the group throughout Rocklin and prompting a request to coordinate the group's live audio during their appearance at the Rocklin Global Carnival—the largest world music festival in the state.

- Produced *Tapestries of Melody* recordings over 5 days in a secluded mountain retreat. Captured unique feel of the group by experimenting with the use of microphones designed to capture the band, while eliminating extraneous household and instrument sounds. Devoted more than 50 hours to mixing 22 songs at both the retreat and in studio, and 10 hours editing the biography showcase.

Other Projects

- Entrusted by folk rock band *Fergus Settee* to resolve quality issues surrounding poor mix and distorted kick drum sound in separate tracks produced during a "rush job" by another sound engineer. Went back to basics and remixed songs to the band's satisfaction.

- Recorded studio songs and mixed live music tracks for *Fergus Settee* entitled *The Fisherman, Brown Cow, Mystery Train, The Letter, The Recliner,* and *Holding On.* Resolved flawed vocals and misplayed notes during mixing process. Musical compositions mixed have since received frequent radio airing.

- Recorded 8 songs for a classical group from India with 40 members, including 5 solo vocalists, a 30-person choir, and instruments including flute, guitar, veena, harmonium, violin, Jews Harp, and percussion section. With all group members new to studio environments, addressed all members on control-room protocols, procedures, and expectations of the recording sessions.

- Coordinated equipment hiring and mixed songs for 3 bands for a live community event. Overcame power-line electrical noise through the PA to deliver a sound performance commended by all bands as *"the best on-stage sound they have ever had."*

Casual Work Experience

Radio 3KY Rocklin   2003
Production Assistant
Independently networked among contacts to secure rare work experience opportunity with prominent radio station, Radio 3KY Rocklin. Reporting to the Manager of In-House Promotions, gained first-hand knowledge of operations, equipment, and broadcasting through observation and limited "hands-on" tasks.

- Contributed to round-table discussions on upcoming promotions for on-air personalities as well as strategies for marketing the prominent sports events.

- Trained in the use of RCS Selector and the Yamaha O2R digital mixing desk connected to DSP editing software where promotional clips were produced.

PATRUN STUDIOS, Rocklin   2001/2002
Work Experience/Assistant to Senior Sound Engineer

Company: Post-production specialists in television and radio advertisements.
Equipment: O2R, DSP, Drawmer DL 241 compressors, EMU e-Synth ultra, Sony PCM-7030 DAT recorder

Experience/observation engagement that provided insight into the technical aspects of compression. Learned methods for communicating with clients and talent to convey a genuine commitment to achieving the best outcomes possible.

- Edited raw-voice recording, adding sound effects and mixing it to DAT format. The production was considered superior with the artist using it as a talent showcase for securing new projects.

- Produced sound designs in studio that were included in an advertisement development project.

MICHAEL MOSBACH

■ 5575 Maureen Lane ■ Dublin, Ohio 43016 ■ Home: 614.793.4416 ■
■ Cellular: 614.374.1106 ■ Email: Michael@osu.edu ■

FOCUS: ELECTRICAL ENGINEERING

■ Service Engineer ■ Sales Engineer ■ Reliability Engineer ■

Significant capability managing all phases of R&D from analysis and requirements definition to design and implementation. Able to balance multiple priorities, manage change, and effectively handle the most challenging situations. Strong team player, able to successfully address and collaborate with laymen as well as technical professionals. Fluent in written and spoken Farsi.

Education:

MIAMI UNIVERSITY
Oxford, Ohio

Bachelor of Science
Electrical Engineering
Graduated: 2004
Major G.P.A. 3.94 – Dean's List

Courses of Study:

- **Circuit Design**
- **Logic Design**
- **Signals and Systems**
- **Micro Controllers**
- **Switch Circuit/Circuit Lab**
- **Material Science**
- **Semiconductor Devices**
- **Microelectronic Circuits**
- **Electromagnetics**
- **Digital Circuit Design**
- **Mixed Signal VLSI**
- **Digital VLSI Design**
- **Analog Integrated Circuits**
- **Engineering Economy Analysis**
- **Reliability**
- **ISE**
- **Energy Conversion Lab**
- **Electron Circuits Lab**
- **Calculus**
- **Ethics in Engineering**
- **Electric Machines**
- **Power Electronics**
- **Industrial/Commercial Power Systems**

Proficient with Magic, Cadence, Matlab, VLSI, Auto CAD, Basic C++ and Microsoft Office.

Engineering Projects:

- **DC Motor System:** As 1 of 5 team members, designed and tested entire motor drive system, employing forward/backward capable H-Bridge converter, within 3 months.

  Project initiative specified DC motor must be operable at multiple speeds and cost less than $80 total. Personal responsibility included location of transformer and bridge rectifier within both budget parameters as well as technical specifications. Final results and project progression detailed in full and presented to professor and peers.

- **Op Amp Project:** Contributed as 1 of 3 members tasked with design of 2-stage MOSFET Op Amp using cadence software.

  Objective included provision of higher gain than single-stage differential operational amplifier. Defined project layout and formulas, determined transistor width, length, and current flow, and developed scheme of amp employing cadence software. Personal responsibility included determination of layout and mathematical equations needed to locate parts specifications.

- **Audio Signal Manipulation:** Project involved turning analog signal into digital signal employing A/D converter, sent through communication link (IR link), and reconstructed into analog form using D/A converter. Employed 2 voltage regulators and oscillator to generate signal, filter, level shifter, and amplifier. Project completed with music sent from audio source through circuit path and connected to speaker with minimal distortion.

Professional Experience:

Rhonda's Pizza ... Columbus, Ohio (1995 – Present)
Popular chain of family pizza restaurants with 120 retail outlets.

Delivery Driver
Expedite product delivery, assure security of cash receipts, and demonstrate excellent customer service. Recognized for adhering to high company standards.

Train new associates providing insight into order processing, quality and logistics. Assume responsibility for effective and efficient resolution to customer complaints resulting in win-win situation for both customer and company.

- **Awarded "Employee of the Month" several times for demonstrated honesty, commitment to excellence, and fast-paced work style.**
- **Recognized and valued by all General Managers for ability to outperform colleagues during high-demand delivery periods;** average twice as many deliveries per hour over other drivers, enabling reduction in drivers during slow periods and saving company labor costs.
- **Participate in product promotion, using suggestive selling techniques during phone-in orders.**

ANDREW T. FRANKLIN

860 Wisconsin Lane • Elk Grove Village, Illinois 60007
Home: 847.555.2982 • Cell: 847.444.3827
E-mail: Andrew_Franklin@anyisp.com

ENGINEERING DESIGN AND DRAFTING PROFESSIONAL
Architectural, Civil, and Mechanical Engineering Applications

---

Comprehensive experience in architectural, civil, and mechanical engineering disciplines gained through formal education and paid internship in civil engineering firm. Well-versed in federal, state and local safety regulations and building codes. Background also includes 4+ years in the retail sector, with 2 years in management. Known for completing assignments in a prompt, accurate manner. Articulate communicator with management, peers, clients, and subordinates. *Areas of strength & skill sets include:*

- Residential & Commercial Projects
- Blueprint Reading
- Site Plan Preparation
- Storm Water Management

- Drafting & Technical Writing
- Interpretation of Working Drawings
- Highway Designs
- Parametric Modeling Design

- Computer & Technical Proficiencies: AutoCAD 2000-02-04; Bentley Microstation; ProEngineer; AutoDesk Inventor; Mechanical Desktop; AutoDesk Architecture; 3D Rendering; Model-making

---

ACADEMIC ACHIEVEMENTS

UNIVERSITY OF ILLINOIS (CIRCLE CAMPUS) – Chicago, Illinois   *May 2004*
Bachelor of Science Degree – Engineering Graphics & Design – GPA: Major, 3.31; Overall, 2.79
- Core Classes: Design & Graphic Communication; CAD Applications; Manufacturing Processes & Materials; Architectural Drawing & Residential Planning; Computer Graphics & Design; Engineering Graphics; Construction Systems; Strength of Materials; Statistics for Technology; Machine Tool Processes; Architectural Drafting/Multi-Family Design; Machine Drawing; Plant Layout & Material Handling; Advanced Study in CAD; Fundamentals of Management; Engineering Economy

---

PROFESSIONAL INTERNSHIP

ABC DESIGN GROUP – Chicago, Illinois   *May 2003 to May 2004*
(Civil engineering consulting firm providing site plans, surveying, waste management, storm water management, and highway design services for client companies. Employs 15.)

Draftsman– Internship
Worked under supervision of licensed civil engineers. Supported commercial and residential project assignments throughout Illinois and Wisconsin. Created site plans, engineering designs/layouts, and storm water management configurations (limited to preparation on the Bentley Microstation system), and performed surveys.

ANDREW T. FRANKLIN

860 Wisconsin Lane • Elk Grove Village, Illinois 60007
Home: 847.555.2982 • Cell: 847.444.3827
E-mail: Andrew_Franklin@anyisp.com

PAGE 2

Key Projects:

- *Highway Design (10 miles, 4 lanes, 5 exit ramps and cloverleaves, located in Chicago, IL):* Used Bentley Microstation to implement highway design, drainage of surrounding creeks and rivers as well as existing utilities and property. Implemented plan revisions per red-marked instructions from supervisors and co-workers.

- *Indoor Tennis Facility (10,000 sq. ft. on a 3-4 acre lot located in Chicago, IL):* Surveyed portion of the lot, set future building corners, and prepared facility site plan, including the future building, parking lot, and storm water management configurations.

- *Fifth Third Bank Building (3,000 sq. ft. on 1-2 acre lot located in Chicago, IL):* Prepared key sections of site plan.

- *Church buildings (4 structures total; average lot size: 2-3 acres; Chicago, IL):* Created site plans to set property corners and settle boundary disputes. Prepared layout of building corners.

- *Habitat for Humanity (Residential, low-income housing community):* Performed surveys and prepared site plans for 3 single-family homes located in Cicero, IL.

EMPLOYMENT EXPERIENCE

VALUE-FRESH *(Local grocery chain; 4 locations in Illinois)* – Wheeling, Illinois   *1999 to 2003*

Second Assistant Manager (2001 to 2003), promoted from Cashier and Stock Associate (1999 to 2001)
- Worked part-time while attending school, supporting general manager in all store operations, including sales, customer service, purchasing, merchandising, and training new employees.
- Independently managed the chemicals/cleaning items department.

CUB FOODS *(National retail grocery store chain)* – Arlington Heights, Illinois   *1998 to 1999*

Customer Service and Stock Associate (Part-time)
- Set up merchandising displays, stocked shelves, carried out purchases for customers, and trained new associates.

EXCELLENT REFERENCES WILL BE PROVIDED UPON REQUEST

RYANNA M. ZANTON

82870 Brannon Station Drive
Charlotte, North Carolina 29867
704.980-5528
rzantonr@nc.rr.com

MULTI-LINGUAL SOFTWARE PRODUCT DEPLOYMENT STRATEGIST

Critical, multi-year internship experience in product development management, deploying project and products in software, Internet, and Web-based application service provider areas.

* *Software Product Development*	* *CTO/VP Level Relations/Communications*
* *Reengineering/Process Improvement*	* *Business Dependencies/Impact/Cause-Effect*
* *High-Visibility IT Project Management*	* *Direct Customer/Vendor Administration*
* *Software Product Release Management*	* *Cross Product Line Software Releases*
* *Risk Management Solutions*	* *Web-Based Application Service Provider*
* *Staff Selection and Training*	* *Company Visioning/Direction Leadership*
* *Cross-Functional Group Mediation*	* *Team-Focused Coach/Leader/Motivator*
* *International/Worldwide Product Focus*	* *ASP Software Space*
* *Creative Resource Leveling*	* *Multi-lingual: French, Portuguese, German, Spanish*

- *Key player in the design and implementation of offshore development projects. Successfully collaborated with national and international teams to plan and execute development projects. Successes include high-visibility, high-risk project management. Effectively manages offshore development resources (India, Pakistan, Turkey).*
- *Successfully implemented company's globalization processes with a focus on continuous improvement practices. Strategic focus has been on internationalization, globalization, localizability, and localization processes.*
- *In-depth understanding of dependencies, impacts, cause and effect related to projects and product releases.*
- *Leader of high-profile projects, managing project teams that include software developers, QA testers, business analysts, architects, data center engineers, and management teams.*

EDUCATION

UNIVERSITY OF CHARLOTTE, Charlotte, NC
Bachelor of Science in Electronic Engineering Technologies, August 2004
- **Minor in Language Studies**

PROFESSIONAL EXPERIENCE

CHARLOTTE LINCOLN DEVELOPERS, Charlotte, NC
Project Support Director- Intern (4/02 – 5/04)
In Support of Project Director:
- Identified and implemented company's globalization processes with a focus on continuous improvement practices. Promoted education at an enterprise level, influencing future product features, solutions, and service decisions.
- Utilized language skills (Spanish, German, English, Portuguese, French) for global client base.
- Developed new partner relationship with a software product globalization vendor. Achieved simultaneous delivery of the base product and the first localized product.
- Analyzed product internationalization and localization readiness; advised company's products and services globalization plans for short- and long-term strategies..
- Project-managed the product-launch process; direct cross-functional national and international representative teams through every functional area of the company.
- Oversaw launch readiness and SOPs that resulted in higher client satisfaction and increased communication.
- Dresdal software development and utilization: XML, C#, C++, HTML, ASP, Visual Basic, .NET technologies, SQL Server 7 and Win 2K, and Active Directory.

DOUGLAS R. HALL

450 Main Street, Mukwonago, WI 53149
Telephone: (262) 363-5555, E-mail: doughall@email.com

EDUCATION

Bachelor of Business Administration, University of Wisconsin, December 2003
- Double Majors: **Management Computer Systems (MCS)** and **Spanish**
- Cumulative GPA: 3.74 on a 4.0 scale
- Member of the following honor societies: Phi Kappa Phi, Golden Key, and Beta Gamma Sigma.

Technical Skills:

Operating Systems:	Microsoft Windows 98/00/XP/NT
Languages:	Java, Pascal, COBOL, SQL
Web Development:	XHTML, Active Server Pages (ASP), JavaServer Pages (JSP), JavaScript
Database Tools:	CAST SQL-Builder, Embarcadero Rapid SQL
Software:	Microsoft Office (Word, Excel, PowerPoint, Access)
Platforms:	PowerBuilder running against a Sybase database

Language Skills:	Fluent in **Spanish**. Studied abroad for three semesters in Monterey, Mexico, Valladolid, Spain, and Quepos, Costa Rica.

PROFESSIONAL EXPERIENCE

DYNAMIC INFORMATION SYSTEMS (DIS), Pewaukee, WI   2002–Present
Intern, Software Development Department/Information Systems (IS) Division

Serve as a member of a five-person software development team to program, implement, and support systems for the Customer Service, Press, and Finishing business units.
- Maintain, enhance, and expand a major production application which was written in-house by our team.
- Serve on cross-organizational teams which leverage resources in order to complete critical projects.
- Perform development for an electronic job-specific production ticketing tool:
  - Ensure consistent data and uninterrupted communication, among more than 11,000 employees at plants in five states, for data entry and reporting purposes.
  - Maintain related views via the customer home page which are accessed by major media clients.
- Support tools for customer service representatives that facilitate customer job information throughout the fulfillment process (scheduling, imaging, pressing, and distributing).

Key Project:
- Participated in a major initiative to implement a new business approach which significantly reduced customer service representatives' input time.

BREWER TEMPORARY AGENCY, Pewaukee, WI   2000-2001
Technical Staff Assistant, City of Pewaukee, WI Department of Human Resources (HR)

Increased across-the-board efficiency for maintaining employee records by creating a relational database which reengineered a decentralized, paper-intensive HR system for the City's 1,500 employees.
- Interviewed HR personnel in order to identify user requirements for a functional database.
- Provided user training to all office personnel and created a systems reference guide.
- Trained a member of the City's IT Department so that he could oversee ongoing database maintenance.

Administrative Staff Member

Completed short-term administrative and clerical assignments at various manufacturing firms.

Juan Gonzalez

2712 Ridge Road   Jackson, MI 49201   juangonz@isp.com
                                                                          517-555-2143

HIGHLIGHTS OF QUALIFICATIONS:

- ❖ **BBA** with concentration in Food Marketing; additional coursework in marketing research, logistics, category management and merchandising.
- ❖ Demonstrated initiative and leadership qualities; able to creatively problem-solve and adapt to challenges.
- ❖ Hands-on experience in the field leading to understanding of the industry's needs and its relationship with customers' perspectives.
- ❖ Experienced in making presentations to decision makers. Strong team player.
- ❖ Technology: Microsoft Office • Access • Publisher • SPSS Analysis • AC Nielsen • IRI • Spectra • Apollo Space Management

EDUCATION:

Eastern Michigan University • Ypsilanti, Michigan   2004
Bachelor of Business Administration
- • Major: Food Marketing
- • Kmart Stores Food Marketing Scholarship (2003-2004)

PROFESSIONAL EXPERIENCE:

General Foods Co. • Detroit, Michigan   2003-2004
Sales Representative/Merchandiser/Intern
- • Coordinated the availability, placement, and appearance of approximately 44 General Foods and its partnering brand products in 16 Kroger accounts across Michigan.
- • Made cold calls and pre-sell presentations to Kroger in-store order writers to ensure adequate product volume for advertised sales and unadvertised promotions.
- • Merchandised product, built displays, and applied signage and point-of-sale materials.
- • Performed category resets, adhering to pre-negotiated shelf diagrams.
- • Independently tracked and documented weekly advertisements for General Foods, its partnering brands, and competitor products for sales analysis.
- • Negotiated the placement of freestanding displays with store management.
- • Converted internship position into part-time employment following graduation.

Vernors Beverage Company • Detroit, Michigan   2003
Sales Intern
- • As direct sales distributor, merchandised inventory on shelves and displays in chain and independent grocery stores. Acted as liaison with store management.
- • Monitored and reported on market condition changes to facilitate accurate sales goals.
- • Conducted category resets through implementation of plan-o-grams and other merchandising aids such as point-of-sale material.
- • Assisted category manager with obtaining and analyzing performance measurements.
- • Conducted category field audits to assess performance.

Bavarian Inn • Frakenmuth, Michigan   2002-2003
Retail Sales Team Member – Schnitzelbank & Royal Gift Shops
- • Assisted customers with merchandise selection and purchase in boutique-style gift shops.
- • Displayed inventory according to established visual standards and guidelines, applying cross-merchandising techniques to increase profitability.

Laura L. Petersen

2896 Wheeler Road
Bloomfield, New York 14469
(585) 657-8346
LaLePetersen@frontiernet.net

NYS Provisional Certification - Elementary Education (1-6)

Education:

New York State Teacher Certification Examinations:
LAST Examination - Score: 268; EAST-Written Examination - Score: 255
Multi-Subject Examination - Score: 246

Bachelor of Arts, Elementary Education   **May 2004**
Nazareth College of Rochester; Rochester, New York

Significant Courses:

- Special Needs Elementary Classroom
- Teaching Culturally Responsive Language Arts
- Psychological Foundations of Elementary Ed
- Social Foundations of Elementary Education
- Exploring Educational Issues

- Using Media in Education
- Basic Reading Instruction
- Learning Elementary Math
- Teaching Elementary Science
- Children's Literature

NYS Regents Diploma   **June 1999**
Our Lady of Mercy High School; Rochester, New York

Teaching Experience:

Board of Cooperative Educational Services (BOCES); Fairport, New York
Per Diem Substitute Teacher's Aide   **2000 - Present**
Have spent approximately 200 days in Special Education classrooms over the past four years. Work one-on-one and in small groups with students from pre-school to adult, supporting them in learning motor skills and activities of daily living (ADL). Students include those with emotional and behavioral disabilities, physical disabilities, autism, and other developmental disabilities.

Lake Ontario Elementary School; Watertown, New York
Student Teacher - Fifth Grade   **Mar.-May 2004**
Instructed 24 students in an inclusion environment, during this seven-week assignment.
- Developed and taught science units on matter and the periodic table.
- Created and implemented lesson plans and learning strategies for poetry and literature.
- Led two different reading groups, based on students' skill levels.
- Supported implementation of IEPs to address the needs of individual students.

Student Teacher - First Grade   **Jan.-Mar. 2004**
Instructed 19 students over a nine-week period.
- Developed and implemented lesson plans for phonics, addition/subtraction, and social studies.
- Designed various hands-on activities to engage students in the learning process.
- Led reading groups at various skill levels.

Maurice Sendak Elementary School; Kingston, New York
Practicum / Observation (Block II) - Kindergarten   **Oct.-Nov. 2003**
Observed classroom management techniques and developed/delivered lessons for 20 students in all-day kindergarten class.

Eric Caryle Elementary School; Kingston, New York
Practicum / Observation (Block I) - Fourth Grade   **Mar.-May 2003**
Observed classroom techniques and taught lessons in reading and writing to a class of 25 students.

Placement File Available Upon Request

90

MARCUS BLACKMARR

2323 Hopetown Road
Rocklin CA 95677

Email: blackmarr@opto.com

Telephone: (916) 555-0442
Mobile: (916) 443 5532

CONSTRUCTION MANAGEMENT & ECONOMICS STUDENT

Award winner: Johnson Martin Heritage Prize for Excellence
Student Member: American Institute of Quantity Surveyors • California Institute of Building (CIB)

TARGET: PROJECT MANAGER • CONSTRUCTION MANAGER • QUANTITY SURVEYOR • CONTRACT ADMINISTRATOR • SITE MANAGER

Accomplished Construction Management and Economics student distinguished from peers through superior academic performance and broad, real-world experiences in technical troubleshooting environments. Praised by peers, lecturers, and managers for solutions-focused and service-oriented approach; a pragmatic, commonsense professional adept in achieving genuine results—either as a team collaborator or solo performer. Keen to fast-track knowledge through hands-on industry experiences.

Professional strengths include:

Building Measurement • Project Cost Control • Critical Problem Solving • Strategy Development • Team Leadership • Client Relationship Management • Contract Administration • Technical Troubleshooting • Information Dissemination/Research

EDUCATION | TRAINING

Bachelor of Construction Management & Economics
University of California (2004)

INDUSTRY PLACEMENT | WORK EXPERIENCE

MCDONALD CONSTRUCTION SERVICES   2/2004–4/2004
Project Bluestream: 2 apartment complexes, San Diego. 25 apartments and 7 office suites.
2-month industry placement. Prepared tenders and quantity estimations and negotiated best price on vendor services and materials. Supported site/project managers, administered contracts, and performed on-site labor.

MALBERG GAS & POWER PTY LTD   5/2002–11/2002
Provider of environmentally friendly "green power" servicing 10,000 homes.
7-month paid internship. Monitored across-the-board business compliance to protocols surrounding systems, security, and operational control standards across all power stations. Provided technical support to all users of the network, and ensured back-up and activity log processes were consistent and error-free.

• Spearheaded electronic engine fleet maintenance scheduling system that virtually eliminated human error and boosted organizational efficiencies.

UNIVERSITY OF CALIFORNIA   6/2001–4/2002
Network Support Analyst, Faculty of Medicine & Dentistry
Progressed problematic network to new professional level that eased the administrative burden on all faculty staff. From a congested, error- and virus-prone system, the infrastructure was transformed through the implementation of a Windows 2000 standard operating environment. Personally conducted staff training, configured all services and devices, and trouble-shot hardware and software issues.

Susan J. Davenport

527 Glenview Avenue, Apt #115, Los Angeles, CA 90024
(858) 555-5555 / susand@net.net

ENTRY-LEVEL CASTING · FILM PRODUCTION · DEVELOPMENT

Value Summary

High-energy professional eager to make a positive contribution to a production company. Known for willingness to go "over and above," working long hours in challenging circumstances to get the job done. Experience includes casting, production, development, and talent agency work – all while studying full-time and writing an award-winning screenplay.

Educational Achievements

University of California, Irvine - **B.A., English and Film Studies** (December 2004)

Honors & Awards
Dean's Honor's List
Recipient of 2004 Junior Writer's Guild Screenplay Award for *Leaving David*
Finalist in 2003 Cinematric Annual Screenwriting Awards for *Leaving David*

Entertainment Industry Experience

Casting Intern – MELDER-BROWN CASTING, Los Angeles   **March 2004 – Present**

Assist five casting directors in this busy office. Review actor submissions, schedule audition appointments, correspond with agents, and assist in audition sessions. Also provide phone coverage and general administrative support to casting directors.

Acquisition and Development Intern – iLEVEL, Los Angeles   **May 2003 – Sept 2003**

Screened and read incoming scripts for the development director. Assisted with marketing activities, including compiling media kits, in addition to performing clerical tasks and running frequent errands.

Talent Agency Intern – MNP, Los Angeles   **June 2002 – Aug 2002**

Provided full support to three agents. Accountabilities included the distribution of breakdowns, compiling submissions, contacting talent, screening query letters, organizing tape library, and handling general administration for all three agents.

Production Intern – CINEMAKERS, Los Angeles   **June 2001 – Aug 2002**

Reported directly to the Producer of *Hats Off*, a long-running CBS TV series. Conducted online research for storylines, provided support to the casting director, and assisted writers with clerical work and errands. Worked directly with the CEO on proposals for potential investors.

Endorsements

"Susan will never let you down. She always reminded me of the Energizer bunny ... it doesn't matter how late it gets or how overwhelming the task ... Susan just keeps going and going."
Joyce Mays, Casting Director.

"I can't thank Susan enough for her contributions to my talent agency. She is just as willing to make coffee and run errands as she is to take on the glamorous assignments."
David Braine, Talent Agent

"Hire Susan and hire her now! She is an absolute burst of energy and a truly talented writer. She has a big future ahead of her in this industry. Mark my words ... hire her now or someone else will!"
Emily Parr, Retired Producer

JANE RUALANA

Career Target: Researcher - Bali Primate Research Center	*809 Everpines Way, Edmonds, Washington, 98106* *425.777.9999 - email: macque99@hotmail.com*

Qualifications

- Dedicated, durable, detailed, caring team player with genuine interest in primates and cultures.
- Undaunted by and adaptable to harsh surroundings. Lived in Bali in rustic conditions.
- Learn languages quickly. Bilingual in Spanish. Some sign language gained during CWU research.

Education

Central Washington University, Ellensburg, Washington

B.S., Primate Behavior and Ecology, and B.A., Anthropology, 2004, cum laude. GPA 3.6.

Review Session, Human Variation Class – Chosen by professor to lead mid-term review.

Top Classes: Human Variation, Long-Term Primate Studies, Primate Social Behavior, Primatology Lab, American Sign Language, General Ecology, Introduction to Evolutionary Psychology

Research Experience

Chimpanzee and Human Communication Institute, Central Washington University

- *Intern - Weekend Docent, Chimposium Program, September 2001 – June 2004*
  Joined program as one of 22 interns, remaining as one of 11 to finish. Worked 10 hours a week in addition to classroom studies, cleaning, preparing meals, doing laundry, and answering phones. Logged notes on behavior and socialization patterns. Used special notation to keep journals. Updated database. Maintained sign logs.

- *Studies & Tests*
  — Took Chimp ID and Chimp Taxonomy test to qualify for Chimpcare, ranking in top 10%.
  — Post-Conflict Interaction Study – Observed chimps in 1-hour intervals, recording proximity of chimps to one another. Recorded conflictive behaviors while second researcher timed events.

- *Selected to participate in Chimpcare, April, 2003*
  Initially assisted trainer, serving meals, providing interaction/playtime, and asking chimps if they wanted to play. Promoted to feeding and interacting with chimps independently while trainer stayed in the kitchen. Administered vitamins and medicine when chimps were sick.

Field Experience in Bali, Indonesia with Professor Agustin Fuentes, Anthropology

- *Volunteer – June 2002 – July 2002*
  Selected to participate in international field training co-sponsored by Univeristas Udayana and CWU. Lectures included: Balinese Religion and Conservation – Infectious/non-infectious diseases in monkey with emphasis on athropozoonosis – Primatology in Source Countries. Gained knowledge and experience in:
  — Methods and theories of videography in behavioral research
  — Theories and methods of behavioral observation
  — Survey and census techniques
  — Observational data collection of macaque groups at various free-ranging and semi-free ranging sites around the Island of Bali

Other Experience

October 2002 – present – Bartender, Private Parties and Catered Events.
Summer 2000 – Hostess – Held two jobs – Mama's Cantina & Lounge and Westin Seattle Hotel

BELINDA A. LINCOLN

672 Blackberry Crescent / Pittsford, New York 14534 / (585) 248-7749   BALincoln@yahoo.com

OBJECTIVE: *A position leading to a career in Botany and/or Environmental Sciences.*

EDUCATION:

May 2004   **Bachelor of Science, Biology (Minor: Environmental Studies)**
State University of New York College at Stony Brook; Stony Brook, New York
Cum Laude Graduate / Dean's List / GPA: 3.70
Tri-Beta (Biology Honorary) / Golden Key / Senior Plant Biology Award

Significant Courses:

- Environmental Management
- Taxonomy of Vascular Plants
- Evolutionary Ecology
- Conservation & Resource Management
- Principles of Ecology

- Hydroponics
- Plant Physiology
- Plant Diversity
- Analytical Physics
- Organic Chemistry

RELEVANT EXPERIENCE:

Summer 2004   **Research Associate, SUNY Stony Brook, Stony Brook, New York**
Served as Taxonomist for grant-funded study entitled "Proposal for Initial Analysis of Macrophyte Growth in Keuka Lake."
- Collected and identified aquatic plant species.
- Assisted in measurement and analysis of macrophyte biomass.
- Prepared graphs of transect depth profiles and biomass changes.
- Assisted scuba divers with sample collection and field observations.

Spring 2004   **Lab Instructor / Lab Assistant, SUNY Stony Brook; Stony Brook, New York**
Accountable for instructing 12 freshman biology students in laboratory setting.
- Lectured students on theory behind lab experiments.
- Monitored students during lab sessions and offered assistance as appropriate.
- Prepared and graded quizzes; contributed to preparing final quiz.
Assisted in Plant Physiology lab course with 20 students.
- Answered students' questions; guided students in lab procedures.
- Prepared materials for labs and assisted lab instructor as needed.

Summer 2003   **Internship, NYS Department of Environmental Conservation; Geneseo, New York**
Supported DEC staff on a variety of projects.
- Assisted in wetland delineations and establishing mean high-water marks.
- Reviewed Article 15 Permit applications and participated in compliance inspections.
- Developed and delivered educational presentations to community groups.
- Constructed waterfowl nesting structures and worked on improvements to Pleasant Point Nature Center trails.
- Conducted plant inventory of unique communities at Pleasant Point Nature Center.
- Assisted state forester with timber marking activities.

COMPUTER SKILLS:

Microsoft Office (PowerPoint, Excel); Delta Graph.

ADDITIONAL WORK EXPERIENCE:

2003 - Present	**Waitress, Tia Maria's Mexican Restaurant; Pittsford, New York**
2002 - 2004	**Customer Service / Plant Care, Forsythia Florists; Stony Brook, New York**
Summer 2002	**Customer Service, Captain Tony's Pizza; Pittsford, New York**
Summer 2001	**Waitress, Hawthorne's Restaurant; Pittsford, New York**
2000 - 2001	**Customer Service, Petersen's Flower Shop; Rochester, New York**

References Available Upon Request

Josie Vargas
cell: 810.444.4550 · jvargas@bigfoot.net

CANDIDATE: Critical Care / ER / Cardiology / ICU / Medical-Surgical / Trauma Nurse
FOCUS: To provide comprehensive quality patient care in an acute care unit/department

---

Qualifications Profile – Patient advocate with advanced knowledge, professional drive, and high motivation. Dedicated medical professional committed to quality care and ongoing education. Excellent problem-solving skills demonstrated through physical assessment of chronically ill patients, use of multiple types of equipment, and general knowledge of nursing procedures.

Fluent in Spanish (spoken and written); Good computer skills (Microsoft applications, Internet)

Registered Nurse License *(in process)* – State of Michigan

EDUCATION

WAYNE STATE UNIVERSITY; Detroit, MI
Bachelor of Science Degree in Nursing · December 2004 – *Summa Cum Laude*

MICHIGAN STATE UNIVERSITY; East Lansing, MI
Bachelor of Science Degree in Biopsychology & Cognitive Sciences · December 2000

CLINICAL TRAINING/RELEVANT EXPERIENCE

September-December 2004
Critical Care (ICU / Cardiac) – University Hospital; Detroit, MI
Community / Home Care – McCasland Home Care; St. Clair Shores, MI

May-August 2004
Pediatrics (Renal, Oncology, Hematology) - Children's Hospital; Chicago, IL
Obstetrics – Chicago Hope Hospital; Chicago, IL

January-April 2004
Mental Health – Providence Hospital; Southfield, MI
Medical/Surgical (Adult Inpatient) – VA Hospital; Detroit / Seaway Hospital; Redford, MI

September-December 2003
Geriatrics – St. Matthew Elderly Living Center; Detroit, MI
Urology / Renal – Martin Memorial Hospital; Dearborn, MI

August 2001-October 2002
Emergency Room Assistant – Joseph Trace Hospital; Ypsilanti, MI

OTHER EXPERIENCE

NOVI ATHLETIC CLUB; Novi, MI
Certified Fitness Instructor · April 2002-present
Taught group fitness classes and promoted exercise and proper diet to health club members. Educated individuals and explained special training programs. Led martial arts and taught barbell toning class. Trained other instructors in choreography techniques.

FRAMINGHAM FIELD HOCKEY CAMP; Framingham, CT — **Staff Coach** · 2002

MSU FIELD HOCKEY CAMP; East Lansing, MI — **Coach** · 2001 & 2003

AWARDS & RECOGNITION

Golden Key Honor Society · 2001-04 / **Sigma Theta Tau Nursing Honor Society** · 2004

All Region-All American · 2002 / Field Hockey Big Ten Championship · 2002 / Big Ten Defensive Player of the Year Candidate · 2002 / North-South Senior All Star · 2002

Michigan State University Alumni Association **Senior Leadership Award** · 2000

Latino Academic Scholarship Recipient · 1999

Recipient of **Michigan Competitive Scholarship** – Varsity Athlete · 1998-99

CARLA SAAKS

24583 Canvas Street No. 133-7
Agua Dulce, California 91350

805 694-1537
saaks@socal.rr.com

BUSINESS DEVELOPMENT / PRODUCT DEVELOPMENT
BIOMEDICAL ENGINEER

Unique understanding of both business and science issues

Recent bachelor's degree in Biomedical Engineering with emphasis on business development. Technical skills include extensive laboratory and field research as well as participation in business assessments and creation of economic plans. Excel at strategizing and logical thinking. Read and understand grant submissions. Natural team leader, yet also participatory team member. Self-starting in implementation. Traveled extensively; understanding of cultural diversities; fluent in conversational Spanish.

Creative, proactive, process-oriented and marketing-focused. Ability to develop rapport and build relationships with customers and clients through attention to detail in defining needs and providing service and solutions to meet those needs. Keen organizational, analytical, problem-solving and decision-making ability. Articulate communicator with effective interpersonal and presentation skills.

Easy interaction with people at all levels (R&D, engineers, senior management, clients, community) whether communicating in business or in science. Committed to high ethical standards; reputation for tenacity, honesty, and integrity.

EDUCATION

Bachelor of Science, Biomedical Engineering, University of Southern California, May 2004

Relevant Coursework

Biology	General Biology, Molecular Biology, Quantitative Physiology, Quantitative Neuroscience, Biological Computer Simulation Methodology
Chemistry	General Chemistry, Organic Chemistry
Laboratory	Microscopy, Centrifugation, Distillation, Reflux, NMR Spectroscopy, Gas Chromatography
Clinical	Initial History and Examination Interview, Basic Physical Examination
Electrical	Linear Circuit Analysis and Design, System Analysis and Design
Mathematics	3 levels of calculus including Multivariable and Multidimensional, Differential and Linear Equations
Physics	Newtonian, Electricity, Magnetism, Optics, Quantum, Relativity
Computer	C Programming, MatLab, Mathematica, LabView, Microsoft Office Suite (Word, Excel, PowerPoint), PhotoShop

Certificate, Business Program, University of Washington, Summer 2003

Relevant Courses and Course Work
Finance, Accounting, Organizational Behavior, Marketing, Human Resources Management, Business Law, Strategy. Attended numerous seminars conducted by senior executive managers from various well-known companies.

Project: Microsoft X-Box Division
As participatory team member, analyzed product and people, studied organizational structure and financials, and performed SWOT analysis of team and market analysis. Upon project completion, provided Microsoft with recommendations and a business plan for this product.

WORK EXPERIENCE

STUDENT RESEARCHER, USC - Los Angeles, CA   Spring 2004

Wrote computer program and studied cardiac output. Analyzed scientific data from past research.

INTERN, Coltech - Monterey, CA   Summer 2003

Scope of responsibility was three-fold:
- **Assisted CEO** with business and research plans. Learned how money was allotted. Observed interviews when PhDs presented their research.
- **Worked closely with Senior Project Leaders:** participated in brainstorming and problem-solving sessions; contributed ideas to development process.
- Lab: **Gene Cloning Project** contributing to a larger arthritis study. Compiled and analyzed data and performed separation process. Held discussions with academic specialists (advisors) and followed through on advice and decisions.

STUDENT ENVIRONMENTAL RESEARCHER - Atenas, Costa Rica   Summer 2002
School for Field Studies

One of 7 team members to **write an economic plan** for Volcan Poas National Park which was implemented in January 2003 and is currently still in place. Park offers various services among which are guided hiked tours and a gift shop. The plan was to provide efficient pricing and use of resources to increase profits. Project required tremendous community interaction, tourist and employee surveillance (2500 people). Used strategy, organizational behavior, marketing and financial analyses to provide a comprehensive plan.

One of 5 team members to **write a case study** concerning the biological reserve. Studied Costa Rica's methods for environmental sustainability, conducted field research into the flora and fauna of the rainforest, analyzed the area, and acquired knowledge regarding economics behind logging, cattle, agriculture. Reserve accepted recommendations made. Analyzed possible implementation in the U.S.

Gained trust though understanding; coordinated functions to promote interaction between the people of Atenas and School for Field Studies' students.

MEDICAL ASSISTANT, San Fernando Center for Pain Management - San Fernando, CA   2000 - 2002

Business   Managed front office. Handled all administrative duties: scheduled appointments, prepared invoices; dealt with patients and insurance companies.

Medical   Performed initial history and physical examinations. Assisted physician with patient examinations and performed injections. Consulted with patients about health-related matters.

RESEARCH ASSISTANT, UCLA Center for Reproductive Health, Valencia, CA   Fall 1999

Observed medical procedures in removing and replacing follicles and ovum, participated in semen analysis, and assisted with labor procedures for in-vitro fertilization. Brainstormed better methods for the procedure to improve retrieval methods and achieve higher success rates.

CHAPTER 6

Best Resumes to Highlight Athletics, Volunteerism, and Leadership Achievements

Overview

For many graduating students, their greatest selling point (in addition to their college degree) is their active participation in competitive athletics, their long record of volunteerism, and/or their demonstration of outstanding group, team, or personal leadership skills. Each of these communicates a message of top performance, integrity, and commitment, all of which are essential for a company to make a good hire. In turn, your objective is to write a resume where this information is the foundation around which you build everything else.

If you fall into this category of college graduate, the focal point of your resume should be:

- Your involvement in high school, collegiate, community, recreational, or professional sports; any honors or awards you or your teams received; any sports leadership activities or positions; personal athletic achievements; and more.
- Your record of volunteering, whether community-based, school-based, or otherwise; the particular organizations and their missions; your assignments, activities, contributions, and achievements; and more.
- Your experience in leading organizations, teams, and other groups; what your specific role was in each group; your most notable contributions and achievements; professional skills you acquired through these activities; and more.

Whether listed at the top of your resume in your Professional Skills Summary, in your Education section, under Employment Experience, or in a separate section (e.g., Athletic Achievement, Volunteer Contributions, Leadership Experience), these skills and experiences should be prominently highlighted on your resume to get the most impact and the best results. Companies want to hire people that are energetic, enthusiastic, and committed, with strong communication, team-building, and leadership skills. Let them know that you're that candidate!

Index of Resumes Featured in This Chapter

Objective: General business position, preferably with an international organization

Strategy: Focus on unique international and cross-cultural educational opportunities

Resume: David Reese, page 109

Writer: Eva Mullen, CPRW

Objective: Professional position in architecture and/or environmental design

Strategy: Focus on volunteerism within the art and architecture community

Resume: Hillary Elaine Snow, pages 110-111

Writer: Arnold G. Boldt, CPRW, JCTC

Objective: Entry-level professional position in a general business capacity

Strategy: Combined emphasis on volunteerism, leadership, education, and community outreach to allow this graduate (with no clear objective) to apply for a cross-section of positions

JEANNA AYRES

9099 Meadowbrook Lane #204 • Novi, MI 48374 • 248.380.6101
jlagymteacher@hotmail.com

Career Focus	**SALES • MARKETING • ACCOUNT MANAGEMENT • SALES REPRESENTATION**
Competencies	Self-motivated communicator with experience dealing with diverse populations through background in the public marketplace, professional coaching, and team competition
Studies in	Advertising Communications • Brand Strategy • Electronic Media • Press Releases • Competitive Analysis • Creative Writing • Marketing Statistics • Consumer Research

EDUCATION AND TRAINING

MICHIGAN STATE UNIVERSITY; East Lansing, MI
Bachelor of Arts in Business Administration with Marketing Specialization • 2004

Hands-on projects included:

Advertising: Planned a comprehensive advertising strategy for Ford Mustang, including media plan and advertising budget.

Business Administration: Generated a business plan for Northwest Airlines; researched competition, analyzed market niches, investigated viable marketplace strategies, and learned business record-keeping.

Marketing: Analyzed retail merchandising at Aeropostale; examined loss prevention, sales projections, and sales trends.

Certified Gymnastics Trainer and Coach
2004 Michigan State All-Around Gymnastics Champion

Competed in state and nationwide competitions; State (Michigan) Medalist 3 years; All-American 3 years; Scholar Athlete; National Honor Society in High School

Gymnastics Judge at State Level

EXPERIENCE

ABERCROMBIE & FITCH; Troy, MI
Manager Trainee • 2003-current
Responsible for day-to-day operations in a support capacity for retailer of youth-driven apparel. Oversee sales associates, manage customer service issues, and handle merchandising and marketing concerns for store that is positioned in the top 10% of sales nationwide. Attend training meetings.
- Member of team that exceeds plan regularly (March 2004 – 117% of plan).
- Assisted in preparations for annual inventory.

MILFORD GYMNASTICS; Milford, MI
Instructor/Coach • 2001-current
Train and mentor young athletes (7- to 18-year-olds) in gymnastics fundamentals and competitive requirements, from levels of pre-training through regional team competition.

LANSING HIGH SCHOOL; Lansing, MI
Assistant Gymnastics Coach • 2002-04
Managed practices and training for competition; conducted motivation sessions; set personal and team goals.

SOUTH LYON GYMNASTICS CENTER; South Lyon, MI
Instructor/Coach • 1996-2000 (seasonal)
Trained and mentored youth athletes from levels of pre-training through national team competition.

Additional Experience: Held other various positions to help fund college expenses (Server/Hostess: Chili's, Starbucks, On The Border)

Lyndee Rosslander

NE 333, Rainbow Place S
Bowland, WA 98333

Cell Phone: (909) 321-4412
rossla@cole.edu

Sports Marketing and Promotion

- Dynamic, energetic, industrious, and goal focused — a sports enthusiast from an early age — participant and supporter of high school soccer, basketball, and softball, children's clinics / camps, fundraisers, coaching, and work crews.
- Marketing and Promotion internships with Seattle Mariners, Fresno Falcons, and Bellingham Bells provide rich experience, including ballpark management, contract negotiation, sponsorship procurement, media blitzes, and event planning.
- Recognized for focus, drive, positive attitude, team spirit, and achievement.
- Demonstrated multi-tasking, prioritizing, time management, and organizational abilities.
- Highly creative and innovative, conceived and implemented precedent-setting, record-breaking marketing and promotion schemes.

"… a contributing member of our procurement team immediately accepting challenges and producing results … far exceeded our expectations…." — S.F., CPM, Director of Procurement, Softball Team

"…always had a smile on her face … never complained and took on each challenge with enthusiasm … has strong customer service skills …." — S.C., Director of Merchandise and Promotions, Professional Hockey Team

"… able to communicate effectively with persons from diverse backgrounds … well-liked and respected …." — M.R., Coordinator, National Student Exchange Program, CSU

EXEMPLARY PROMOTIONAL SUCCESSES

- College State Blood Drive Beach Party broke all records in number of donors.
- "Western Idol" Search for a Campus Star revitalized interest in COLE Mascot.
- "Mascot Night" for the COLE Basketball and COLE Baseball involved community, drew spectators, and promoted local businesses at half-time.
- Theme-based sponsorship BBQs generated revenue while providing innovative publicity at games.
- "Youth Games" at half-time—YMCA, Boys and Girls Clubs, and community youth participate in half-time activities.
- "Helmet Races" — designed gigantic helmets — races involved fans and generated excitement.

EDUCATION

B.A., Business Administration, COLE University, June 2004
Concentration: Marketing

RELEVANT EXPERIENCE

Marketing and Promotions, Softball Team, Bowland, WA	4/2003–present
Web Design Intern, COLE University	1/2004–present
Marketing and Promotions, Athletic Department, COLE University	9/2002–present
Marketing and Purchasing Intern, Professional Baseball Team	5-9/2002
Gym Attendant, Fitness and Aquatics Center, Bowland, WA	5-9/2002
Marketing and Promotions, Professional Hockey Team, City, CA	1-5/2002
On-Field Ballgirl, Professional Baseball Team, Bowland, WA	2-8/2001

OTHER WORK EXPERIENCE

Waitress, Fig Garden Retirement Home, Bowland, WA	8-12/2001
Grocery Hostess/Bagger, Albertson, City, WA	1-4/2000
Barista, Blue Ribbon Espresso, Elko, WA	9/1999–1/2000
High Board Member, Bon Marché, Elko, WA	9/1998–6/1999

Angela Goodness
30-01 Dreyvus Avenue W. • Seattle, WA 98122
Residence: 206.888-8888 • E-mail: good1234@aol.com

OBJECTIVE: SOCIAL SERVICES POSITION
Seek staff position with nonprofit/foundation that promotes empowerment of young women

- Articulate, dedicated, high-energy sociology student with ability to support and staff programs that promote positive self-esteem and anger management among adolescents and children through sports and recreation.
- Six years of experience organizing and participating in sporting events. Top student, athlete, and team member.
- Excel at teaching, coaching, supporting peers and clients, aiding program operations, and problem solving.
- Compassionate and client-focused advocate who can reach, motivate, and create results across diverse groups.
- Proven ability to prioritize tasks and lead projects. Internationally traveled. Speak Swahili and some French.

Education

Gonzaga College, Spokane, WA
Named one of the 15 best liberal arts colleges in the country for the past 15 years, U.S. News & World Report.

B.A. Program, Sociology • Honors Student. GPA 3.3 • Graduation: June 2004.

Study Abroad Program. Tanzania, Africa. University of Dar es Salaam.
Qualified to tutor as Student Assistant, 2004.

Relevant Projects

Researched female body builders and social construction of female athletes. Completed project that developed strategies for addressing aggression expressed between children (inspired by Odd Girl Out). Presented strategies and secured buy-in from Iowa School Board. Ideas are to be incorporated into future curricula.

Leadership, Honors and Awards

Team Captain, Gonzaga College Frisbee Team • Organizer, Gonzaga Ultimate Tournament • 2002 - present
Member, Ski Racing Team – Soccer Captain – Lacrosse Captain

Experience

Lead Student Dispatcher. 2003 • **Student Dispatcher** 2002, Gonzaga College, Spokane, WA   2002 - 2003
Report to Head of Security, 24/7 on call. Handle hiring, scheduling, and training of student dispatch team.

Head Women's Counselor, 2003 • **Counselor, 2002,** YMCA Camp Orcas, Blaine, WA   2002 - 2003
Support lead for female staff. Co-led teen leadership hiking trips. Coached using climbing wall. Lifeguard duties.

Server • Hostess • Dishwasher • Expediter, Olive Garden, Seattle, WA   2001 - 2002

Camp Cook • Camp Powder, Mt. Baker, Concrete, WA   1997 - 2001
Participated annually in ski camp during high school. Grew from role as Camp Cook to aiding the Girls' Counselor.

Hobbies and Interests

Biking, Skiing (12 years racing), Rollerblading, Running, Tae Kwon Do Karate (Red Belt), Working Out, Reading
Certifications: Lifeguard, CPR, First Aid, Defibrillator

OLIVIA L. TYLER

5555 Sunflower Drive • Prairie Hills, Michigan 48473
Phone: 810-666-6789 • Cell: 810-730-4239 • livtyler54@aol.com

Career Goal

An **INFORMATION TECHNOLOGY** position used as the first professional opportunity
to launch a career in Programming, Systems Analysis, or Networking.

Education

Bachelor of Science,
Ferris State University,
Big Rapids, Michigan 2004

Major: Computer
Information Systems
Minor: Finance

Computer Skills
(Coursework completed)
Operating Systems:
Windows XP/98
Software:
Microsoft Office (Word, Excel,
Access, PowerPoint, Outlook)
Programming Languages:
Java, COBOL, Coldfusion,
Visual Basic, and SQL

Relevant Coursework

Networking Essentials and
Administration

Database Design and
Implementation

Client/Server
Implementation

Systems Analysis & Design

Midrange Online Program
Development

E-Commerce Application
Development

Finance Coursework:
Investment Principles

Financial Management

Portfolio Management

Profile

Leveraging coursework in Information Technology and Finance with an analytic mind, strong work ethic, team spirit, and natural leadership ability. As part of a four-member Systems Design and Implementation class project team, designed an online voting website with backend database.

Key Qualifications

√ **President, Financial Management Association (2004)**

Leadership: Revitalized an inactive campus organization. Increased participation from three to ten members in one year by creating a direct marketing campaign for recruitment.

Teamwork: Teamed up with International Business Association president to present a successful funding proposal before the 15-member Student Government Finance Board.

Planning & Organization: As part of a two-person leadership team, arranged logistics for first-ever association trip to Chicago financial district.

√ **Vice President of Chapter Operations, Delta Sigma Pi (2004)**

Communication Skills: Served as liaison between national organization and local professional business fraternity. Ensured all paperwork was completed and submitted on time.

√ **Community Service Chairperson, Delta Sigma Pi (2002 – 2004)**

Ingenuity: Arranged 15 community service projects for 25-member business fraternity (more than twice the national requirement), achieving an average 40% participation.

√ **Track Coach / Assistant Freshman Volleyball Coach (2003)**
Prairie Hills Community Schools

Time Management: Volunteered as part of a four-person staff to coach a large junior-high track team. As a freshman assistant coach, taught volleyball fundamentals and provided a positive role model. Balanced volunteer service with a full academic schedule.

PART-TIME Work History

Meijer, Big Rapids, Michigan *Produce Department*	2003 – 2004
American Eagle Outfitters, Flint, Michigan *Sales Associate*	1999 – 2002
Mr. Convenience, Prairie Hills, Michigan *Cashier*	2001
Prairie Hills Community Schools, Michigan *Payroll Office / Co-op Student*	1998 – 1999

104

ALLISON M. WELLMAN

Burlington Blvd., Apt. 356 • Fairfield, CT 97554 • tel: 203.332.1839 • emstewxt@yahoo.com

Accomplished, well-rounded college professional seeking to apply educational training and skills in government and public policy development. Enthusiastic and energetic contributor to student government and mentoring programs, requiring leadership, problem solving and cross-cultural communications strengths. Computer and Internet savvy.

EDUCATION

FAIRFIELD UNIVERSITY, Fairfield, CT, May 2004
- **B.S. Degree in Government and Public Policy; GPA: 3.87**

Courses in International Studies	U.S. Foreign Relations (1890 to the present), Moot Court Honors Class (researching current Supreme Court cases and role-playing as justices or attorneys), Government and Political Communication, Government and Political Policy Process.
Scholarships/ Honors	• Recipient of **Aramark Fellowship**, Spring 2002 Program is designed to tap highly motivated, talented students who represent the next generation of leaders and provide training on governmental processes. • Recipient of **Academic Excellence Scholarship**, 2000 to 2003 • Selected for **Collegium V – Fairfield University's Honors Program**

LEADERSHIP / ORGANIZATIONAL ACTIVITIES

Chair, Academic Affairs Committee - Student Government Association (2001–2004)
- Instrumental in various projects including surveying students and persuading the administration to develop and implement new foreign language curriculum (French, Mandarin Chinese, Arabic, and Vietnamese courses are now offered). Involved in other initiatives such as Advanced Placement credit for selected classes and establishing a campus radio station.

Senator, Executive Committee - Student Government Association
- Twice elected Senator in 2001-02 and 2003–04. Collaborated with the President, Vice President and other Senate Chairs to establish effective processes/procedures both within the committee and in partnering with other campus organizations.

Vice Chair, Multi-Cultural and Minority Affairs - Student Advisory Council (2003)
- Researched university system policies regarding international students and study abroad programs with recommendations to be presented to the Board of Regents.

Orientation Team Mentor - New Students Program (2002)
- Completed preparatory class to become a team mentor that included leadership skills training. Participated in the coordination of all orientation programs to facilitate transition of freshman, transfer and graduate students to the University, as well as at the Freshmen Camp and Emerging Leadership Program. Served as mentor to 5 students and assisted them with transition/academic issues.

FELLOWSHIP

Special Assistant - UNITED NATIONS INFORMATION CENTRE, Washington, DC (Spring 2003)

- Awarded **Aramark Fellowship** as 1 of 2 from Fairfield University. Produce reports on Congressional hearings, conferences and lectures relating to United Nations activities.
- Research nonprofit organizations applying for NGO status with the UN and prepare information updates on the UN conference on Sustainable Finance.

EMPLOYMENT

SAT Tutor - SCORE PREP, Stamford, CT (2003–2004)

- Provided private math/verbal SAT tutoring as well as coaching in Score Prep methods, relaxation skills, vocabulary, and basic math formulas.
- Effectively tutored 35 students to date, including individuals with dyslexia and ADD/ADHD. Results led to increased scores of 100 points or more on each section.

DERRICK N. SNYDER ————————————————————————➤

208 South West Side Avenue ➤ Jefferson, MD 21755   dsnyder@yahoo.com
301.555.0936 (home) ➤ 240.555.8532 (cell)

OBJECTIVE

Business, Service or Brand Development and Marketing

PROFILE

➤ Recent Business Administration graduate with marketing and public relations skills.

➤ Excellent leadership abilities clearly exemplified by a record of athletic and community service achievements.

➤ Competitive, yet flexible; a highly effective team player who capitalizes on individuals' strengths to achieve a goal.

➤ Strong verbal communication skills; confidently connect with people of all ages, academic, professional, and cultural backgrounds.

➤ Computer competent in MS Office applications, Internet research, and email communication.

➤ Amendable to travel and possible relocation; participated in numerous service and athletic events in England and Scotland.

EDUCATION

BS, Business Administration, Catawba College, Salisbury, NC 2004
Recipient of a four-year lacrosse scholarship and the only athletic scholarship recipient for the Jefferson High School class of 1999

HIGHLIGHTS OF EXPERIENCE AND ACHIEVEMENTS

BOY SCOUTS OF AMERICA

Fully participated in numerous service and leadership activities in the Shenandoah Council of Central Maryland.

➤ Achieved the rank of Eagle Scout by the age of sixteen, developing and directing a troop project to refurbish playground equipment for the community of Jefferson, MD.

➤ Worked as a camp Counselor for Camp Sinoquipe, in Gettysburg, PA for four summers.

➤ Elected to the Order of the Arrow and held the rank of Lodge Chief (two terms), Chapter Chief of Elections, and Vice Chief of Programs.

➤ Participated in the international student exchange program, attending the International Jamborette in Blair Atholo, Scotland (summer 1996) and attended in 2000 as a Scout Master supervising five scouts from the Council.

COLLEGIATE AND HIGH SCHOOL LACROSSE

Established an impressive scoring, coaching, mentoring, and leadership record during more than 10 years of team competition.

➤ Competed as a four-year starter at Catawba College; one of the top three scorers all four years.

➤ Team captain senior year.

➤ Participated in the new student mentoring program in junior and senior years.

➤ Led team scoring the first win against the school rival in the college's history.

COLLEGIATE AND HIGH SCHOOL LACROSSE (continued)

- ➤ Invited by the Assistant Coach to play for the Great Atlantic Lacrosse Company in England (1998) against the English National Team.
- ➤ Taught lacrosse fundamentals to high school students in summer camp.
- ➤ Received an exclusive invitation to a Top 75 recruitment camp.
- ➤ Coached the North Frederick High School Lacrosse Team, introducing college-playing strategies to the high-school arena.
- ➤ Established an exemplary high-school record of achievement playing for the Central Maryland Lacrosse Club: four-year starter; four-year all star; three-time all conference.

EMPLOYMENT

Worked various part-time and seasonal positions while pursuing degree, each demanding high levels of customer service, time management, and public relations skills.

Restaurant Server, Arnone's Pizzeria, Frederick, MD   Current
- ➤ Competently manage multiple job functions including food preparation, table service, and off-site delivery.

Valet, Town Park, Baltimore, MD   Summer 2003
- ➤ Professionally represented Town Park Valet Services and the Wyndham Hotel as the first point of contact for hotel guests, while assisting with parking, luggage, and city information.

Sales Associate, Dick's Sporting Goods, Frederick, MD   2001 – 2002
- ➤ Identified as the "lacrosse specialist" in assisting customers with choosing and purchasing appropriate equipment.

Elizabeth P. Drayson

Profile

❖ Mature, high-achieving student with solid academic background and extensive extracurricular involvement in leadership capacities.
❖ Life experience includes educational travel to South America and Europe.
❖ Professional demeanor; outstanding interpersonal and relationship building skills.
❖ A strong written and verbal communicator.
❖ User of Windows and Macintosh operating systems; Microsoft Office, Adobe Illustrator, and Photoshop.

Education

Bachelor of Liberal Arts   Hope College • Holland, Michigan   Spring 2004
  • **Economics** major, **Art** minor
  • Named to Dean's List (2001-2004)
  • Omicron Delta Epsilon Honor Society for Economics; Kappa Pi Honorary Society for Art

Study Abroad/Off-Campus

Dollarization of Ecuador – Ecuador   Summer 2003
Participated in four-week immersion program combining instruction in Spanish language and culture, a service-learning project, and in-depth economic analysis of dollarization and the process/effect of globalization on Latin American nations such as Ecuador. Met with representatives from government, business, and the indigenous population. Taught English, Government, and Economics to students in public and private schools.

Recent American History – University of California at Berkeley   Summer 2002
Completed six-week class focusing on events in the 1940s-1990s, many of which actually occurred on or near Berkeley's campus. Dynamic instructor who experienced this history headed the class.

Art History – England   Summer 2002
Conducted research on Greek Black Figure Pottery in the Victoria and Albert Museum, home of one of the world's largest collections. Authored research paper and made presentation to peers and instructors.

People-to-People Student Ambassadors – Scandinavia   Summer 1997
Traveled to Denmark, Norway, and Sweden to promote international and cultural awareness.

Collegiate Experience

Presidential Advisory Committee - Member   2002-2003
Served as one of two student members elected by the student body. Committee provided counsel and acted as liaison with the college's new president. Addressed relevant issues such as tuition and budget cuts.

Kappa Iota - Treasurer   2002-2003
Managed finances for Alma College's oldest sorority.

Student Congress - Representative   2001-2003
Elected to four single-semester terms. Served on Budget and Finance Committee charged with disseminating funds to student organizations. Reviewed budgets and special requests for funding.

Panhellenic Council - Recruitment Chairperson   2003
Filled elected position overseeing rush activities for five sororities serving 500+ students. Prepared and distributed marketing material. Delegated and reviewed activities of five student assistants.

Tennis Team - Athlete   2000
Competed on Women's Tennis Team which won the MIAA Division III Championship.

Employment

Assistant Manager   Fossil • Rockford, Michigan   Summer 2002
Cashier   D&W Foods • Whitehall, Michigan   Summer 2001

DAVID REESE

8512 Grand Avenue • San Diego, California 92109 • (858) 444-8254 • david.reese@yahoo.com

SUMMARY OF QUALIFICATIONS

Architecture student offering a Bachelor of Environmental Design with hands-on experience creating and reading construction documents. Comprehensive knowledge of construction materials, equipment, and tools. Able to effectively communicate ideas and proposals to clients. Excellent design, graphic design, drafting, and modeling skills. Strong work ethic, organized, and positive.

- Co-created annual Art and Architecture Show where students display work for San Diego architects. 100 students and 20 architecture firms participated in first show.
- Served as fundraising director, tour director, and advertising director of the American Institute of Architecture Students (AIAS).

  ✓ Directed Auction of the Architects and raised $3,000 in two years.
  ✓ Organized 10 tours of firms, construction projects, and buildings.
  ✓ Designed flyers and posters that successfully advertised AIAS events.

- Volunteered for Habitat for Humanity and worked with architects on construction of seven houses.
- Taught high-school students about art and architecture at San Diego Charter School. Worked as volunteer for teacher and former architect.
- Performed research for six months and wrote paper on historic preservation of the San Diego Brewery. Presented findings to the Historic Preservation Panel.

EDUCATION

Bachelor of Environmental Design   May 2004
Major in Architecture
University of California, San Diego, California

Proficient in PC and Macintosh environments, AutoCAD, 3D Rendering, Form-Z, Adobe Photoshop and Illustrator, and all Microsoft applications and operating systems.

WORK EXPERIENCE

UNIVERSITY OF CALIFORNIA, San Diego, California   2002 - Present
Information Technology Services
Customer Support Representative (2003 - Present)
   Analyze and solve technical problems for staff, faculty, and students. Answer questions
   about software, viruses, network connections, telephone networks, and email accounts.

Office of Conference Services
Conference Coordinator Assistant, Liquor Coordinator/Director, A/V Coordinator (2002 - 2003)
   Hosted events for large organizations visiting University. Took charge of billing,
   recordkeeping, ordering, receiving, and transportation.

SAN DIEGO EXCAVATION, San Diego, California   1999 - 2000
Machine Operator, Project Assistant
   Worked for construction foreman. Operated excavators, front-end loaders, bobcats, and
   other construction equipment. Implemented construction plan based on working drawings.

HILLARY ELAINE SNOW

E-mail: hilles@aol.com

1248 Morningside Drive, Rochester, New York 14613

(585) 288-6891

OBJECTIVE:

An entry-level opportunity that will capitalize on human services education, exceptional communication skills, and strong administrative capabilities.

SUMMARY OF QUALIFICATIONS:

- **Strong writing skills, including significant academic study in English.**

- **Excellent understanding of and substantial coursework on important women's issues.**

- **Exceptional ability to understand diverse multi-cultural issues.**

- **Superb research capabilities, including experience in academic and public libraries.**

- **Exceptional attention to detail with strong analytical and problem-solving skills.**

- **Demonstrated administrative support skills, including client relations, filing, and use of Microsoft Word / Excel in office environment.**

HIGHLIGHTS:

Work with multi-cultural, economically disadvantaged group of 10- to 12-year-old girls in a community outreach setting. Lead activities, coordinate field trips, and mentor program participants.

Organized and coordinated multi-cultural and women's events on campus, including Alfred University Women's Leadership Conference (women's issues) and Alfred University Lyrical Unity (multi-cultural event to raise literary awareness).

Served as Resident Assistant in college dormitory setting. Responsibilities included all-night on-call duties 8 to 10 nights each month, with accountability for addressing crisis situations as they arose. Designed and implemented educational programs for dorm residents on relevant issues. Mediated disputes between students. Received training on alcohol/drug abuse, suicide watch, and other key topics.

Assisted JV Librarian and Young Adult Librarian in organizing and implementing New York State Summer Reading Program at Rochester Public Library. Coordinated the activities of 20 volunteers serving over 2,000 children involved in program. Organized book displays based on established school reading lists. Processed, ordered, and labeled books. Helped manage the distribution and redemption of "Book Bucks" in exchange for prizes based on number of books read.

Implemented "Art Factory" program in conjunction with Rochester Public Library. Delivered weekly instruction to approximately 20 children in grades 2-5 on arts and crafts topics. Developed themes and incorporated library books into curriculum.

EDUCATION:

Bachelor of Science, Sociology (Minor in Women's Studies)   **December 2004**
University of Rochester; Rochester, New York
Dean's List / GPA: 3.85 / Alice M. Duffy Scholarship Recipient
Significant Courses: Racial and Cultural Minorities; Social Problems; Marriages and Families; Social Research Design and Methods; Women's Studies (Senior Seminar); Sociology (Senior Seminar).

Alfred University; Alfred, New York   **1999 - 2002**
Major: Sociology (Completed Courses Equivalent to Minor in English and in Women's Studies)
Dean's List / GPA: 3.75 / Omicron Delta Kappa Leadership Circle (2001)
Significant Courses: Deviance and Society; Socialization; Psychology of Women; Creative Writing; Social Theory; Imaginative Writing; Women and Society.

School of the Arts - Rochester City School District: Rochester, New York   **June 1999**
Graduated With Honors / NYS Regents Diploma - Drama and Literature

WORK EXPERIENCE:

Office Manager, Arnold-Smith Associates; Rochester, New York   **May 2003 - Present**
Perform a variety of customer service, office management, and administrative support functions to facilitate efficient operation of this small career transition consulting firm. Manage office operations during brief periods of partners' absence.

Customer Service, Starbucks; Rochester, New York
Jan. 2002 - Present
Maintain knowledge of extensive product line, provide exceptional customer service, and fulfill operational functions.

Library Assistant, Rochester Public Library; Rochester, New York   **Summers 2000 - 2003**
Supported Children's and Young Adult Librarians in coordinating and implementing programs for school-age library patrons. Performed general circulation desk duties.

Library Assistant, Herrick Memorial Library - Alfred Univ.; Alfred, New York   **1999 - 2002**
Reviewed periodical collection to ascertain completeness and weed materials to be discarded. Performed information and circulation desk duties and assisted patrons in locating reference materials. Supported Secretary to the Library Director.

Resident Assistant, Alfred University - Residence Life; Alfred, New York   **2000 - 2003**
Maintained safety and security of dormitory facility on college campus. Served in on-call capacity with accountability for crisis management and for addressing needs of student residents. Developed programs for student residents and counseled individual students on issues affecting their personal and academic lives.

HONORS / AWARDS:

Alice M. Duffy Scholarship Recipient (2003)
Fisher Literary Award (Spring 2002)
Most Outstanding New Resident Assistant (May 2001) / Best RA Programmer (May 2001)
Omicron Delta Kappa Leadership Circle (2001)
Gertz Writing Award - Alfred University (May 2000)
Alpha Phi Omega Scholarship Winner (Fall 1999)
ARC of Monroe County Scholarship Winner (June 1999)
First Prize, Sokol Junior Literary Awards (March 1999)
Third Prize, Leila Tupper Writing Scholarship (March 1999)
The Wellesley Book Award (June 1998)
The Dartmouth Club Book Award (June 1998)
Finalist, Orrin T. Shapiro Memorial Foundation Award (for creative writing) (1998, 1999)

COMMUNITY INVOLVEMENT:

Alfred University Women's Leadership Conference (planned and organized conference; booked facilities).
Alfred University Lyrical Unity (founded/organized multi-cultural event to raise literary awareness).
Monroe County ARC - Youth ARC; Special Sitters (serving the needs of autistic children).

PUBLICATIONS / PERFORMANCES:

Featured poet in *Allusions* – University of Rochester literary magazine (Fall 2002; Spring 2003).
Editor of Alfred University *Review Poièsis* literary magazine (2001-2002).
Poetry Discussion Leader / Contributor for *Review Poièsis* (1999-2000).
Rochester Shorts - Issue #19 (Fall 1998 / Fall 1999).
99 Cent Special and *Cuneiform* (School of the Arts literary magazines).
Monarc and *Archive* - Monroe County ARC newsletters (Summers 1996, 1998).
Reckless, Women & Wallace, and *Scapin* (Fall 2001-Fall 2003).
American College Theater Festival (Winter 2002).

References Available Upon Request

CHAPTER 7

Best Resumes for College Graduates With Advanced Degrees

Overview

For those of you graduating with master's and doctoral degrees, your resume challenge may be a bit different than students with four-year degrees. Why? Because you often have substantially more experience which may have been acquired through paid employment, internships, clinical rotations, volunteer activities, research studies, and more. And for many of you, let's not forget the thesis or doctoral dissertation that you "knocked out" in your spare time!

Because of the depth of your experience, it is not unusual to have a two-page resume (versus the traditional one-page resume for most undergraduate students). In fact, your resume may even be three pages in some instances, and that's okay. It is critical that you include all of your experiences – whether paid or unpaid – for they have provided you with a wealth of skills and qualifications that must be communicated on your resume. They are of paramount importance in positioning you strongly within the job market and demonstrating that you are a well-qualified professional. Don't let anyone ever tell you that you must keep your resume to one page!

You will find two rather distinctive styles of resumes in this chapter:

- What you would traditionally think of as a resume – a document that begins with some type of summary section and then includes both education and experience sections (which one of those two comes first will depend on your specific experience and which of the two is your stronger selling point).
- A document that is more appropriately referred to as a curriculum vitae (CV) – tends to be a bit more academic in writing and presentation style, and is considered somewhat more conservative.

Which style is right for you – resume or CV, or a combination thereof – will depend on the type of position you are seeking, the kind of organization you would like to work for, and your geographic preferences (U.S. or abroad). Do your research, find out which style is appropriate for your target audience, and then move forward.

Index of Resumes Featured in This Chapter

Objective: Consulting position with a management consulting firm in the Asia-Pacific region

Strategy: CV-style, one-page resume accentuates project management experience and client relations skills in a format readily acceptable within the target international market

Resume: Peter T. Betancourt, pages 125-126
Writer: Arnold G. Boldt, CPRW, JCTC
Objective: Position in finance, operations, or sales and marketing with a US firm doing business in Latin America
Strategy: Equal focus on US/Latin American education, professional experience and internships to position graduate for immediate entry into the world of international business and commerce

Resume: Samantha Fowler, pages 127-128
Writer: Martin Buckland, MRW, CPRW, JCTC, CJST, CEIP
Objective: Research-based position in academia, with a nonprofit or foundation, or with some other type of institutional organization
Strategy: Highlight wealth of educational qualifications and professional experience (spanning two continents) directly related to professional objective

Resume: Joana M. Wesley, pages 129-130
Writer: Beverly Harvey, CPRW, JCTC, CCM, CCMC
Objective: Career opportunity in international health care administration/management
Strategy: Traditional CV-style format with conservative visual presentation complemented by excellent presentation of professional experiences directly related to current career goals

Resume: Allison Bristow, page 131
Writer: Don Orlando, MBA, CPRW, JCTC, CCM, CCMC
Objective: Position as an Attorney with an established law firm
Strategy: Unique resume style and format for a JD graduate, customized to the firm she's applying to (see "Capabilities" section at top of resume) and presenting a wealth of experience and competencies

Resume: Sophia K. Mersino, page 132
Writer: Carolyn Braden, CPRW
Objective: Professional position with a nonprofit or government agency
Strategy: Solid, one-page presentation using headline format to communicate core skills, highlighting the education section to note recent MPA degree, and creating high-impact content for both paid and volunteer positions

Resume: F.E. Toner, pages 133-134
Writer: Nicole Miller, IJCTC, CCM, CRW, CECC
Objective: Position as a Clinical Psychologist
Strategy: Distinctive CV-style format with strong focus on educational credentials, projects, and achievements, and extensive residency, internship, and professional work experience

STANLEY STARZ

Recent graduate with a **Master of Fine Arts Degree in Film and TV Producing.** Served as the producer of two films and provided broad administrative support to film and television productions by NBC and Rightway Entertainment. Skilled at working independently and collaboratively on diverse projects. Accustomed to working with a broad range of individuals and arranging all pre-production considerations in a timely and cost-efficient manner. **Fluent in English, French, and Spanish.**

EDUCATION

MFA, Film and TV Producing, University of Southern California (USC), Los Angeles, CA   2004
MA, Political Science, Sociology, Pepperdine University, Malibu, CA   1999

Produced the following thesis film projects in satisfaction of degree requirements:
- *"House of Cards,"* a 35-mm, sync-sound film directed by a fellow student.
- *"Uncommon Thievery,"* a super 16-mm, color sync-sound film directed by a fellow student.
  - ➤ Identified and secured prime locations and negotiated all contracts with city officials in a timely manner, resolving all legal issues in advance of filming.
  - ➤ Arranged for insurance, placed print media advertisements to promote casting calls, coordinated casting sessions, assembled crews, and arranged catering.
  - ➤ Obtained corporate sponsorship in the form of film donations.
- Thesis: Developed a comprehensive proposal for a social drama, science-fiction film project addressing all aspects of production, casting, and budget.

PROFESSIONAL EXPERIENCE

Production Assistant (PA), *"Heros In Exile"* (Short Film), Rightway Entertainment, Los Angeles, CA   2004
    Produced by Darden Kyle, producer of *"Up In Arms,"* and starring Tina Tolliver and Monty Bluemont.

Administrative Assistant (Intern), Script Coverage, Rightway Entertainment, Los Angeles, CA   2003

Administrative Assistant (Intern), *"Days of Our Lives,"* NBC, Los Angeles, CA   2002
    Sorted mail, ran errands, and provided support between the production office and the sets.

Lab Assistant, Academic Computing Department, USC, Los Angeles, CA   2001
    Assisted students with computer troubleshooting and provided user support via the computer hotline.
Administrative Assistant, USC, Los Angeles, CA   2000–2001
    Scheduled appointments, monitored testing for students with disabilities, and maintained confidential files.

Resident Advisor, USC Language Academy, Los Angeles, CA   2000
    Assisted with intake/departure of 250 international students, enforced hall policies, and mentored students.

COMPUTER SKILLS

Proficient in Windows and Mac environments with the following applications: Movie Magic Budget and Scheduling, Final Draft (screen writing software), and Microsoft Word and Excel.

GABE CONNOR DAVIDS

684 Lawnside Villa 5, Magna Trad Rd, Km6
Samut Prakarn, 10540, Thailand
Home: 02 333 3333-2 ▪ gcdavids@yahoo.com ▪ Mobile: 01 222 2222

QUALIFICATION SUMMARY

Proven performer with an exceptional academic record in international trade law, gaining vital knowledge in both commercial and legal aspects of international trade. Talented negotiator with keen cultural awareness, possessing strong communication, interaction, leadership, and relationship-building skills. Outstanding cross-cultural skills developed through overseas study and travel, with worldwide travel throughout Southeast Asia, Western Europe, the United States, Australia, and New Zealand.

Fluent in verbal and written Thai and English.

EDUCATION

NEW YORK UNIVERSITY COLLEGE OF LAW – *New York, NY*   2003 to 2004
Master of International Trade Law

- **Courses included:** Commercial Law, International Trade Law, International Business Law, International Law, Telecommunication and Media Law, Negotiation, International Dispute Resolutions, Common Law, Economics. Received **Distinction** level average for all courses.

    - ☑ **Achieved academic honors** level over fellow students who were professional lawyers through a personal commitment to continued learning and improvement.

    - ☑ **High Distinction** for research project and presentation on Free Trade Agreement between Thailand and the United States.

    - ☑ Appointed as **Project Leader** for research project (topic: **Negotiation Strategic Skills**) and one-hour presentation about the possible construction of New Jersey's second airport, supervised up to 5 students and assisted team members.

    - ☑ **Received a Distinction** for research projects: "Liberalization of Thai's market under the WTO Regime" (project and presentation), "Dispute Resolution System in East and West Society," "Legality of the War in Iraq," and "Mineral, Oil and Seabed Mining."

NEW JERSEY STATE UNIVERSITY – *New Brunswick, NJ*   2000 to 2003
Bachelor of Media Communication

- **Courses included:** Introduction to Digital Technologies and Design, Directing Information Programs, Production Planning, Professional Writing, Fundamentals of Design, Digital Media, Media Communication and Globalization, Project Management, Advertising.

    - ☑ Acknowledged for strong production-related skills and for assisting students in **problem diagnosis and troubleshooting** in post production of film projects.

    - ☑ Appointed as Head Editor and Sound Designer for "The Columbian," a film project involving 10 team members. Received an **Encouragement Award** at the Fox Studio Film Award in 2002.

CHELTENHAM COLLEGE – *England*
G.C.E 'A' Levels in English Literature, Economics, and Music   1996 to 1998

G.C.S.E's in Music, Design Technology, Economics, English, History,   1994 to 1996
Biology, Chemistry, Physics, and Mathematics

GABE CONNOR DAVIDS   CONFIDENTIAL   1

117

WORK EXPERIENCE

Interviewer/Recruiter (part-time)   2003 to Present
LAKE BUTLER DONALDSON – *Fairfield, Connecticut*

Highly valued team member for one of Connecticut's leading market research companies. Responsible for recruiting participants from the company's database to conduct face-to-face and over-the-phone interviews for generating public opinion polls on political issues, consumer products, and advertising campaigns.

Key Contributions:

> - **Fast-track promotion** from Interviewer to Recruiter within 4 months due to proactive, decisive, and action-driven leadership.
> - Appointed to conduct specific research for one of the company's largest clients, HP Limited.
> - **Built productive partnerships with key client contacts** in research projects, ensuring all business objectives were met. Clients included the Attorney General's Office, Johnson and Johnson, Kraft, HP Invent, and Dell.

Marketing Trainee   2002
COLUMBIA TRI STAR PICTURES – *Sydney, Australia*

Valuable team member for one of the industry leaders in feature films within the Australian marketplace. Developed publicity strategies and campaigns for the launch of new-release movies.

Key Contributions:

> - **Developed publicity and promotional strategies** for the launch of two movies: Triple X and Spider Man.
> - Worked collaboratively with marketing team to identify publicity opportunities and **implement marketing strategies** to achieve production objectives.

Research Trainee   2000 to 2001
BURGMANN-ONG TOURISM – *Thailand*

Recruited at this Web-based tourism company to conduct extensive research on Internet advertising and Web page listings before the official launch of the company's website.

Key Contributions:

> - Completed a **comprehensive marketing plan and business strategy analysis** that identified the impact of Internet advertising on major search engines and led to the implementation of recommendations.
> - **Conducted qualitative and quantitative research** to evaluate the bidding strategies of other websites and examine how each of the major search engines operates.

Recording Artist   1996 to 1998
SONY MUSIC - *Thailand*

Member of Ice-Cube Shock, a rock band that played concerts across the country with many national television and radio broadcasts through a contract with one of the world's leading music companies.

Key Contributions:

> - **Collaborated with band members** on the music production and publicity for the band prior to the release of the album, ensuring the correct image for the band.
> - Appointed as a Personal Assistant Manager for Australian guitarist Tommy Emmanuel during his two-week tour in Bangkok. Driving force behind successful tour.

PERSONAL INTERESTS

Tennis, Water Skiing, Kite Boarding, Sailing, Music, Film Productions, and Travel

GREGORY MILLER, M.S.

67 Barkette Road
Tarrytown, New York 10098

(914) 664–9099
martin234@yahoo.com

PROFILE

ORGANIZATIONAL DEVELOPMENT / CHANGE MANAGEMENT PROFESSIONAL with training and experience that provide a foundation for partnering human resources/OD initiatives with strategic business units to enhance productivity, performance, quality, and service. Core skills include:

Project/Program Management—Five years of project management experience that encompasses conceptualization, needs assessment and planning through execution, post-intervention assessment, feedback, and closure. Ability to integrate broader corporate values into functional project plans that yield deliverables aligned with enterprise objectives.

Training ans Facilitation—Versed in OD interventions: training, coaching, process improvement, team dynamics, meeting facilitation, performance assessments, 360° feedback instruments, change management models, and human factors issues.

Research—Experienced in researching, formulating and conducting group training including development of presentation materials. Competent researcher, utilizing electronic databases (InfoTrac) and survey methods; trained in performing data analysis using SPSS, ANOVA, and T Tests.

EDUCATION

NEW YORK UNIVERSITY, New York, NY:
Master of Science in Industrial and Organizational Psychology, May 2004

Selected Projects and Research:

- Transformational leadership and change management study.
- Peer review and organizational citizenship behavior in relationship to TQM and organizational satisfaction.
- Study of lean manufacturing, participative management, cell concepts, flexible structures, and related concepts.
- On-site studies of workplace safety, human factors, and ergonomics issues.

Bachelor of Science in Psychology, *graduated magna cum laude,* May 2002

Awards/Honors: Provost's Awards (1998, 1999); Outstanding Social Science Award (1999); Psi Chi Honor Society (1999). Self-financed 100% of college tuition and expenses.

EXPERIENCE

KENWORTH CORPORATION, New York, NY
Intern: Organizational Development Consultant (2002–2003)

Assisted the internal Senior Organizational Development Consultant in providing proactive OD consulting and interventions to enhance operational and human resources effectiveness, efficiency, and quality in a Fortune 500 enterprise with 5,000 employees. Supported corporate training and development initiatives in coordination with the Human Resources Service centers, Learning and Development Unit, Corporate Library and Learning Centers, Corporate University offerings, and customer service training.

Program Management, Training and Facilitation

- Planned, managed, and facilitated Manager Information Network, a management peer group from 5 business units sharing best practices and fostering company's commitment to excellence. Initiated group's Intranet-based communication vehicle. Developed an organizational structure to allow group to become self-perpetuating.

- Reviewed literature and developed modules on a range of business topics for management development programs. Designed and trained managers on effective use of quantifiable employee performance assessment tools. Recognized for exhibiting a group facilitation style that places participants at ease and encourages willingness to share information.

Program Management, Training and Facilitation continued...

♦ Served as co-facilitator for customer service training program for new hires. Demonstrated ability to energize training participants through enthusiasm and creativity.

♦ Participated in various phases of serving clients, from responding to requests, to researching and observing several interventions.

♦ Collaborated on the remodel of the Learning Center to enhance usability, physical environment and selection of resource tools available for managers. Managed the Center's grand reopening project, including recommending and implementing ergonomic changes, project planning, budget administration, and other related activities.

UNICARE HEALTH, INC., New York, NY
Program Director - Intern (2000–2001)

Conceptualized, planned, executed, budgeted, and directed a successful intergenerational pilot program at a health care organization. Demonstrated creativity in theme development and designing unique activities to maximize impact among multifunctional levels. Program became an ongoing event.

COMPUTER CAPABILITIES

Microsoft Word, Excel, PowerPoint, Outlook, Publisher, Word Pro, Netscape and Explorer browsers; the Internet; SPSS statistical methods; desktop publishing, including development of brochures and newsletters and other materials.

LEE JUNG

ORACLE
Certified Professional

204 George St
Columbia, MD 21045

Mobile: 410 666 555
Residence: 410 444 211
Email: hall_f@hotmail.com

PROGRAMMER • DATABASE ADMINISTRATOR

SAP R/3 BASIS ADMINISTRATOR • SAP ABAP/4 PROGRAMMER • ORACLE 9i DATABASE ADMINISTRATOR

Masters Graduate with independent work habits, an analytical mindset, and the versatility to resolve multifaceted issues despite the challenges of changing priorities, imminent deadlines, and differing team agendas. Characterized throughout employment and academic life as a self-starter; an individual committed to delivering solutions and possessing the ability to apply complex technologies that translate business needs into a practical reality. Bilingual—English and Chinese (Mandarin).

EDUCATION

Masters of Information Technology
Major: Information Systems
Maryland University of Technology
(2004)

Bachelor of Information Technology
Major: Information Systems
Thailand Technology College
(2003)

Diploma of Electrical Engineering
Major: Power Electronics
Polytechnic, Singapore
(2002)

TECHNOLOGY SUMMARY

- Oracle Developer/2000 Forms
- Oracle 9i PL/SQL • Oracle SQL *Plus*
- SAP R/3 4.6C BASIS Administration
- SAP ABAP/4 Programming
- Macromedia Coldfusion MX, Dreamweaver MX, Flash MX
- Microsoft Visio
- Microsoft Visual Studio.NET
- Microsoft Office Professional
- Microsoft FrontPage
- JavaScript • HTML
- ARIS Toolset 5.0
- Database Design
- Windows NT/2000/XP/ME/98/95

ACADEMIC PROJECT HIGHLIGHTS

The Subject: *Case Studies in Enterprise Wide Systems*

The "Client": *Maryland Health*

The Project: *Team project to act as "Business Analysts" implementing SAP Enterprise Buyer Professional 3.0 (EBP)—a Web-based procurement solution to be used throughout all state hospitals.*

Personally selected by academic supervisors to contribute to a 13-week team project to support Maryland Health's e-Procurement *Proof of Concept* pilot project. Working from a framework of existing issues, produced costing and process models encompassing proof-of-concept, business process reengineering recommendations, expected functionality, feasibility of technology for long-term expandability, and forecasted investment returns.

Using ARIS Toolset 5.0, mapped business processes and gathered data via a series of interviews with cost center general managers, supervisors, and key employees. As appointed Communications and Time Manager for the team, presented meeting minutes outlining issues delegated, discussed, and resolved.

- Volunteered to preside over performance measurement issues. Conducted research and produced recommendations that compared the value of implementing or not implementing EBP functionality.
- Added value by introducing idea to interview vendors for feedback on an EBP implementation. Project managers were delighted with positive responses from Johnson & Johnson and Pfizer.
- Introduced idea of interviewing other organizations such as Maryland Rail currently implementing the solution to facilitate meaningful exchanges for improved implementation.
- Gathered information from focus group meetings at the Maryland Base Hospital. Collated responses for the Excel-based "Issues Register" offering short-, medium-, and long-term recommendations to concerns raised.
- Presented formal e-procurement solution findings before audiences of 30-plus attendees on two separate occasions.
- Estimated and "sold" the benefits of a new e-procurement solution citing cost savings of 35%.

PROJECT HIGHLIGHTS
c o n t i n u e d

The "Client": Investigative Center for Technology Advancement

The Project: Created a Web-based survey program for enhanced data collection capacity

The Technologies: Macromedia Coldfusion MX, Macromedia Dreamweaver MX, Microsoft IIS 5.0, Microsoft Access 2002, Adobe Photoshop 7.0, Macromedia Flash MX

Awarded *Distinction* for this academic project conducted during post-graduate studies. Planned 13-week work schedule complete with project milestones and met deadline for the main program—later adding enhanced functionality.

The program, written in Macromedia Coldfusion MX, consisted of 125 code files and was designed to function seamlessly with most Internet browsers. Processing was performed primarily on the server side.

- Transformed expensive and protracted mail-based data collection method with a faster, cheaper Web-based base survey instrument that was "instant" and accessible to a global audience.

- Software enabled the surveyors to insert, modify, and delete survey questions; monitor responses via graphical presentation; monitor average time taken by respondents to answer the survey; import email addresses and send invitations, thank-you notes, and reminder messages; export data in a variety of formats; and alter surveyor permissions.

EMPLOYMENT CHRONICLE

ASIA INTERNET PTE LTD, Thailand   1/2001–2/2001
Largest Internet communications service provider in the Asia Pacific region with representation in Singapore, Hong Kong, the Philippines, Australia, India, Thailand, and Malaysia.

Technical Support Executive

High-pressure help desk call center environment assisting customers with Internet connectivity issues across multiple operating system platforms.

- Deflected atmosphere of staff discontent by displaying a positive attitude and initiating ideas that served to boost personal productivity and circumvent the outdated and unsynchronized computer environment.

- Boosted personal productivity by using own laptop, an idea that elevated call rates by 30%. Improved productivity decreased customer-waiting times by 30 seconds, lowering the levels of customer dissatisfaction.

- Consistently surpassed call targets of 45 to 55 calls per shift by average of 30 to 35%.

MINISTRY OF CIVIL TECHNOLOGY, Thailand   6/1996–7/1996
Singapore government body overseeing infrastructure development (schools, government buildings, bridges)

Assistant Electrical Engineer

Reported to: Electrical Engineer

Two-month industrial internship during electrical engineering studies. Designed ISO standard electrical and power systems for major buildings including fire alarm placement, lighting, speakers, power switches, back-up generators, and more.

MILITARY

THAILAND ARMED FORCES   1998–1999/2003
Unit Intelligence Clerk

- Represented army unit in the annual *Army Half Marathon*.
- Selected to attend training exercises with defense force representatives of Singapore and Indonesia.
- Awarded *"Company Best Shot"* honor.
- Won *"Gold Award"* for all physical fitness tests.
- Conducted course to trainees.

Lee Jung   Page 2

122

Cassandra Vanderbilt

16 Terryville Avenue   E-mail: cassievanderbilt@email.com   Phone: 203-555-1111
Bristol, CT 06010   Cell: 203-555-0011

GRAPHIC DESIGNER / WEB DESIGNER

Experienced in **website design and development**. Skilled in Adobe Photoshop, Image Ready, Illustrator, Macromedia Flash, Dreamweaver, Director, Coldfusion, Homesite, Painter and QuarkXPress (Mac), and MS Word, Excel and PowerPoint (PC). Additional proficiency in digital photography. Competent public speaker. Quick and eager learner with excellent interpersonal and communication skills and a strong customer focus.

EDUCATION

PEABODY UNIVERSITY, New Haven, CT   2004
Master of Science: e-Media   GPA: 3.95
Studies have included: New media technologies (digital graphic design; image, animation and sound production; hypermedia and Web page design), relationship of content to form, and the ideological role of new media technologies in contemporary society.

CONNECTICUT COLLEGE OF ART, Hartford, CT
Bachelor of Fine Arts: Graphic Design   GPA: 3.4   2003

PROFESSIONAL EXPERIENCE

Web Designer, Illuminated Images (IlluminatedImages.com)   2002 – Present
Designed websites for:
- yourbusiness.com: graphic design, HTML and JavaScript
- First World Express (firstworldwide.com): HTML
- Military Museum (mpi.us.mil/units/museum/index.htm): graphic design, HTML and JavaScript
- World War II retrospective (in process): graphic design, HTML and JavaScript
- The Best Online Yellow Pages (inform_all.com): graphic design, HTML and JavaScript

Design Consultant, Home Decor, Berlton, CT   2000 – 2003
Received extensive technical and customer service training at Kitchen U, including use of a customized AutoCAD kitchen and bath design application. Learned quickly and gained the trust of customers purchasing high-ticket remodeling and interior design packages. Assessed customer needs; prepared cost quotes for materials and labor; negotiated with customers for best value. Mentored new hires.

- Personal sales reached $500,000 in first full year; sold approximately $675,000 in 2002.
- Selected to design all marketing / merchandising signs for seasonal specials throughout store.
- Created graphic design used on promotional t-shirts for employees participating in 2002 Diabetes Walk-A-Thon.

LYN CHEN

tel: (703) 750-4478

443 Nestor Road
Alexandria, VA 22003
e-mail: lchen@comcast.net

■ OBJECTIVE

Seeking to apply skills and knowledge of e-business, e-government, and telecommunications markets in the Asian-Pacific Region, project management and cross-cultural communications (Western and Asian) acquired through experience in diverse business environments. Fluent in Chinese (Mandarin and Shanghai Dialect) and English.

■ EDUCATION

M.B.A. with concentration in e-Commerce Marketing, 2004
AMERICAN UNIVERSITY, SCHOOL OF BUSINESS, Washington, DC

Management Consulting Projects

- **Redman, Brotter & Williams Communications, Washington, DC:** Conducted comprehensive assessment of the business practices of the Washington DC-based public relations firm. Designed a detailed e-business plan for a focusing on process improvement and communication strategies, integrating order fulfillment, service delivery and customer relationship management, and resulting in significant reduction in daily operating costs.

- **ADI Management Institute, Alexandria, VA:** Conducted an on-site analysis of the organization's management information systems requirements and designed procurement system that integrated contracting, accounting, and receiving processes, resulting in more responsive, user-friendly system with real-time trackable data.

- **PacSystems Inc., Arlington, VA:** Analyzed existing business model and global expansion opportunities for a B2B e-marketplace serving the U.S. packaging industry. Conducted extensive research of major international packaging markets in Asia and Europe. Designed and presented to senior executives the region-specific sales/marketing plan to effect market positioning and entry. Commended on research and dynamic presentation style.

Awards

- Case competition winner out of 10 teams in the Managers in International Economy class on Steinway's entry strategy to the China market. Professor's comment: *"You made the best presentation on that case ever; no one else was even close."*

B.S. in Communications, graduated summa cum laude, 2002
UNIVERSITY OF NORTH CAROLINA, Chapel Hill, NC

■ INTERNSHIPS

MYRON INTERNATIONAL, Washington, DC (2003-2004)
ELLISON CORPORATION, Washington, DC (2003-2004)

Intern—During MBA program, completed internships related to business outreach, e-commerce marketing, and e-business/e-government analysis.

Client Engagement Projects

Myron International—Conducted market risk analysis on telecom, Internet and e-commerce development throughout the Greater China Region (China, Hong Kong, and Taiwan). Identified global market trends, growth areas, and investment opportunities for Aster Technologies, a client of the international investment and consulting firm. Results were published for senior decision makers on Aster's Intranet.

Ellison Corporation—Assessed e-business policy/leadership and e-government readiness in the China market for the global technology and policy consulting firm and clients, including Dunston-Patterson, Jones Smythe and Hamden. Contributed research and analysis to company publication, *"Risk E-Business: Seizing the Opportunity of Global E-Readiness."* Utilized contacts in China and acted as liaison between firm and Chinese Ministry of Industry Information that regulates Internet and telecommunications development.

PETER T. BETANCOURT, MBA

Current Address:
2803 Southside Drive
Atlanta, Georgia 30302
(404) 279-1033 / ptgill@aol.com

Permanent Address:
509 Jacaranda Court
West Palm Beach, Florida 33404
(561) 525-6190 / ptgill@aol.com

FINANCIAL ANALYST / OPERATIONS MANAGER / SALES & MARKETING

MBA Graduate with demonstrated management and business analysis skills. Proven track record of developing and managing new business ventures, including establishing strategic partnerships, identifying new markets, developing business opportunities, and managing high-level account relationships. Experience operating businesses in Latin America (Venezuela) and collaborating with international business partners to access Caribbean and South American markets. Bilingual (Spanish/English) with excellent capacity to interact productively with Hispanic cultures in the Southeastern US and throughout the Latin American region. Strong public speaker with excellent presentation skills.

EDUCATION

Master of Business Administration (Corporate Finance and Operations Management)   **May 2004**
Georgia Institute of Technology - College of Management; Atlanta, Georgia
GPA: 3.60

Significant Courses:

- Corporate Finance
- Financial Analysis
- Case Studies in Corporate Finance
- Product Management

- Monetary Policy
- Micro Economics
- Macro Economics
- Forecasting

Bachelor of Business Administration (Management)   **April 1998**
Simón Bolívar University; Caracas, Venezuela
Course Sampling: Accounting, Business Management

MANAGEMENT EXPERIENCE

Operations Manager / Sales Manager, Gas Natural del Sur; Caracas, Venezuela   1996 - 2001
Established strategic partnership with European manufacturer to provide equipment for converting gasoline-powered engines to natural gas fuel in the Venezuelan market. Responsible for accounting and financial management, sales and marketing, and operations management for this $2 million company.
- Collaborated with Italian partners to develop and implement financial policies and business strategies.
- Engendered support of municipal governments and petroleum firms for fuel conversions as part of comprehensive energy conservation policy.
- Made major presentations to high-level decision-makers in corporate and municipal government positions.
- Built customer base from zero to more than 900 clients, exceeding established goals by 75%; recognized by firm's CEO with promotion based on outstanding performance.
- Facilitated bank financing for clients to fund conversion of fleet vehicles to natural gas fuel.
- Developed market analyses of the Latin America region and recommended business strategies for expanding into other South American and Caribbean countries.
- Chaired a 20-person cross-functional problem-solving team that focused on improving internal processes, tailoring services for existing clients, and identifying new business prospects.

Co-Owner / General Manager, Las Vacas Ranch; Valencia, Venezuela   1992 - 1996
Managed operations and stock sales for this family-owned livestock ranch grossing $1 million, annually.
- Increased profit margin by 230% over a five-year period.
- Implemented process improvements and breeding programs that enhanced herd's adaptability to its environment and increased revenues and profits.

MANAGEMENT EXPERIENCE (continued)

Co-Owner / General Manager, Simplemente, S.A..; Maracaibo, Venezuela   **1992 - 1996**

Managed business operations for this "convenience store" business grossing $800,000.
- Controlled inventory levels and managed supplier relationships to secure favorable credit terms.
- Developed marketing strategies generating sales revenues up to $800,000 and net profit exceeding 16%.

INTERNSHIPS

UBS/Paine Weber; Miami, Florida   **Spring 2004**

Accountable for business development activities for this leading financial services firm. Supported sales and marketing teams in improving product support and customer support programs.
- Conducted telesales-based prospecting and cold-calling to generate potential leads for financial planners.
- Developed business opportunities for the firm in the Hispanic community throughout Florida.
- Observed financial planners analyzing client portfolios and developing financial plans to meet client goals.

Petroleos de Venezuela (P.D.V.S.A.); Puerto Ayacucho, Venezuela   **1998**

Worked part-time in local airport fueling service division of this third largest oil company in the world.
- Analyzed, redesigned, and improved internal processes of the airport fueling service division.
- Conducted market research projects for oil industry in Latin America.

ADDITIONAL SKILLS

- Foreign Languages: Spanish (Native Speaker), English (Business Fluent).
- Computer Literacy: Solver, Microsoft Project, Microsoft Office (Word, Excel, PowerPoint, Access).
- Multicultural experience gained through studies and extensive travel.

Excellent Business and Personal References Provided on Request

Samantha Fowler, B.A., B.S.W., M.S.W.

40 Blue Pond Lane, Leeton, Oxford, OX4 THB, England
Phone: 011.44.1865.744762 Cell: 011.44.7791.567899
E mail: Samantha.fowler@nbd.ox.ac.uk

RESEARCH ANALYST

Spirited, motivated, solutions-oriented professional with a creative outlook, seeking to utilize education to further career in social research. Thrives on challenge, disciplined and industrious in approach; able to gain the trust and respect of various stakeholders. Effective and tactful communicator; culturally and ethnically sensitive; well-traveled; establishes profitable rapport with persons of all levels and backgrounds. Confident, decisive; exudes energy; committed to creating top-quality work. Presents material in a manner which engages readers. Core expertize includes:

- Welfare Dynamics
- Constructing Data Sets
- Deprivation Mapping

- Statistical Analysis/Modelling
- Economic, Social & Cultural Disadvantage
- Longitudinal & Administrative Data Analysis

- Report Preparation
- Population Estimates
- Social Policy Analysis

Education

University of Oxford, Department of Social Policy and Social Work, Oxford, England   1999 – 2005
D.Phil. Candidate, Doctoral student in Social Policy
Thesis: *"Prospective Workers? Benefit Dynamics Among Lone Mothers of Different Ethnic Groups"*

McMaster University, Hamilton, Ontario, Canada   1998
MASTER OF SOCIAL WORK (Analysis of Social Welfare Policy) Dean's honor list
Thesis: *"Redistributive Impacts of Globalization"*

McMaster University, Hamilton, Ontario, Canada   1997
BACHELOR OF SOCIAL WORK – Dean's honor list
Recipient of the Masters Graduate Entrance Scholarship

McMaster University, Hamilton, Ontario, Canada   1997
BACHELOR OF ARTS in Sociology – Dean's honor list

Professional Experience

University of Oxford, Department of Social Policy and Social Work, Social Disadvantage Research Centre, Oxford, England
RESEARCH OFFICER   2003 – present

- Manage and analyze large administrative data sets and small area statistics. Projects have included: "The English Indices of Deprivation in 2004."
- Played a key team role in creating population estimates for The English Indices, a Commission for the U.K. Deputy Prime Minister's Office.
- Selected to assist in undertaking other projects including welfare spending and benefit transition analyses in Kent, analyzing longitudinal dynamics of ethnicity, health, and poverty in Slough, geographical mapping of worklessness dynamics across certain areas of England, and extracting and creating data sets for the development of the Health Poverty Index 2004 for England.
- Currently compiling data sets based on the 2001 U.K. Census of Population.

University of Oxford, Department of Social Policy and Social Work, Oxford, England   1999 – present
DOCTORATE STUDENT IN SOCIAL POLICY
- Manage and analyze large Housing Benefit/Council Tax Benefit administrative data sets.
- Scrutinize benefit dynamics and deprivation at the small area level, including longitudinal, demographic, and multivariate statistical analyses.

Lombard Canada, Toronto, Ontario, Canada   1998 – 1999
RESEARCHER, Human Resources Department
- Created job descriptions for all company employees on behalf of the Human Resources Department to be utilized for pay equity responsibilities.
- Worked in partnership with cross-functional and multi-cultural staff to successfully achieve mandate.

McMaster University, Hamilton, Ontario, Canada
APPLICATION READER   1998 – 1999
- Reviewed applications for the 1998 – 1999 Master of Social Work degree.

TEACHING ASSISTANT   1997 – 1998
- Marked examinations for first-year Bachelor of Social Work students; provided one-on-one guidance and assistance throughout the school year.

Lombard Insurance Companies, Toronto, Ontario, Canada   1995 – 1999
RESEARCH ASSISTANT
- Assisted with a variety of company- wide projects in Planning and Marketing Departments.

Publications

Noble, M., Wright, G., Dibben, C., Smith, G., McLennan, D., Anttila, C., Barnes, H., **Fowler, S.,** Noble, S., Gardner J., and Braswell, S. 2004 **The English Indices of Deprivation 2004, Office of the Deputy Prime Minister. Pp 181.**

http://www.odpm.gov.uk/stellent/groups/odpm_urbanpolicy/documents/page/rtpm_urbpol_028471.pdf

---

Community Involvement

Community Action Program for Children   1996 – 1997
- Provided services and assistance to children from low-income families.

Affordable Homes Action Association of Ontario   1995 – 1996
- Met with persons trying to obtain sheltered and low-income housing.
- Worked with multi-agency and inter-governmental persons to secure housing.
- Tasked with investing and implementing a plan to remove housing barriers for low-income families.

Computer Skills

Highly computer literate in the MS Windows environment. Program knowledge includes:

Statistical programs: SPSS, SAS, STATA, SASPAC, Supertable, GIS
General Software: MS Word, Excel, PowerPoint, Endnote

Joana M. Wesley

45 W. Greenview Avenue
Bowie, Maryland 20721

(240) 741-7411
jmwesley@aol.com

OBJECTIVE

International Health Care Management & Administration Position

International health care professional with two master's degrees in health care administration and management plus five years of work experience. Committed to quality public health programs worldwide. Conscientious, dedicated, and extremely organized. World traveled and fluent in Spanish and Italian.

EDUCATION

Bocconi School of Management, Milan, Italy
MSc, International Health Care Management, Economics, and Policy, 2004

    Professional Memberships: American College of Health Care Executives
                                     National Association of Health Service Executives

University of Maryland, College Park, Maryland
MSc, Health Care Administration, 2002

    Professional Memberships: American College of Health Care Executives
                                     Institute for Health Care Diversity

University of Maryland, College Park, Maryland
BA, Government and Politics, 1999

PROFESSIONAL EXPERIENCE

Taylor Research Consultants, Inc., Washington, DC   May 2002 to Present

Dr. Martha Taylor guides U.S. and international organizations in planning, designing and evaluating employee assistance programs (EAPs) and work/life programs. Dr. Taylor's clients include: Pfizer, Bristol-Myers, IBM, U.S. Postal Service, American Management Association, IRS, Merrill Lynch, U.S. Department of Health and Human Services, Substance Abuse Mental Health Services Administration and many others.

Executive Assistant to the President / Research Consultant

    Offered full-time position by Dr. Taylor upon completion of internship. Assist with Employee Assistance Program (EAP), Managed Mental Health (MMH), AIDS In The Workplace, Drug-Free Workplace, and Workplace Violence programs/projects developed for Fortune 500 corporations, government agencies, and international work/life organizations.

- Assisted Dr. Taylor with a commission to develop international guidelines for mental health in the workplace for strategic partners worldwide. Guidelines have been copyrighted and are being presented for adaptation in various countries worldwide.

- Conducted a comparative study of various world organizations for the development of a composite of guidelines on which Dr. Taylor could base the new international guidelines. Researched the guidelines of: The Council on Accreditation Standards, European Network on Occupational Social Work (ENOS), Employee Assistance Professional Association (EAPA), Federal Association of Occupational Social Work, International Council on Alcohol and Addictions, and International Labor Law Organization-Management of Alcohol and Drug-Related Issues in the Workplace.

- Assisted with EAP customer satisfaction survey analyses, performance guidelines, outcome measurements, and cost-benefit studies.
- Interacted daily with senior-level executives, directors, doctors, and professionals, and managed confidential paperwork, records, and communications.
- Presented a segment at the 2004 University of Maryland, Baltimore School of Social Work Second Annual Advanced EAP Management and Proactive International Satellite Conference presented to an international audience situated at 11 sites around the world.
- Participated in the 2003 Joint National Conference on Mental Health and National Conference on Mental Health Statistics in Washington, DC.

Oakland Memorial Hospital, Washington, DC   May to August 2001

Administrative Intern, Executive Office

- Provided administrative support to CEO for nonprofit, full-service, 328-bed acute care community hospital and 104-unit assisted living facility.
- Conducted targeted research to support departmental budgets; compiled a comparative study on the allocation of volunteer hours in patient care versus non-patient care departments.
- Conducted independent research of current health care issues and products, and presented findings at the Hospital's board of director meetings.
- Assisted the Medical Director with a Medical Error Prevention research project. Conducted an evaluation of the drug ordering and distribution process, and developed and presented recommendations that were implemented by the staff. Recommendations resulted in a 75% reduction in medical errors.

University of Maryland, School of Public Affairs, College Park, Maryland   May 1997 to May 2001

Administrative Assistant – Institute for Philosophy and Public Policy (a research center focused on the conceptual and normative framework of public policy formulation.)

Administrative Assistant – Center for International and Security Studies at Maryland (a research center focused on a broad range of security issues facing the U.S. in the global arena.)

- Provided administrative support to internationally recognized philosophers, policy makers, analysts, and other highly respected public affairs professionals who conduct research through the School of Public Affairs.
- Edited researchers' publications, provided technical assistance regarding layout and publication, and processed credit transactions.
- Executed numerous projects requiring extensive knowledge of several different Excel databases.
- Managed a diverse range of special projects, and coordinated meetings and events.

SKILLS

Computer: Microsoft Office Suite (Word, Excel, Access, PowerPoint, Access, Outlook), Adobe Photoshop, Dreamweaver, ACT!

Cultural: Traveled throughout Germany, France, Switzerland, Seychelles, Africa, Trinidad, Tobago, and Okinawa, Japan. Lived in Jamaica, London, and Italy.

ALLISON BRISTOW

323 Coldstone Court   Montgomery, Alabama 36100   ab102@net.net   ☎ [334] 355-5398

SITTING FOR BAR EXAM: Jul 05

CAPABILITIES DONNELLY & SHOREDITCH CAN USE NOW:

○ **Communications skills** tested by uninformed clients

○ **Research skills** tested by practicing attorneys

○ **Presentation skills** tested in court

LAW-RELATED EXPERIENCE:

○ **Law clerk** *later* **Legal Intern** Smith & Hawken, L.L.C., Wetumpka, AL   Jan 03 – Present

EXPERIENCE AS AN ADVOCATE FOR CLIENTS IN COURT

• Bond reduction hearings • Pendente lite hearings • Juvenile court hearings • Sentence reviews • Arraignments • Probation revocation hearings • Administrative hearings • District criminal, civil, and traffic courts • Dependency hearings • Sentencing hearings • Plea hearings

EXPERIENCE PREPARING FOR COURT

• Investigations • Drafting and filing motions • Writing briefs and memoranda • Negotiating plea bargains • Interviewing • Evaluating worth of civil cases • Legal research • Explaining legal rights and evidence

○ Successfully defended client in suit against real estate attorney with a decade of practice. Handled case after only four months of internship.

○ Proved in court my juvenile client was not guilty in assault case, even though experienced law officers were witnesses for the prosecution.

○ Carried the argument before a tough judge that my client's probation should not be revoked – even though he had tested positive for drugs. Had 15 minutes to prepare this case.

EDUCATION AND PROFESSIONAL DEVELOPMENT:

○ **Candidate for J.D.**, Archer of Law, Montgomery, Alabama   Expect graduation: 05
Pursued at night while working up to 45 hours a week.

○ B.A., Broadcast Journalism, University of Southern Arkansas, Littleburg, Arkansas   01

○ B.S., Business Administration (**Industrial Management**), University of Arkansas, Fayetteville, Arkansas   99

○ "Alabama Mediation Training," Resolution Resources, Birmingham, Alabama   99
Self-funded, 21 CLE hours.

PROFESSIONAL AFFILIATION: Future Trial Lawyers Association   Since 01

OTHER EXPERIENCE:

○ More than 13 years in various positions in sales, broadcasting, manufacturing, and public relations.

131

SOPHIA K. MERSINO, MPA

4175 Allerton Circle
Nashville, Tennessee 37217

Cellular: (615) 355-2296
Email: skmersino1@aol.com

Career Focus: FUNDRAISING – GRANT WRITING – PUBLIC POLICY ANALYSIS
for a government agency or nonprofit organization

> ➤ Recent graduate with master's degree in Public Administration plus bachelor's degree in Political Science. Career interest in associating with a DC-based government agency or nonprofit organization as a grant writer, fundraiser, or public-policy analyst.
> ➤ Key strengths include project management, research and information gathering, networking, and volunteer development. Excellent communication, writing, and analytical skills.
> ➤ Computer proficiency includes Microsoft Office (Word, Excel, Access, PowerPoint), PeopleSoft, Internet navigation and research, and email. Confident in learning and using new applications.

Education

MASTER OF PUBLIC ADMINISTRATION – 2004
Vanderbilt University, Nashville, Tennessee

BACHELOR OF ARTS IN POLITICAL SCIENCE – 2002
Florida A&M University, Tallahassee

Professional Experience

DECCA INSURANCE COMPANY – Nashville, Tennessee...2002 – Present
Policy Owner Services Specialist, Long-Term Care Department

Research and provide information to field agents regarding benefit changes to policy owners' long-term care coverage. Prepare benefit illustrations that reflect policy changes. Assist with special LTC projects.
- ▸ Examine policies and suggest alternate plans of care. Review applicant's medical assessment and assign appropriate rating (standard or preferred).
- ▸ Keep apprised of legislative changes and tax-qualified benefits relating to long-term care policies.
- ▸ Train and mentor new employees regarding long-term care issues and company procedures.

REPRESENTATIVE DONALD BYRD, DISTRICT 23 – Tallahassee, Florida ....2001 – 2002
Receptionist, Legislative Delegation Office

Provided assistance with legislative office activities. Interacted with constituents, the mayor's office, nonprofit organizations, and the Leon County Board of Education.
- ▸ Responded to inquiries from citizens regarding a wide array of issues related to Florida law.
- ▸ Assisted with Rep. Byrd's reelection campaign by networking with area voters and city officials. Recruited volunteers to post yard signs, assist with bulk mailings, and other campaign activities.
- ▸ Reviewed grant applications from nonprofit organizations to determine funding eligibility.

SIMPSON & GREY LEGAL CLINIC – Ocala, Florida ....2000 – 2001
Law Firm Assistant

Furnished administrative support to a team of two attorneys handling bankruptcy, divorce, and Social Security litigation.
- ▸ Collected and compiled data for clients filing Chapter 13 and Chapter 7 bankruptcies.
- ▸ Compiled client information, summarized and prepared case files, and scheduled appointments.
- ▸ Organized corporate filings and followed up on deadline requirements for SSA filings.

F.E. Toner, PhD

12 Saint Boulevard #54, Orlando, Florida 34690
321-524-7781 ♦ ftoner@yahoo.net

CLINICAL PSYCHOLOGIST
Newly Graduated Professional Focusing on Mental Health and Long-Term Care.

Empathic, effective, and motivated professional who combines clinical experience with compassion to meet the challenges facing today's health care organizations. Clear awareness of diverse backgrounds; alert to widely varied patient needs and circumstances. Collaborative team player, acting as key resource to colleagues and allied health professionals. Licensed psychologist and registered nurse. Specializations include:

Assessment Techniques (MMPI, RIAP)	Statistical Packages (SPSS, SAS)
Behavioral Medicine / Health Psychology	Cognitive Behavioral Interventions
Practice-Based Research	Clinical Outcomes Measurement
Evidence-Based Practice	Commitment / Competency Procedures

Thorough experience within emergency / urgent care psychiatric services.

SPECIALIZED EDUCATION

DOCTOR OF PSYCHOLOGY, Clinical Psychology, 2004
MASTER OF SCIENCE, Clinical Psychology, 2000
State University, Department of Psychology and Neuroscience, Orlando, Florida

Bachelor of Science ♦ Master of Science, Psychology / Statistics *(magna cum laude)*
University of South Carolina

NURSING EDUCATION:
- ✓ Chemistry, Nursing *(University of Central Texas, Dallas, Texas)*
- ✓ Graduated 1st in class – Nursing *(Dallas City General, Victoria Hospital School of Nursing, Dallas, Texas)*
  Pediatrics: City Memorial Hospital for Children, Washington, DC
  Psychiatric: Grand Central Hospital, New York, NY

DISTINCTIVE PROJECTS AND ACHIEVEMENTS

- ♦ Dropped smoking rates from 52% to 23% by pioneering innovative tobacco cessation program for veteran populations, culminating in receipt of "Best Practice Award."

- ♦ Spearheaded writing and submission of no less than 16 research grants, resulting in hundreds of thousands of dollars in monies to a variety of medical centers.

- ♦ Involved in private practice dealing with pain management and health psychology, servicing Department of Industry and DealCare patients for both brief and long-term modality.

- ♦ Serving as Chair of Medical Center's Institutional Review Board (IRB), achieved full federal and state regulatory compliance for health establishment and full NCQA accreditation.

- ♦ Utilized superior leadership abilities to motivate, teach, and supervise psychological trainees, externs, interns, and residents within American Psychological Association pre-doctoral program.

PROFESSIONAL AFFLIATIONS & MEMBERSHIPS

Canadian Psychological Association ♦ Ontario Psychological Association ♦ American Psychological Association ♦ Florida Psychological Association ♦ American Pain Society ♦ Texas Nurses Association

F.E. Toner, PhD

EMPLOYMENT HISTORY

VETERANS HEALTH CARE SYSTEM *Orlando, Florida*

(A two-division teaching hospital, affiliated with State University, servicing over 46,000 veterans along the entire Florida coast.)

POSTDOCTORAL RESIDENCY (2004)

Participated as part of a multidisciplinary team in an APA-accredited postdoctoral clinical psychology program in health psychology / behavioral medicine within full service outpatient and acute medical inpatient service. Ailments spanned range of acute and chronic psychological/psychiatric conditions frequently including concurrent acute, chronic, and/or life-threatening medical problems. Provided case management, psychotherapy, and assessment.

- Specialized in crisis intervention, couples therapy, smoking cessation groups, women's issues groups, transplant assessment, depression and stress/anxiety management groups, pain management, diabetes, cardiac rehabilitation, and stroke support.
- Presented "Outstanding Psychology Resident Award" based on performance.

PREDOCTORAL INTERNSHIP (2002-2003)

Chief Resident within APA-accredited predoctoral clinical psychology internship program. Specialty included emergency and crisis intervention, with subspecialty in primary care. Carrying a caseload of 40-50 patients, provided case management, psychotherapy, and assessment, as well as up to 10 full neuropsychological batteries per year.

ADDITIONAL CLINICAL WORK EXPERIENCE

Family Children's Home, *Dallas, Texas* (July 2001)

Practicum involving residential basic care facility for children, ages 6-17. The majority, victims of physical, emotional, and/or sexual abuse, presented with concerns such as attachment and separation issues, oppositional behavior, conduct disorders, relational problems, substance abuse, ADHD, learning disabilities, adjustment disorders, coping deficits, poor socialization and interpersonal skills, and poor academic and achievement skills.

EARLY HEALTH CARE EXPERIENCE   1987 – 1994
REGISTERED NURSE

Telemetry, Medical/Surgical, ER, ICU, CCU, and acute care, with minor experience in chronic or long-term care. Primary work with adults.

TEACHING / SUPERVISORY EXPERIENCE

- Adjunct Professor of Psychology, University of South Carolina, September 1999 to February 2000

- Department of Veterans Affairs, Orlando, Florida. Minority Summer Psychology Apprenticeship Program, 1998

- Adjunct Professor of Psychology, State University, Orlando, Florida, 1998

INDUSTRY RELATED PRESENTATIONS

Invited guest speaker at following associations speaking on a variety of professional topics:
- *Texas Board of Nursing* ◆ *Florida Psychological Association* ◆ *University of Dallas*
- *University of South Carolina* ◆ *Veterans Affairs Medical Center* ◆ *Hallmet Conference*

CHAPTER 8

Best Resumes for College Graduates Earning Degrees to Advance Their Existing Careers

Overview

Maybe you've worked in your current profession for 10 or more years, or perhaps only a couple of years. Either way, the fact that you can now add a four-year degree to your resume is virtually guaranteed to make a difference in your "employability factor" (equivalent to the number of companies, recruiters and others interested in hiring you). In fact, you're in a most advantageous position because not only do you have your bachelor's degree, you've got the experience. That's a great place to be!

To optimize the effectiveness of your resume, follow these recommendations:

- Be sure that your resume does NOT look like or "feel" like that of a traditional graduating student, someone with a degree but little if any experience.
- Consider starting your resume with a section titled Professional Profile, Qualifications Summary, or Professional Skills Profile, using that space to highlight your relevant professional skills, achievements, awards, and notable affiliations.
- Be sure to write strong job descriptions, perhaps using the Challenge-Action-Results format which communicates the challenge of each position, the action (what you did), and the results (your achievements).
- Don't worry if your resume is two pages long. There is no one-page rule!

If you follow these recommendations, focus your resume on your professional skills and experience, and leverage your degree to further promote your candidacy, you'll find that you are well positioned in the market against other qualified professionals. Your degree is one more notable achievement that you've just added to your career portfolio.

Index of Resumes Featured in This Chapter

Strategy: Another "traditional" professional-style resume with an entirely different format, tone, and presentation, and emphasizing notable workplace achievements and development projects

Resume: Dean M. Smith, pages 147-148
Writer: Ellie Vargo, CPRW, CFRWC
Objective: Undecided; open to a diversity of business opportunities
Strategy: Heavy emphasis on diversity of skills since graduate is uncertain of specific career direction; comprehensive, but succinct, job descriptions to demonstrate cross-functional qualifications

Resume: Maxwell T. Mason, pages 149-150
Writer: Sharon McCormick, MS, NCC, NCCC, CPRW
Objective: Management position in the financial services industry
Strategy: Dynamic presentation of professional skills with an emphasis on notable achievements and corporate contributions; supported with heavy focus on both collegiate and high school education, leadership, and athletics

Resume: Martha Lenin, page 151
Writer: William G. Murdock, CPRW
Objective: Position in outside sales and account management
Strategy: Excellent presentation of previous sales career with emphasis on achievements; utilizing all appropriate keywords to position graduate for a higher-level opportunity within a field sales organization

Resume: Aqueline M. Forana, page 152
Writer: John O'Connor, MFA, CRW, CPRW, CECC, CCM
Objective: Position in the institutional food sales and service industry
Strategy: Unique visual presentation and format supported by years of related work experience and a summary rich with the right skills and qualifications

Resume: Frank R. Pennington, pages 153-154
Writer: Ross Primack, CPRW, CEIP, GCDF
Objective: Position in the field of transportation management
Strategy: Primary emphasis on leadership and team-building competencies which, when combined with newly acquired bachelor's degree, positions client for a large leap in level of professional responsibility within current industry

Resume: Noreen Filbert, pages 155-156
Writer: Gail Frank, NCRW, CPRW, JCTC, CEIP, MA
Objective: Management training position in banking and finance industry
Strategy: Great format and structure to demonstrate competency across all core functional requirements for a management position within targeted industry; further utilizing references and testimonials to communicate level of performance

Resume: Terry Black, pages 157-160
Writer: Annemarie Cross, CEIP, CPRW, CRW, CCM, CECC
Objective: Prominent position as a Programmer/Developer of leading-edge IT solutions
Strategy: Very unique and detailed presentation of IT qualifications acquired through both professional experience and educational training; supported by one-page addendum detailing all major development projects to give this candidate unique and competitive distinction

Felicia Bowman

**Corporate Trainer
Available Immediately!**

Summary of Qualifications

1 Bachelor's degree in Adult Education/Training with hands-on delivery and development.

2 Experience in training and program development for major corporation.

3 Delivered dozens of workshops for team building, technical training and other workplace topics.

4 Conducted analysis of work teams, job and task components. and presented findings.

5 Excellent computer skills. including development of on-line training and tools.

6 Member: ASTD (national and local), SHRM, and ISPI

555 Wilshire Road
Tampa. Florida 33624
(813) 555-0248
fbowman@hotmail.com

Educational history and degrees

For Felicia Bowman

University of South Florida
Adult Education-Training-Human Resource Development, B.A.
Tampa, Florida in 2004

Leto High School
Graduated with Honors
Tampa, Florida

Key Strengths

Creativity – Ability to create unique solutions, analogies, and illustrations for complex problems.

Patience – Ability to work with all departments with all levels of employees.

Knowledge – Ability to use extensive insights in Adult Learners' understanding and information processing.

Structured – Ability to plan and prepare programs and workshops in a long-term, time-based critical path schedule in order to meet targeted launch dates.

Communication – Ability to express complex ideas and important points in a way that is understandable and simple for the majority of Adult Learners.

Professional Experience

Training and Documentation Specialist, Lockheed Martin
Lakeland, FL 2002–Current

Team member of highly creative Training Group for corporate offices and 3 major business sectors of this $27 billion company.

✓ Completed 12 major job and task analysis projects to document technical work processes.

✓ Designed 4 training programs, each in multiple forms of media, including the Internet, CD-ROM, PowerPoint and NetMeeting.

✓ Used interactive team development processes to assess the functionality of teams in the Shared Services division.

✓ Delivered 3 specialized training modules for highly technical computer systems.

✓ Facilitate team-building exercises, communication enhancement workshops, and general business meetings.

✓ Offer constructive and strategic input on organizational structural changes.

✓ Participate in business development projects and strategic planning.

Continued on Page 2

139

Program Assistant, Counseling Center for Human Development, University of South Florida
Tampa, Florida 1996–1999

Created policies, procedures and training for clients of USF's Counseling Center. Also provided administrative and computer troubleshooting support.

✓ Produced detailed publications and handbooks, including the Counseling Center's Handbook, internship materials, and brochures.

✓ Designed promotional materials and presentations for professional workshops for clients and university administration.

✓ Trained staff on Internet usage and software programs such as Microsoft Word, Excel, PowerPoint and Scheduler.

✓ Resolved client issues and provided customer service. Took incoming calls and provided referrals to other resources.

✓ Provided computer support for staff in the areas of software support and system troubleshooting.

✓ Conducted administrative support for the campus-wide Employee Assistance Program.

Program Assistant, University of South Florida, Veteran Services
Tampa, Florida 1994–1995

Performed administrative and financial services in USF Office that serviced Veterans in their search for Continuing Education and Employment.

✓ Reported directly to the Veteran Services Coordinator and ran the office when she was not present.

✓ Supervised 3 employees and ensured that reports and forms were properly filled out.

✓ Provided training in office procedures and policies.

✓ Handled all travel and budgeting administration.

✓ Solicited assistance from other campus offices in providing opportunities for work placement openings.

✓ Counseled veterans on their education and work options, and helped them define goals.

✓ Coordinated VA Work-Study Program for USF.

Professional Associations

Member of top local and national training organizations

National Chapter of American Society for Training and Development (ASTD)

Suncoast Chapter of American Society for Training and Development (ASTD)

Society for Human Resource Management (SHRM)

International Society for Performance Improvement (ISPI)

College Courses Completed During Program

Adult Education in the United States | Program Management

The Adult Learner | Foundations of Research

Methods of Teaching Adults | Consulting Skills

Instructional Design | Group Processes

Trainers in Business and Industry | Personnel Policy

Sample Presentations & Projects Completed During Program

Experiential Learning in Adults

Presentation Skills Workshop

Future Trends in Adult Learning

Book Review: The Adult Learner, A Neglected Species

Andragogy Versus Pedagogy: Adults Are Different Than Kids

2

Wyatt L. Frisch

213 Linn • Minnetonka, Minnesota 50248
(515) 733-9666 • wyatt_frisch70@hotmail.com

CAREER GOAL: PARK RANGER

Profile:

Story County Conservation Technician with five years of full- and part-time park-aid experience with the Skunk River Unit, Minnetonka, Minnesota.

Patrol and enforce Story County rules and regulations. Maintain, repair, and improve over 750 acres of park, prairie, and marsh; 10 miles of trails; and a beach surrounding a 3-acre lake.

Strong customer service and listening skills, calm demeanor, and sound judgment used to diffuse volatile situations and work side-by-side with County Sheriff's department personnel.

Qualified and ready to participate in law-enforcement certification.

Skills:

Prairie Burns... Park Rule Enforcement... Equipment / Building Maintenance... Park Security... Dock Management... Crime Prevention... Area Inspections... Truck, Tractor, Mowers, Power Tools, and Special Equipment Operation... Wood and Concrete Construction Techniques...

WORK EXPERIENCE

STORY COUNTY CONSERVATION, MCFARLAND PARK, Minnetonka, Minnesota   **1998–Present**

Conservation Technician (2002–Present)
Summer Park Aid (2000 & 2001)

- Maintain, repair, and improve Skunk River County conservation lands and facilities and handle park rule enforcement decisions quickly and safely. Patrol areas include McFarland Park (200 acres/5-acre lake); Peterson Park (200 acres/3-acre lake); several pothole prairies with habitat for wetland wildlife; Wakefield Woods, a 10-acre oak/hickory woodlands; Jim Ketelsen Greenwing Marsh; and Larson Marsh.

- Provide maintenance, cleaning, harrowing, and patrolling of Peterson Park swimming beach. Maintain popular hard-surfaced Touch-a-Life Trail with handicapped access to fishing dock, picnic areas, and deck overlooking the lake.

- Organize and build approximately 100 bird feeder and bat house kits yearly as requested by naturalist.

- Participate on five-member Safety Committee, setting up summer training schedule and curriculum. Check first-aid boxes and fire extinguishers.

- Operate and repair all equipment including mowers, truck, tractor, skid loader, backhoe and power tools.

Accomplishments:

√ Continued project to build 60-70 wood duck, goose, and mallard boxes from recycled mailboxes vs. wood structures, reducing costs by over 86%. Maintained over 100 habitats, even through dry, adverse weather conditions, while serving as part of Wildlife Nesting Structures Committee.

√ Served as "burn boss" on area prairie fall burn. Helped build and replant numerous prairies. Held lead role in pesticide spraying program to reduce trees in prairie.

√ Helped design, build, update, and rebuild approximately 8 of 30 footbridges covering more than 10 miles of trails. Constructed docks and decks, prepared land for parking areas, and helped remodel ranger's on-site house.

√ Invented and implemented successful night-camera project to monitor and record night activity of animals. Prepared and taught a class showing people how to build a night camera for their own use.

√ Bid on vehicle purchases, remaining well under budget.

EDUCATION / LICENSES

BS, Fisheries & Wildlife Biology, Rasmussen College, Minnetonka, Minnesota (2004)

Commercial Driver's License with Air Brakes (CDL)

Pesticide Applicator License (Class 1A & 6)

Wild Prairie Fire Certification (S130 & S190)

First Aid / CPR Training

PHIL BREHMEN

Marketing ■ Music Promotion ■ Public Relations

■ PROFILE

Entrepreneurial, high-energy marketer known for generating and implementing a constant stream of new and creative strategies. Proven track record of creating media "buzz" and generating free publicity /advertising using guerrilla marketing combined with persistence and outstanding communication skills. Conceptual wizard with a gift for exciting marketing and PR campaigns that get results.

Guerilla Tactics ... Brand Experiences ... Buzz Creation ... Permission Marketing ... Street Teams Lifestyle Campaigns ... Grassroots Promotions ... Viral Marketing ... Sponsorship Development

■ SELECTED HIGHLIGHTS

Campaign Management: Coordinated promotions, events, and marketing efforts for creative leaders including EMI, VH1, The Marketing Company, Juicy Records, Media Blitz Entertainment, and Tactile Records. Promoted events, festivals, and concert tours in the US and Australia.

Guerrilla Marketing: Spearheaded highly successful guerrilla marketing campaign for MCA recording artist, *Hope Dies*. Penetrated radio stations in several US markets using grassroots marketing and guerrilla tactics. Tour-managed and successfully promoted the band in California.

Music Promotion: Founded and marketed *Up Close and Personal*, a successful acoustic concert series featuring emerging acts and established independent bands. Produced shows, secured corporate sponsors, negotiated contracts, established partnership with the major arts magazine *Jive Weekly* and attracted top-notch performers for a fraction of their normal fee.

"Buzz" Generation: Conceived, designed, and managed PR campaign for annual Halloween festival which grew into one of Vermont's largest seasonal attractions and raised thousands of dollars for local and national charities. Garnered print, TV, and radio coverage in addition to significant corporate sponsorship.

■ PROFESSIONAL EXPERIENCE

VH1, New York, NY, Talent Assistant | Winter 2003 – Spring 2004
Primary contact for visiting celebrity talent. Worked closely with managers, agents, and publicists to ensure that everything was prepared as requested by the artists. Liaised with show producers on specific artist requests. Assumed additional responsibility for assembling daily entertainment news reports and scouring the Internet for unusual information and story angles.

Tactile Records, New York, NY, A&R/Marketing Assistant | Winter 2003 – Spring 2004
Assisted both the A&R and Marketing departments, juggling multiple responsibilities including reviewing demos, implementing Internet marketing campaigns, conducting market research, and assembling press kits.

Splash!, Philadelphia, PA, Founder and President | 2002 – 2003
Developed concept and comprehensive business plan for an innovative poster-based entertainment publication targeting the college demographic. The magazine, which attracted interest from numerous corporate advertisers, was to be distributed to dormitory bathrooms throughout the US.

PHIL BREHMEN

Marketing ■ Music Promotion ■ Public Relations

■ EXPERIENCE (continued)

Juicy Records, White Plains, NY, A & R/Marketing Intern | Summer 2003
Worked closely with A&R Director to identify new and undiscovered talent, including soliciting/reviewing demos and attending live showcases. Also assembled press kits, created marketing plans, photographed artists, and managed general office logistics.

EMI Australia, Sydney, Australia, Creative/Marketing Intern | Spring 2003
Compiled master directories of potential imaging, fashion, and creative clients. Assisted with in-store retail promotion and tour marketing. Attended live shows and recommended artists to A&R.

Media Blitz Entertainment, New York, NY, Marketing & Promotional Assistant | 2002 – 2004
Developed marketing and promotional strategies for MCA recording artist *Hope Dies*. Consulted on image, instituted innovative promotions, aggressively targeted radio stations, solicited and secured TV and print interviews, and placed the band on various music websites and other media outlets. Managed all aspects of the band's California appearances.

Mercedes World Festival, Bethesda, MD, Tour Marketing Assistant | Summer 2002
Promoted this unique summer tour package to various retail outlets, colleges, restaurants, and on the street through postcards, flyers, posters, press releases, and counter cards. Also worked on-site.

CollegeCentral.com, New York, NY, Marketing Manager, Pennsylvania | 2000 – 2001
Researched and identified sites for on-line/cross promotion. Successfully tested and promoted site which attracted the second highest number of hits for a territory. Managed Pennsylvania market.

Additional related experience includes event management at several concerts and festivals in the US and Australia. Guerrilla marketing and promotional campaigns for emerging bands and musicians. Journalism for school newspapers in Vermont and New York. Interviews with national artists such as *Dave Matthews* and *Smashing Pumpkins*.

■ EDUCATION AND PROFESSIONAL DEVELOPMENT

BA, Communication with Marketing Emphasis, New York University, New York, NY | May 2004
Dean's List ▪ Student Council ▪ President, Class of 2004 ▪ President, Communication Club

Professional conferences and workshops included: SXSW-South By Southwest, CIC-Concert Industry Consortium. CMJ Convention, Virgin Megastore/MTV2 Developing Artists Panel, Australian Music Week, Atlantis Music Conference, NACA-National Association for Campus Activities National Convention, Millennium Music Conference, The Media Workshop, College Media Convention, NACA Summer Workshop on Contemporary Concert Promotion & Mgt, Association for the Promotion of Campus Activities Conference.

Computer skills include MAC/PC, Word, Excel, PowerPoint, digital photography, advanced Internet skills.

■ AWARDS AND HONORS

Frank Jacobs Memorial Prize for "unusual tenacity in pursuit of a goal"
Vermont Spirit of Community Awards, Bronze Medalist – selected from over 35,000 entrants

CHRISTINE MICHAELS

813-632–1834 ▪ michaels@email.com

14 Driftwood Lane, Tampa, FL 33601

Career Goal	**Reporter ... Producer** qualified by superior communication, writing, and storytelling skills. Creative and personable, with the ability to remain calm and collected under pressure. Fluent in French and Creole.
Education	**Bachelor of Science** – May 2004 *Telecommunications (Specialization News) with an outside concentration in French* University of South Florida, Tampa, Florida

Professional Highlights

→ *Selected from among 20 applicants for the role of News Producer* on WUFT-TV 5, a Public Service Broadcasting (PBS) affiliate serving 20 counties.

→ *Recognized for writing and producing pieces on relevant issues* including housing funding for the homeless and the effects of holiday depression.

→ *Interviewed high-profile personalities* including Lt. Governor Frank Brogan and gubernatorial candidate Bill McBride.

→ *Volunteered with the Radio Reading Service* reading newspapers on the air for the visually impaired.

→ *Instrumental in positioning the local Eye on Entertainment series to feature national entertainers.* Personally interviewed David Copperfield and Comedy Central comedians David Attel and Daniel Tosh.

Related Experience

WUFT-TV 6 (PBS Affiliate), Tampa, Florida – since 2002
News Producer for the noon news show; assign stories, write teases, design boxes and graphics, and ensure a smooth-flowing program. *Reporter* for the evening news show and tasked with writing, shooting, and editing packages.

Cable News Network, Atlanta, Georgia – 2002
Producer tasked with *field production of special projects.* Aided in producing segments, coordinated with PR agencies in scheduling guests, and wrote scripts.

WRUF-AM 850, Tampa, Florida – since 2001
Host and Producer for the weekly radio show "Eye on Entertainment." *Anchor and Producer* for the mid-day news show.

WUFT-Classic 94, Tampa, Florida – 2000 to 2001
Reporter for the evening news.

Selected Leadership Highlights

Official Ambassador, Florida Cicerones
One of 70 selected from an applicant pool of over 650 to promote the University of South Florida to visitors, conduct campus tours, and foster alumni relations.

Recruitment Counselor / Junior Panhellenic Vice President, Panhellenic Council
One of 72 counselors selected from over 200 applicants to serve on the 2002 recruitment team. As Vice President, oversaw the organizational selection process of directors and assistant directors.

Vice President of Administration / Executive Secretary, Kappa Alpha Theta
Held executive leadership roles for two consecutive years.

JEREMY T. WRIGHT

1773 Adams Lane, Princeton, NJ 08540

(609) 730-5555 Home ▪ jtwright@mymail.com

Network Engineer / Network Administrator / IT Support Specialist

Network engineering graduate with experience in project lifecycle management for LAN network administration, MS Small Business Server 2000 architecture, workgroup and website support. Proven troubleshooting skills for corporate LAN and external client network applications. Skilled in:

☑ Network Installation / Configuration	☑ Network Management	☑ Project Management
☑ System Upgrades / Conversions	☑ LAN / WAN Architecture	☑ Peer-to-Peer Networks
☑ Backup / Disaster Recovery	☑ Web Content Upgrades	☑ Customer Service

---

TECHNOLOGY SUMMARY

Networking

Installation and configuration of Cisco 2500 and 1900 routers and switches, LAN/WAN, OSI Model and layered communication, OSPF, RIP, IGRP, EIGRP, BGP, Ethernet cabling, IOS Command-line Modes, Netware 5.1, Novell Directory Services, NDS rights, Windows 2000 Server, Microsoft TCP/IP Protocol Suite, Active Directory objects (users / groups / security) and other administration-based applications.

Operating Systems

Windows 95 / 98 / 2000, Windows 2000 Server, Cisco IOS, Netware 5.1, Linux Red Hat 7.3

Applications

MS Word 2000, FrontPage 2000, PowerPoint 2000, Excel 2000, MS Outlook, MS Publisher, Visio

---

EDUCATION

Diploma in Network Engineering, The Chubb Institute, New York, NY – 2004
Concentration: Windows 2000 Server, Netware 5.1, Linux 7.3, Cisco 2500 and 1900 routers and switches

Bachelor of Science, Communications, Rutgers University, New Brunswick, NJ – 2003
Concentration: Small Group and Marketing Communications

EXPERIENCE AND ACCOMPLISHMENTS

COMMUNICATIONS COMPLIANCE SERVICES, Princeton, NJ   2000 – present
Start-up company providing eCommerce subscription service to life sciences and regulated industries for FDA submissions and compliance research via database-driven website (www.compliance.biz).

Systems and Support Analyst (Report to CIO)
Project management, network engineering and troubleshooting 24X7 for servers, network integration, security/backup, and hardware/software supporting internal and external clients such as Janssen Pharmaceuticals. Built and maintain LAN, manage users and groups, and create client email accounts.

- **Networking.** Upgraded Microsoft Small Business Server 4.5 to Microsoft Small Business Server 2000 in two days, rather than the projected five-day period, resulting in zero downtime for business.

- **Website Support.** Created and upgraded content on production server for 8,000-page eCommerce website (www.compliance.biz), built customer database with 2,000 entries, managed workflow for free trial accounts, and provided first-level contact via support emails in response to customer inquiries.

- **Customer Service.** Designed and implemented innovative process for addressing customer support requests, effectively reducing response time from two hours to less than one hour.

145

Robert Taylor

1228 Buckingham Drive ◆ Schaumburg, IL 60193
(847) 555-5555 ◆ rtaylor@mydomain.com

Professional Summary

Visionary **IT BUSINESS ANALYST** with over eight years' experience in technology project management and assimilating business intelligence targeting efficiency and optimization. Expertise includes budget development and management, resource planning, team building, vendor selection and negotiation.

Ability to produce framework for delivering high-value enterprise-level intelligence leading to improved decision-making and cost-reduction measures. Highly effective in promoting productive work environments, with commitment to team building, empowerment, and quality control. Exceptional attention to detail with regard to development, cost control, planning, and implementation.

Consistently successful in strengthening organization's value, reducing operating costs, and improving bottom-line profitability through innovation and strategic organizational leadership. Extensive experience in strategic planning and project management.

Additional expertise in Request for Proposal process and Cisco Network design and implementation.

Education

Bachelor of Science in Business Administration/Information Technology   2004
MARQUETTE UNIVERSITY ~ Milwaukee, WI

Experience

Senior Business Analyst   2002 – Present
ACME FOODS, INC. ~ Chicago, IL
Designated Project Manager for Network Implementation Team, responsible for budgeting and cost control, resource planning, communications, and team leadership.

- **Improved corporate infrastructure** by analyzing existing communication needs and developing wireless network framework currently being implemented. Network unites 95 remote nationwide locations by providing access to secured internal information, and an Internet gateway.
- **Championed business processes** of corporate Wide Area Network solutions provider, **reducing order fulfillment** from six months to one month.
- **Spearheaded development of *Just in Time* (JIT) methodology** for managing and deploying WAN capacity to remote locations, ensuring adequate distribution of bandwidth across multiple locations and optimizing cash flow.
- **Reduced associated deployment costs approximately 50%** by defining Wireless Local Area Network (WLAN) standards supporting all current and future wireless-based applications.
- **Served on integration team** responsible for merging acquisitions into corporate infrastructure.
- Instrumental in **site-to-site Virtual Private Network development**, resulting in 60% cost reduction relating to remote location connectivity charges to main network.
- Primary promoter of Network Services Group's benefits to corporate end users, **improving communication flow** and general employee knowledge of group's capabilities.

Associate Business Analyst   2001 – 2002
Developed and marketed new business service ensuring newly created applications exceeded client expectations prior to initial deployment.

Network Analyst   1996 – 1999
BUSINESS CONSULTING GROUP, INC. ~ Atlanta, GA
Installed and supported Local Area Network (LAN) systems at client locations.

DEAN M. SMITH

6453 Wydown, Apt. E-4 • Clayton, MO 63105
314.555.8222 • 716.555.4587/cell • deanmsmith@sbcglobal.net

Energetic, entrepreneurial Business Professional with proven results in business analysis, process/efficiency improvement, new business development, marketing, and sales.

SUMMARY

- ➢ Critical thinker with a strategic, big-picture focus.
- ➢ Organized, meticulous planner.
- ➢ Focused and creative project manager; adept at generating ideas and orchestrating effort to deliver better-than-anticipated results.
- ➢ Skilled relationship manager, effective in building productive working relationships based on empathy, accurate needs assessment, problem-solving expertise and trust.
- ➢ Articulate communicator.
- ➢ Tough, but fair, negotiator.
- ➢ Hands-on, demanding team leader; aggressive in goal attainment.
- ➢ Logical, collaborative, and diplomatic problem solver; skilled in facilitating integrated, efficient, and profitable business solutions.
- ➢ Computer literate: proficient in MS Office products, FrontPage, and the Internet.
- ➢ Dynamic contributor with proven leadership potential and a passion for growth.

EDUCATION

B.S.B.A., Major: Finance, Minor: Political Science, Saint Louis University, St. Louis, MO, May 2004
- • Cumulative GPA: 3.50; Dean's List.
- • Attended school while fulfilling a co-op work assignment with Emvee Corp.
- • Vice President, Social Secretary: Alpha Epsilon Pi social fraternity.

EXPERIENCE

GREEKDUDS.COM, St. Louis, MO   2002-present

Partner
Developed business plan and started online retail business offering apparel and accessories to college Greek organizations. Formulated marketing, purchasing, pricing, and customer-relations strategies.
- • Achieved immediate profitability.
- • Carried no inventory; purchased direct from Emvee Corp.

EMVEE CORP., St. Louis, MO   2001-2002

Director of Operations 9/01-07/02
Directed operations for manufacturer/wholesaler generating multi-million dollar annual sales of licensed apparel and accessories marketed to chain drug, department store, mass merchandiser and food wholesaler accounts including JC Penney, Kmart, Wal-Mart and Walgreen. Assessed operations to identify cost-reduction opportunities and developed strategic initiatives to deliver efficiency and process improvements. Hired change managers to continue positive momentum.
- • Changed primary emphasis in hiring decisions from qualifications to attitude.
- • Initiated "all-channel" communications.

- Sourced, planned, and implemented IT infrastructure upgrades. Integrated accounting, purchasing, inventory control, sales, order entry, and data processing functions using Great Plains Dynamics software. Vastly expanded and improved system functionality for data retrieval, order selection, inventory management, and performance reporting.
- Created new numbering and bin systems to facilitate locating finished inventory items.
- Formulated standard operating procedures and automated purchasing, receiving, order-to-invoice, return authorization, new account, new vendor, and new item information.
- Created weekly sales programs and closeout lists; initiated profitable disposal of overstocked and out-of-season merchandise by promoting and selling these as "collectibles" via Internet.
- Researched and instituted new employee health insurance package.
- Attended trade shows nationwide – including Men's Apparel Guild in California (MAGIC) – to establish and enhance account relationships.

Account Manager *1/01-05/02*
Concurrent with position below, established account relationships with major retailers nationwide.

- Participated in Times Square ToysRUs store opening. Designed and executed 40-sq.-ft. planogram instrumental in gaining national account status.
- Orchestrated Super Bowl 2002 merchandise sales effort. Engaged local printer to apply NFL logos; hired trucks and drivers to deliver Super Bowl XXXV merchandise to 100+ Baltimore-area Kroger supermarket locations.
- Opened casino market: added Harrah's and Caesar's Palace in Las Vegas.
- Consistently exceeded sales forecasts.

Cost Analyst *1/01-9/01*
Established and analyzed manufacturing costs. Developed new pricing strategy and expanded price structure for different customer groupings based on inbound/outbound shipping requirements.

- Dramatically reduced pricing time: developed Excel spreadsheet with cost, margin, and quantity data; built and integrated Access database to facilitate and streamline the pricing process while also making it accessible to colleagues.
- Created style and item numbers for new products; apprised Sales via sell sheets and sales updates.
- Reformulated item and style numbers; reduced 17,000 items to 4,250, simplifying inventory, dramatically reducing picking and delivery times, and increasing inventory turns.

Freight Analysis (Logistics) *1/01-9/01*
Initially researched freight charges to detect past discrepancies. Illustrated discrepancies for vendors and freight resources and collected refunds on billing errors. Participated in co-op learning with other shipping managers to better understand the National Motor Freight Classification System which defines product classifications for truck and rail shipment.

- Cut shipping costs $40,000 in six months.
- Developed and enforced new Vendor Information Agreement form and Purchase Order Confirmation procedures.
- Renegotiated shipping contracts and quotas with UPS, ABF, Roadway, Pilot Air, and FedEx.
- Integrated WorldShip (UPS) software with internal system to increase efficiency and reduce turnaround time.

MAXWELL T. MASON

1818 Sunshine Drive   Houston, Texas 72345   Home: (915) 555-8240
Cell: (915) 555-3334   Email: mmason@hotmail.com

CAREER PROFILE

RESULTS-ORIENTED MANAGEMENT PROFESSIONAL with **7+ years** of solid experience in the financial services, construction, and agricultural industries. Experience includes a **Fortune 500** international billion-dollar world leader in the securities industry, a multi-million dollar agricultural company, a million-dollar development company that contracted with the Federal Emergency Management Agency and a highly respected construction company. Proven track record of success as a cost- and quality-conscious manager who leads by example and inspires staff to achieve maximum performance. Strategic thinker with excellent analysis and problem-solving skills who interacts well with all levels of employees. Superior administrative, follow-through, and organizational skills with a strong hands-on approach to management. Driven and self-motivated professional with excellent mechanical aptitude and troubleshooting skills.

PROFESSIONAL OBJECTIVE

Seeking to drive a company's profitability as a Financial Services Representative in a team-oriented environment that values dedication and results.

PROFESSIONAL EXPERIENCE

MERRILL LYNCH, AUSTIN, TEXAS
Financial and Investment Services Intern (2004)
- ❖ Learned extensively about the financial services industry from an international world leader in securities, investments, and commodities.
- ❖ Researched financial portfolios which included securities, life insurance, corporate and municipal bonds, mutual funds, certificates of deposit, annuities, and other investments.
- ❖ Called companies to provide troubleshooting and problem resolution for accounts worth millions of dollars.
- ❖ Learned and interpreted financial statements and symbols and thoroughly explained account information to clients.
- ❖ Assisted in creating and compiling business presentations for current clients.
- ❖ Researched prospectuses and provided financial information as needed for brokers.
- ❖ Successfully completed all aspects of the internship.

BIG SKY FARMS, HOUSTON, TEXAS
Assistant Manager, Aerial Spraying (2001 To 2004)
- ❖ Worked as an Assistant Manager for a company worth **$8MM** to help manage the additional **$1.5MM** aerial spraying business that sprayed **100,000+** acres of sugar beet farmland per year.
- ❖ Oversaw up to **$500,000** in chemical inventory and responsible for the chemical mixing and loading operations for three industrial-sized planes which sprayed up to **50** loads per day. Each load sprayed **90** acres; a quarter section, or **180** acres, is worth approximately **$200,000.**
- ❖ Drove forward successful cash sugar beet crop yields by mixing chemicals precisely and accurately while other competing aerial spraying businesses experienced chemical accidents that ruined their crops.
- ❖ Performed general maintenance on the planes and on the farm's 13 tractors (**$150,000+** apiece).
- ❖ Managed millions of dollars worth of chemicals and equipment inventory and completed extensive documentation and paperwork to account for every item purchased and used on the farm.
- ❖ Supervised three employees who assisted in all aerial spray operations.
- ❖ Consistently worked 12-hour days while working up to **1,300** hours throughout the year to fund college costs.
- ❖ Flown to Minnesota by the owner to help with the sugar beet harvest by driving a semi tractor-trailer truck.
- ❖ Praised by the owner and staff for professionalism, dedication, dependability, technical knowledge, and integrity.

FIRST RATE HOMES, HOUSTON, TEXAS
Crew Chief (1997 to 2000)
- Worked 12-15 hours per day managing the development and set-up of temporary mobile homes for this million-dollar mobile home sales company. Construction was funded for flood victims through Federal Emergency Management Agency (FEMA).
- Acted as a liaison between FEMA, company owners, builders, and residents.
- Operated all heavy equipment and machinery including backhoes, bobcats, forklifts, front-end loaders, and dump trucks.
- Gained broad exposure to the housing industry by assisting in many different areas of the business such as basic construction, equipment operations, excavation, general maintenance, landscaping, sales, and service.
- Praised for mechanical/technical aptitude, managerial, interpersonal, and relationship-building skills, solid dependability, and quality results.
- Saved money for college and was able to attend full-time.

EXCAVATION SERVICES, CORPUS CHRISTI, TEXAS
Rebuilding Specialist (1997)
- Assisted in cleaning both public and private property damaged from severe flooding.
- Worked independently and as part of a team by coordinating with other workers throughout the county.
- Self-taught skills in learning to operate heavy equipment and machinery required for clean-up duties.
- Recruited to work with First Rate Homes in a management capacity.

CONSTRUCTION SERVICES, DALLAS, TEXAS
Construction Worker (1996)
- Learned all aspects of repairing and maintaining underground crude oil and natural gas lines.
- Moved to Corpus Christi to accept Excavation Services position for the experience.

COMPUTER SKILLS

Windows 3.1, 95, & XP   Office 97 & 2000   Internet Research   Microsoft Outlook Express
Crystal Ball   Ibottson   Real Options Analysis Toolkit   SPSS
Proprietary Agricultural & Financial Services Software

EDUCATION

B.S., BUSINESS ADMINISTRATION, THE UNIVERSITY OF TEXAS, HOUSTON, TEXAS (2004)
MAJOR: FINANCIAL MANAGEMENT
MINOR: ECONOMICS
- G.P.A. : 3.5 / 4.0
- Worked all through college and full-time during the summers to fund **90%** of college expenses.

DALLAS CITY HIGH SCHOOL, DALLAS, TEXAS
- Won second place in the State in an investment game started by the local newspaper.
- Invested **$100,000** of theoretical stock and made **$30,000** the first week.
- Completed one year of high-school Spanish courses.
- Worked part-time while in high school and full-time during the summers to save for college expenses.
- Active in a local band and jazz band by playing the alto saxophone.
- Active in football and golf for three years.
- Volunteered at the County Fair for five years during the summers.

REFERENCES AVAILABLE UPON REQUEST

MARTHA LENIN

1418 Avenue G., Unit 203
Seattle, Washington 98911
204.711.8223
Martha.Lenin@yahoo.com

CANDIDATE: OUTSIDE SALES / ACCOUNT MANAGEMENT
Relationship Management / Account Penetration / Product Presentations

An exceptionally strong sales performer, gaining accolades as a top national producer in a 25-store chain offering exclusive and proprietary products. A consistent employment record of excellence and top performance.

Bachelor of Arts – Speech / Organizational Communications (May, 2004)
<u>UNIVERSITY OF WASHINGTON</u> – Seattle, Washington
Note: Two years academic study at Madison College, Switzerland. Socially fluent: Spanish

Marcy D's – Seattle, Washington
2003 to Present
Sales Representative – Part Time

Market an exclusive and proprietary line of luxury lounge wear (women's, men's, children's) in the prestigious Snoqualmie Heights Shopping Village. Additional responsibilities as 3rd Key (Assistant Manager) for daily operations.

- Completed a one-year march to national sales dominance as the top-producing non-managerial salesperson. Ranked 10th in the company for total revenues out of a corporate staff of 260. Produced $205,000 in gross sales.
- Averaged 11% above goal in total Units Per Transaction and an average ticket of $227.
- Adept at phone prospecting for return business, achieving 85% of all sales from return customers by the end of the first year.

Ron Abrams Showrooms / Seattle Market Center – Seattle, Washington
2003 (July, October)
Sales Representative

Selected for two one-week contract assignments during the regional Apparel Mart's seasonal markets. Initially represented the Kay Celine line with the manufacturer's representative; then personally represented the Noun line at the October market.

- Presented the line to buyers from a wide variety of apparel retailers – small family boutiques to large regional multi-unit chains. Discussed technical differences for over 100 pieces of clothing per line.
- Achieved a higher than anticipated call-back ratio with up to 25% of all buyers placing purchase orders within 60 days of the market.

The Ultimate Closet – Seattle, Washington
2001 to 2003
Sales Representative – Summers / Part Time

Gained two years of strong sales experience in women's apparel, accessories, and jewelry. Consistently ranked second in client volume and first in total ticket revenues.

- Produced six-to-eight sales tickets in excess of $500 per month, double-to-triple the average of the other four producers.
- Completed ongoing client follow-up contact, averaging up to 30 contacts daily depending on the season and floor activity.
- Implemented in-store and vendor promotions, provided strong customer service and oversaw merchandising and displays.

AQUELINE M. FORANA

1298 Bless'd New, Lafayette, LA 27612
aqueline@no.rr.com / 980.065.9556

VENDING SALES / FRANCHISE DEVELOPMENT

NUTRITION/FOODS

SALES

CONSUMER SCIENCES

PROJECT PLANNING

NUTRITIONAL ASSESSMENT

INSTITUTIONAL FOODS

CATERING

FOOD SERVICE

MERCHANDISING

MARKET RESEARCH

EVENT PLANNING

CUSTOMER SERVICE

PROCUREMENT

BUSINESS FOUNDATION

HOSPITALITY

EXPERIMENTAL FOODS

PROFILE OF TRANSFERABLE SKILLS

- *Strong training and transferable skills for various professional opportunities in regional sales of nutrition, foods, and related areas that will utilize training and related business training and volunteer experiences. Seeking an aggressive compensation package in the sales of institutional foods.*
- *Understand techniques, technology and the most current literature/research within the foods and nutrition field.*
- *Professional skills include high level of responsibility in the areas of marketing, public relations, sales, account management, finance, and related functions with Master Merchandising based in New Orleans, Louisiana. Position required extensive travel and the learning/application of multiple aspects of the business, its merchandising functions and other work on behalf of professionally licensed sports products. Additional experience in this area includes event and people management.*
- *Able to conceive and develop new methods that expedite troubleshooting processes and reduce costs.*
- *Demonstrated ability to accept diverse responsibility as well as a strong commitment to community through volunteer experiences. Understand the need to communicate and promote communications with those associated with businesses and the community.*
- *Able to troubleshoot problems that slow or hamper efficiency of team members.*
- *Continuous working experiences and ability to communicate with all levels of decision makers, from the worker in the field to the functional department head to the upper management level.*

PROFESSIONAL WORK HISTORY

MASTER MERCHANDISING, New Orleans, LA; *Institutional Food Representative (2000 – Present)*
Perform multi-task marketing and merchandising duties; facilitate key clients and events including New Orleans Saints Institutional Foods and New Orleans Hornets.

BRINNA CATERING, New Orleans, LA; *Food Service Representative (1996 – 2000)*
Key member of the food service preparation team; worked events including weddings, bar/bat mitzvahs, corporate events, private functions, and fundraisers for various city events.

EDUCATION & VOLUNTEER EXPERIENCE

UNIVERSITY OF NEW ORLEANS, New Orleans, LA
Bachelor of Science in Foods & Nutrition, August 2004
Volunteer Work:

* Meals on Wheels	* Camp Eberhart (Summer 2000)
* Cinderella USF Service Project	* Meridian Wellness Clinic (July 2003 – August 2003)
* Nutritional lesson plans for USF diabetes specialist	

SPECIFIC TRAINING OBTAINED THROUGH COURSEWORK – Meredith College

- ➤ Training in Anthropometrics Sales
- ➤ Presentation about Purchasing in the Food Service Industry
- ➤ Role of Creatine Supplementation for the Athlete
- ➤ Project Work in Sales to Professional Sports Teams and Institutions
- ➤ Presentation on the Blood Urea Nitrogen (BUN) Pathway
- ➤ Food Demonstration – Presentation on Group Discussion Methods

FRANK. R. PENNINGTON

900 West Highland Avenue ◆ San Diego, CA. 91702 ◆ 555-555-9547 ◆ frpennington@aol.com

-DYNAMIC TRANSPORTATION MANAGEMENT PROFESSIONAL-

Fleet Management	*Freight Consolidation*	*Intermodal Transportation*	*Cargo Handling*
Carrier Management	*Customer Delivery*	*Dispatch Operations*	*Freight Forwarding*
Outbound Transportation	*Regulatory Compliance*	*Safety Management*	*Traffic Planning*

PROFILE

Team builder offering proven ability to motivate staff to achieve peak performance. Highly effective and persuasive communication skills. Resourceful troubleshooter adept at rapidly identifying/addressing problems and implementing solutions to ensure operational efficiency. Well-organized and proficient at multi-tasking, prioritizing, and goal setting. Superior customer service aptitude with a forte for meeting and exceeding expectations. Proficient in Microsoft programs including **Word, Excel, Access,** and **Outlook**.

REFERENCE EXCERPT

"Frank has proven that he can lead and manage diverse work groups. He understands the importance of meeting corporate goals and tailors his actions to help achieve them. As a leader, he appropriately challenges substandard performance as well as rewarding achievement. Frank does not shy away from making the necessary tough decisions."

Steven E. Mason
Director of Customer Service – MARINGOLA NATIONAL

EDUCATION

UNIVERSITY OF PHOENIX, Phoenix, AZ
Bachelor of Arts in Business Management (G.P.A. 3.90) – 2004

CAREER HISTORY

MARINGOLA NATIONAL   Los Angeles, CA   3/95 to Present
Served in increasingly responsible positions for Santa Barbara-based provider of premium truckload and intermodal services with 32 locations in the United States and Canada, 19,000 associates, and $3.8 billion in annual revenues.

Senior Service Team Leader – Intermodal Division (12/03 to Present)
- Orchestrate and troubleshoot operations for company's largest truck-rail hub and intermodal division.
- Coordinate daily activity transfer of freight from rail yards to customers.
- Oversee and monitor driver assignments, schedules, and progress. Process accident and incident reports. Administer driver payroll.
- Supervise activities, efforts, and performance of 33 drivers and an administrative assistant.
- Administer personnel functions including interviewing, hiring, referral for termination, new hire orientation, and annual performance appraisals.
  - ❖ Steered over 73% growth of intermodal fleet that improved and ensured achievement of customer service standards. Consistently maintain 98% efficiency rating.
  - ❖ Met Kmart direct-to-store service requirements – 100% for 3 consecutive years.
  - ❖ Initiated truck-rail specific driver orientation to eliminate frequent issues faced by new drivers.

153

Service Team Leader - Regional & Intermodal Division (6/00 to 12/03)

❑ Administered all facets of fleet operations including managing 112 drivers and 3 administrative associates.
❑ Ensured fleet achievement of customer service and goals.
❑ Monitored and maintained performance and safety standards.
❑ Assisted with on-going efforts to retain drivers by maintaining open communication.
❑ Served as key member of Operations Center Training Focus Group.
❑ Assisted with drafting Regional and Intermodal procedure manual.
❑ Trained 5 new Intermodal Division managers along with 4 administrative associates.
  ❖ Acknowledged for superior service by major clients including Blander Paper and McTaver Reed.
  ❖ Increased Western region utilization from 432 to 597 miles per day.
  ❖ Decreased unbilled miles from 83 to 74 per load, resulting in savings of $0.88 per mile.
  ❖ Corrected administrative reporting oversight, resulting in $13,000 annual savings.

Service Team Representative (3/95 to 6/96)

❑ Handled monitoring and troubleshooting of driver communications including macro messages and phone calls.
❑ Processed driver log forms and maintained spreadsheet of mileage and transfers.
❑ Chosen by supervisor as Service Team Committee Chairperson.
❑ Contributed articles and photographs to monthly *On the Road* publication.
  ❖ Within first six months of employment, nominated as "Rising Star Employee of the Month."
  ❖ Recognized for consistently processing more macros and completing more calls than any other representative.

MILITARY SERVICE

UNITED STATES ARMY
Honorable Discharge   May 1994

VOLUNTEER SERVICE

SAN DIEGO PARK AND RECREATION DEPARTMENT – **Baseball Coach** (1997 - Present)

BARTON CHILDREN'S HEATH CENTER – **Fundraising Volunteer** (1994 – Present)

References Furnished Upon Request

Noreen Filbert

555 Drakewood Avenue   Brandon, Florida 33702   (813) 555-7901   nfilbert@yahoo.com

Over 12 years of experience in banking and finance. Dependable and conscientious professional who is attentive to detail and produces quality work. Ambitious team player who enjoyed increasing responsibility levels during NationsBank/Huntington Bank career.

Attending college at night to get B.A. degree with specialization in Management and Quality tracks. Previous entrepreneurial experience as 6-year owner and business manager of small business. Ready and eager to assume management training duties in Finance Department.

Skills and Accomplishments

Analytical and Detail-oriented	☑ Conducted analytical procedures on financial data, spread financial data and tax returns, and calculated financial ratios to determine compliance.
	☑ Researched media sources such as Wall Street Journal to gather external data on large corporate borrowers.
Cash Management	☑ Provided service and help for 50 Cash Management Program accounts pertaining to set-up, wire transfers, and disbursement of funds.
Customer Service	☑ Resolved 10–15 customer problems per day due to changing corporate customer requirements and product limitations.
Trustworthy	☑ Created brand new position as Credit Associate to provide continuity and attention to detail in monitoring loans >$500,000.
Credit Policies	☑ Prepared Credit Review Committee meeting minutes and compiled essential reports for senior management.
Reports	☑ Significantly refined, improved, and regimented reports used by loan officers and senior management to determine when borrowers were out of compliance.
Accounting	☑ Completed Accounting I and Principles of Banking through American Institute of Banking (AIB).
	☑ Mastered Financial Accounting for Managers, Management Accounting and Control (Cost Accounting), Financial Management, and Investments during B.A. program.
New Accounts	☑ Wrote procedures, communicated, and corresponded with new statewide accounts to set up customized account profiles and requirements.
Budgets & Financial Statements	☑ Grew small business to profitable status and managed operations as Business Manager. Developed annual budget, administered payroll and banking, coordinated mailings, managed purchasing, and developed advertising and public relations strategies.
Management	☑ Hired, trained, and managed 8 employees in addition to teaching 20 one-hour classes per week.
	☑ Managed all aspects of annual and quarterly art shows: secured facility, sold advertising, contracted with artists, and created programs.
Presentations	☑ Earned designation as Competent Toastmaster (CTM) after creating and delivering a number of successful oral presentations.
Office Management	☑ Coordinated physical move of entire banking department with minimal downtime: directed movers and utilities, developed floor plan and requirements, and notified employees about plans and progress.

Decision Making	☑ Thoroughly interpreted and made recommendations regarding financial position of borrowers.
Total Quality Management (TQM)	☑ Completed TQM training, including Foundations of TQM, Quality Implementation, Operations Management and Quality Enhancement, and Advanced Quality Management.
Leadership	☑ Voted "Educational Vice President" of Toastmasters group due to strong organizational skills and trustworthiness.
Problem Solving	☑ Created system for loan officers to monitor financial loan covenants through design and implementation of standard compliance reports.
Computer Literate	☑ Competent in Microsoft Word and Excel, Lotus 1–2–3, Ami Pro, WinFast, and WordPerfect. Familiar with Paradox and Word Pro.

Performance Review Excerpts

Is very meticulous.
Meets deadlines.
Makes sound decisions.
Maintains excellent documentation.
Has easily met the targets set for her.
Reports are readable and to the point.
Has been proactive in obtaining what is needed.
Is quickly able to serve as a resource to credit analysts.
Has very high standards regarding the accuracy of her work.
Does a good job recognizing unclear requirements and obtaining clarification.
Demonstrated increased confidence in completing assignments that are not always "routine."

Professional Experience

HUNTINGTON BANK (formerly NationsBank)　　**TAMPA, FLORIDA**　　**1984—PRESENT**

Credit Reporting Analyst, Credit Policy Administration	2002—PRESENT
Credit Associate, Commercial Credit Department	1997—2002
Account Coordinator, Corporate Cash Management	1990—1997
Administrative Assistant to Senior Vice President and Branch Manager	1989—1990

MAJESTIC ART GALLERY　　**BRANDON, FLORIDA**　　**1982—1989**

Founder, Co-owner, and Business Manager

Education

UNIVERSITY OF SOUTH FLORIDA	**TAMPA, FLORIDA**	**B.A., 2004**
CONNECTICUT COLLEGE	**NEW LONDON, CONNECTICUT**	**2 YEARS**
SPRINGFIELD HIGH SCHOOL	**SPRINGFIELD, DELAWARE**	**HIGH SCHOOL**

TERRY BLACK

154 S.E. Bottom O'Rylie Circle
Seattle, Washington 42541   terryblack@hotmail.com   555.478.526 (Home)
555.698.321 (Cell)

Focus
BUSINESS ANALYST • DEVELOPER/PROGRAMMER

Results-driven professional utilizing sophisticated development and programming skills to secure an outstanding record in the creation of applications and solutions across diverse industries. Combines sincere passion for resolving complex issues and business challenges through technical foresight. Employs outside-the-box thinking to achieve outcomes that surpass client expectations and bottom-line performance. Proficiency in working independently or collaboratively. Demonstrated competency for rapid assimilation of technical information.

AREAS OF STRENGTH & EXPERTISE

- Process Redesign & Automation
- Complex Analysis & Problem Resolution
- Consolidation & Streamlining Procedures
- Applications Development & Programming
- Systems Innovation & Implementation
- Solutions-Based Development & Programming
- Troubleshooting & Client Support
- Interpersonal Relations & Communications
- Teaching & Knowledge Growth Enhancement
- Customer Relationship Management

EDUCATION & TRAINING

Bachelor of Applied Science, Major: Computer Science *(2004)*
Colorado State University

Foundation Studies, Major: Information Technology *(2002)*
Colorado State University

Macromedia Flash Seminar ▪ Macromedia Washington *(2002)*

COMPUTER TECHNOLOGIES

LAN/WAN ▪ HTML (Web Design) ▪ Database Design ▪ OO Design ▪ Internet ▪ Email

Applications: *MS Word, MS Excel, MS Access, MS PowerPoint, MS Outlook, MS FrontPage, Macromedia Flash MX, Dreamweaver MX, Fireworks MX, Adobe Photoshop 6, CVS (Unix), WinCVS, Allaire ColdFusion Studio, Rational Rose 98i, MSSQL, MySQL*

Languages: *Java, C, PHP, CFML, ASP, Flash Action Scripting, Perl, Python, CGI, SQL, XML, XSL, DHTML, Lisp*

Operating Systems: *Windows NT/95/98/2000/ME/ XP, Unix (4 years), MAC 9/X*

PROFESSIONAL EXPERIENCE - OVERVIEW

COLORADO STATE UNIVERSITY   2/2003 – Present
Course Tutor & Laboratory Assistant – *Intro to Information Technology / Scripting Language Programming*

BLACK INTERNATIONAL (BLACK 3)   3/2002 – Present
Interactive Developer

PRECISION ONLINE ENTERTAINMENT (STREET CINEMAS)   9/2000 – 2/2001
Flash Programmer

PROFESSIONAL EXPERIENCE - AMPLIFIED

COLORADO STATE UNIVERSITY

2/2003 – Present

Course Tutor & Laboratory Assistant

Introduction to Information Technology – Tutor & Laboratory Assistant
Scripting Language Programming – Laboratory Assistant

Tutor 60 students (two classes) providing opportunities for discussion and solving of tutorial questions as submitted by lecturer; elucidate course material; and provide ongoing support as required. Mark student assignments and oral presentations.

Supervise and enhance students' understanding of programming concepts in Perl, CGI, and Python. Demonstrate programming concepts in practice; relay and instruct debugging key points. Channel students' ability to identify key issues through exploration of methodologies to augment learning, and ensure students achieve academic targets.

- Learned, refined, and developed teaching strategies/materials to accommodate different learning styles; enhanced communication, presentation, interpersonal, and teaching competencies, gaining popularity as tutor/lab assistant and securing increase in number of students in classes, particularly with "Scripting Languages Programming" subject.

- Cultivated problem-solving abilities, gaining proficiency in debugging code.

- Identified and advised lecturer within 3rd week of first semester of potentially failing students; strategized and applied innovative turnaround and inspiring teaching methodologies, gaining students' trust, while aiming to increase pass rates in a subject renowned for high-failure rate.

BLACK INTERNATIONAL (BLACK 3)

3/2002 – Present

Interactive Developer

Black International is the fourth largest communications/advertising network on a global scale, with Black International Division receiving projects involving eCRM programs, interactive advertising campaigns, content management systems, digital/technological solutions, and consulting.

Collaborate with Senior Technical Architect and Project Managers to oversee design and implementation of front- and back-end solutions based on defined requirements for clients' websites and internal projects. Solutions encompass custom e-commerce applications, remote administration tools, surveys and games, custom bulletin boards, site search engines, personalized content delivery and website analysis tools. Facilitate diverse programming projects (*refer to projects addendum*).

Analyze and define business systems and requirements to facilitate smooth integration of developed solutions; document all produced code; and develop Web-based solutions using PHP, ASP, CFML, EML, and XSL technologies on server side and MSSQL/MySQL as interactive databases. Implement customer relationship management/support techniques for existing clients to maximize satisfaction.

- Analyzed, identified, and created two applications that automated common coding tasks performed by programming team across two projects that **captured reduction in development time by 15%.** Applications developed:

  Object Builder: Creates object code in PHP within seconds for a given database, in comparison with manual creation/testing code processes taking approximately one hour for each object. With medium-sized project involving around 20-30 tables in a database, **new application saved around 25 hours (13%) of development time**.

  Form Builder: Used for creating Web-based forms (e.g., registration form) with form layout completed visually, **saving approximately 1.5 hours development** time per form. Code is embedded in HTML with server side (PHP or CFML) and client side validation (Javascript), also written automatically by the application.

- Refined and achieved advanced level in PHP, CMFL, ASP, Javascript, XML, and SXL; **improved personal programming time efficiency by 60%**, strategically calculated via timing experiments across various projects and reported/shown to technical director.

- **Proactive change agent continuously identifying procedural weak links** and securing support from project management team to revitalize and improve current methodologies.

158

- **Captured six-month consecutive costs savings of 8-10%** for project development internal expenditure in comparison to Canberra-based programming team.
- **Pioneered creation of reusable code system** and secured support from technical architect to build; developed content management system with capabilities to be sold off-the-shelf with minimal integration or easy customization to meet specific client requirements; **slashed two weeks off development process** that facilitated product's price reduction and on-selling to three existing customers.

SCAPE ONLINE ENTERTAINMENT (VILLAGE CINEMAS)   9/2000 – 2/2001

Flash Programmer

Created animations and games utilizing action scripting in Flash; illustrated characters for animations using Illustrator; pitched innovative game and animation idea designs; and programmed game architectures for Internet integration.

- **Led turnaround of eight animations within quarter of the normal production time** and **reduced animation lead-time by 50%** without compromising overall quality.
- Championed creation of dynamic games and animations featured on the SCAPE site, and delivered numerous high-level quality products all within tight deadlines.
- Conceptualized and sold pioneering cartoon proposal, gaining support from upper-level management to create an animation series.

FURTHER INFORMATION

Fluent written & spoken – Turkish & English
Basic Spoken – Japanese
Basic Understanding of German

~ Willing to travel or relocate ~

References Available upon Request

TERRY BLACK

154 S.E. Bottom O'Rylie Circle   555.478.526 (AH)
Seattle, Washington 42541   terryblack@hotmail.com   555.698.321 (Cell)

PROGRAMMING PROJECTS ADDENDUM

EP (Emergency Performance)   Health care
Document Management System
- The website is used as a company extranet that serves around 150 members of the company to arrange meetings, discuss issues, upload journals and policies.

CPA (Corporate Public Affairs)   Financial Consulting
Consumer Website
Content Management System
Members extranet
HR Tool
- The website provides a comprehensive online knowledge center for members.
- Created a key platform for marketing center activities.
- Assisted in acquiring new members and identifying international markets.

PSC (Portfolio Standards Corporation)   Health care
Consumer Website
Campaign Measurement Tool
Medical Director Animations
- Medical Director is a program that operates on every GP's computer.
- Seretide animation, created by Black International, was an animation utilized within the program to promote the brand.

Absolutely Fabulous   Financial Consulting
Consumer Website
- Web-publishing tool that allowed client to publish and customize websites for its own clients.

Analysis
Web Traffic Management Tool
- Real-time, high-level website traffic measurement tool used for clients such as MediPrivate.

Performance Plus   Retail
Consumer Website
Extranet
- Extranet: a tool whereby Performance Plus head office can communicate with 750 retailers - **solution captured savings of $350,000** for the client, who previously used fax communication with its retailers. The extranet is the main point of call for all communications between head office and retail.

Juniper   Retail
Viral Marketing Campaign
- An email mail-out campaign that specifically targeted the demographic for the product, being sent out to a database of 10,000 people. This campaign was developed to be cross-browser and plug-in compatible. **Overcame major challenge in this project by satisfying the ideas and needs of different stakeholders.**

CHAPTER 9

Best Resumes for College Graduates Earning Degrees to Change Careers

Overview

Writing a career-change resume, whether you're a recent college graduate or not, can be a real challenge. To begin, you must identify the skills, qualifications, competencies, and more that you've acquired through your past experience and academic training, and then highlight those that are most relevant to your current career goals. Think about that carefully . . . you do not want to write a resume that simply highlights the skills and qualifications you've acquired throughout your entire career. Rather, you want to bring special attention to only those skills and qualifications that are most relevant to, and most supportive of, your current career goals.

It is generally recommended for most career changers that you begin your resume with some type of summary – Career Summary, Professional Qualifications, Technical Qualifications, Career Profile, or whatever you call it – that clearly and prominently displays your transferable skills. A bulleted listing of skills is often the best format to quickly communicate a lot of information within a limited amount of space. Plus, the visual impact of seeing all of those relevant skills right at the top of the resume is a great way to merchandise and sell your qualifications.

Most career changers who go to college to earn a degree will want to highlight that degree as the next section in their resume since, most likely, it will tie directly into their current objectives. Be sure to include internships, research projects, honors, awards, affiliations, and more in this section to give it as much substance as possible.

You'll then complete the resume with highlights of your professional work experience – responsibilities, projects, achievements, and more that directly relate to your current objective. Although something may only have been 10% of your job, if it's related to your new career goal, be sure to give it more than 10% worth of attention on your resume. Conversely, something that was 75% of your job, but is not important to your current goals, will get a brief mention and have a significantly lesser impact on your new career-change resume. Re-weight your resume and your experiences to put the emphasis where it needs to be today!

Index of Resumes Featured in This Chapter

Resume: Houston McLean, pages 170-171

Writer: William G. Murdock, CPRW

Objective: Transition from hands-on manufacturing position to new career track in marketing and public relations

Strategy: Dominant presentation of year-long internship presented as a full-scale professional position to create the perception of an already-working marketing and PR professional

Resume: Charles Hadley, pages 172-173

Writer: Don Orlando, MBA, CPRW, JCTC, CCM, CCMC

Objective: Transition from scattered career in sales and security to new career path in retail store management

Strategy: Unique presentation with a heavy emphasis on graduate's ability to solve problems and deliver results in a diversity of professional and academic environments

Peter M. Gattes

1811 Delaney Boulevard
Princeton, NJ 08540

Home: 609-263-5555
Mobile: 609-780-6666
pmgattes@verizon.net

ENTRY-LEVEL MARKETING ASSOCIATE / ADVERTISING ASSOCIATE
Client Relationship Management / Business Customer Acquisition

- **College graduate** with unique blend of experience in customer acquisition, sales/marketing, operations management, client relationship management, and team building in commercial (B2B) marketplace.

- **Creative, energetic developer** of high-level (95%) repeat and referral business. Enhanced revenues, expanded customer account base, and boosted client retention by selling and cross-selling full-service, custom-designed flooring solutions to discriminating buyers within a highly competitive market.

- **Solid customer relationship management skills,** with ability to build on credibility and gain clients' respect and trust quickly. Motivated team player willing to "go the extra mile," partnering with customers and contractors to devise optimal design options for projects ranging from $10,000 to $40,000.

PROVEN SKILLS

- Client Relationship Management
- Operations / Project Management
- Customer Acquisition Strategies

- Consultative Sales
- Communications
- Revenue Growth

- Opportunity Identification
- Account Development
- Training & Team Management

PROFESSIONAL EXPERIENCE

DELANEY & SONS TILE, MARBLE, & FLOORING – Princeton, NJ   1998 – present
Family-owned subcontracting firm (tile, hardwood flooring, and carpeting) catering to upscale construction trade.

Project Manager / Designer (functioning as Operations Manager/Business Developer)
Worked full-time while attending college (GPA 3.4). Promoted to Operations Management in 2001; supervise 8 F/T and 2 P/T employees. Work in tandem with owner, branding and guiding thriving business.

- **Sales Growth.** Key player in propelling business within 5 years from $80,000 to $1.5 million. Initiated direct marketing cold calls with new-home general contractors, growing major contractor accounts from 3 to 10 (single-family home and condo projects increased from 30 in 1998 to 80-100 projects in 2003).

- **Customer Relationship Management.** Collaborate with homeowners and contractors to design and develop elaborate layouts, becoming trusted project advisor. Utilize solution-selling techniques and creative-design skills to deliver added value and extend relationships. Expert in cross-selling and up-selling to generate additional revenues and solidify account penetration.

- **Training & Team Motivation.** Develop, schedule, and motivate 2-3 work crews (3-5 laborers and mechanics each) for custom new-home flooring construction projects. Handpicked to train and supervise employees in new installation techniques, quality production, and top-notch customer service practices.

- **Leadership.** Chosen to run daily operations, including sales and business development, benchmarking streamlined operations processes and innovative marketing strategies to promote best-in-class services.

EDUCATION & TRAINING

Bachelor of Arts, Visual Communications – Richard Stockton College of NJ, Pomona – May 2004
Courses: Interactive Media Design, Photography, Photoshop, Graphic Design, Visual Communications

Technology Summary: Windows XP/ME, Microsoft Office 2000/2003/XP (Word, Excel), QuarkXPress 5, Adobe Illustrator 10, Adobe Photoshop 7, Macromedia Flash 5, Internet, PC and Mac platforms.

BRUCE W. SCOTT

813–745–1994 ▪ scott@email.com

2432 Sea Gull Road ▪ Tampa ▪ FL ▪ 33607

ELECTRICAL ENGINEER

Manufacturing Processes ▪ Operations Management ▪ Project Coordination ▪ Research and Development

Value to Employer	▪ Experience designing, developing, and testing electrical and electronic equipment; proficient in AutoCAD. ▪ Providing technical support and leadership to cross-functional teams working to improve product quality and refine workflow processes within manufacturing environments. ▪ Detailed and analytical competencies, with the ability to solve complex issues. ▪ Proven "take-charge" leadership skills that result in solutions.
Education	**Bachelor of Science in Electrical Engineering** – May 2004 **Minor in Business Administration** Florida State University, Tallahassee, Florida ▪ Upper Division GPA 3.03/4.0 ▪ Relevant coursework: Microprocessors, C++, Electronic Circuits, Technical Writing, Intelligent Machines Design Laboratory, Management, Finance, Accounting, DSP, Communications Systems, Engineering Statistics, Digital Design
Internships	**Robotics Engineer** – August – December, 2003 FREIGHT MANUFACTURING, Atlanta, Georgia *(One of the world's largest manufacturers of advanced technology, components, and systems for all major automakers)* Collaborated with electrical and mechanical engineering teams in designing automated systems used for all product assemblies. Programmed PLCs by configuring process timing, setting tasks, testing, and performing quality checks. **Test Engineer** – Summers 2000 and 2001 JABIL CIRCUIT, INC., St. Petersburg, Florida *(A global leader in the electronic manufacturing services industry)* Liaised with representatives from two major client accounts (Intel and Cisco) in designing code modifications, writing software, testing new and existing products, and improving workflow processes. **Agricultural Engineering Research** – May - August 1998 FSU CITRUS RESEARCH EXPERIMENT CENTER, Tallahassee, Florida *(The world's largest citrus research, teaching, and extension center)* Partnered with agricultural engineers in modifying and testing citrus spray equipment.
Related Experience	**Telecommunications Specialist** – since March 1999 FLORIDA STATE UNIVERSITY – CIRCA, Tallahassee, Florida Selected from among 30 applicants to design and oversee installation of data/video network infrastructure, testing, and network maintenance. Train new hires on installation methodologies and network maintenance.
Memberships	Institute of Electrical & Electronics Engineers (IEEE)
Leadership Positions	Reformed University Fellowship ▪ Eagle Scout

165

ANDREW B. DONNOVAN
ACCOUNTANT
willing to relocate

10033 Bradley Lane
Brookings, WA 98333

(333) 333-3223
andy@ccc.com

- Background and education provide a "big picture" understanding of business; encompasses full knowledge of accounting disciplines and business strategies.

- Personable with innate relationship-building qualities and lead-by-example philosophy; recognized for effective use of humor.

- Passion for analysis; enjoys variety and challenge. Presents very strong problem-solving and communication skills.

- PC proficient — particular expertise with Pro FX (Tax) / GO Systems (Audit) / MYOB (Accounting) software applications

"...An impact player without being loud"

"...Brings to the table a very nice mix of personality traits, aptitude, and intelligence..."

"...Analytical, quick learner, knowledge seeker ..."

"... Thoughtful comments ... refreshingly constructive"

comments taken from evaluations

EDUCATION

MBA, University of Worthington, Big City, WA, June 2004

Graduate, UW Certificate Program in Accounting —Outstanding Student Award, 3.9 GPA
University of Worthington, Big City, WA, August 2003
Accelerated Accounting Course covering Intermediate
Financial Accounting, Cost Accounting, Auditing Standards and
Principles, and Tax Effects of Business Decisions.

Graduate Studies in Mathematics, University of Worthington, 2000–2001

B.S., Mathematics, Mahara University of Management, City, WA, June 1998
Won "Tony Nader Award" in school-wide writing and presentation competition.

MEMBERSHIPS / COMMUNITY SERVICE

Active Member, University of Worthington Accounting Society

Active Member, Beta Alpha Psi — *Honors Accounting and Finance*

Treasurer/Accountant, Brookings Railway Museum—*newly formed (2003) non-profit organization*

Accounting Consultant, Kermit Sampson Realty — *complex franchise / partnership entity*

Volunteer, Habitat for Humanity

EXPERIENCE SUMMARY

Staff/Tax Intern, Large Accounting Firm LLP, Brookings, WA   1–4/04

Prepared tax forms, trial balance sheets, income statements, and journal entries for US and Canadian corporations, individuals, and partnerships. Recognized by management for ideas and workable suggestions, and by co-workers for team spirit.

Instructor, Mathematics Department, City Community College, City, WA   1–8/02

Teacher Assistant, Mathematics Dept., University of Worthington, Big City, WA   9/00–6/01

Instructor, Mathematics Dept, Mahara University of Management, Big City, WA   9/99–6/00

166

Michael M. McCrate

71554 Hardille Circle, Arvada, CO 80003
Cell: (304) 991-7167 | Home: (304) 980-5166

MANAGEMENT CANDIDATE with a strong history of great customer service and employment involving outside sales, business administration, financial analysis, and supplier relations.

Possess a background of supervising a three-shift restaurant with over 60 employees. Handled key facets of the business, from hiring, training, and employee scheduling to customer relations and maintaining stock levels. Extensive history of working with key company logistics while networking with employees and executive managers. Current position requires the handling of day-to-day departmental functions and presenting high-impact sales presentations that focus on product benefits. Noted by a previous manager as "an asset to any company."

Education and Software

B.S., BUSINESS MANAGEMENT, Summer 2004
Red Rocks University, Denver, CO

A.S., Liberal Arts, 1996
Community College of Denver, Denver, CO

Word, Excel, Access, Outlook, and PowerPoint

Scope of Supervisory Skills

Experience collected from the last 10 years; positions held before college

- Supervised a multi-shift operation with 65 staff members and assisted 5 crew leaders and 3 assistant managers.

- Trained employees, in a one-on-one setting, on topics covering customer service, order fulfillment, operational procedures, time management, and customer service techniques.

- Addressed personnel details, from training and scheduling to work performance and employee relations.

- Identified and resolved issues pertaining to order deliveries and communicated with truck drivers, vendors/suppliers, and employees to ensure inventory was handled timely.

- Supervised cash handling and completed the administrative processes associated with daily financial records and cash auditing.

Professional Employment

SALES CLERK/INTERIM MANAGER, 2003 – PRESENT
Adelphia Insurance Company, Denver, CO
Address business-building logistics, from creating marketing and advertising materials to conducting outside sales. Implement contracts on health insurance needs, and communicate with clients concerning underwriting and insurance policies. Develop leads, call prospects, and set appointments to discuss the client's needs and focus the sales presentation around immediate and long-term policy expectations. Answer client inquiries and address policy coverage.

ADMINISTRATIVE ASSISTANT/CUSTOMER SERVICE REPRESENTATIVE, 1999 – 2003
Montana BonTAP, Denver, CO
Delivered supplies to customers before promoted to an administrative position assisting customers with order problems pertaining to store stock and special-order merchandise. Networked between managers and floor reps to answer client inquiries and problems, along with delegating select tasks to the appropriate departments to timely resolve problems.

JOANNE LANGTON

18 Binnak Drive
Chicago, IL 60606

Email: jlangton@bigpool.com

Cell: (999) 456 7898
Telephone: (999) 456 5544

GRADUATE

NUTRITIONIST: RESEARCH AND DEVELOPMENT ~ FOOD SCIENCES

Science graduate distinguished from peers through a history of "real-world" experiences. Extensive background in information technology has honed strengths in finding solutions, applying a customer service focus to challenges, prioritizing demanding workflows, and meeting deadlines. Internship with a prominent flavor-development company heightened sensory skills and elevated proficiencies in acclimatizing to changing workplaces, priorities, and programs. A mature and tenacious worker with a meticulous approach to detail, "outside-the-box" thinking, and creative flair.

Comprehensively trained in:

- Product Development
- Food Research
- Meal Design & Management
- Nutrition Education Techniques

- Flavor Applications
- Food Composition
- Experimental Food Science
- Elements of Chemistry
- Nutrition in the Lifecycle

- Nutrition
- Sensory Evaluation
- Food Composition & Scientific Preparation
- Organic Chemistry

EDUCATION | TRAINING

Bachelor of Science (Food & Nutrition)
Majors: Human Ecology, Food & Nutrition
Graduated Magna Cum Laude
Chicago State University (2004)

French Regional Cuisine
Rue Léon Delhomme, Paris, France (2003)

RELEVANT INDUSTRY EXPERIENCE

MARK & GLENN, NJ, USA (4/2001–9/2003)
Food Technologist Internship—Sweet Flavor Applications

***Reported to**: Senior Food Scientist • **Clients included:** M&M Mars, Nestlé, Glaxo Smith Kline, Pepsi*

Summary: International flavor and fragrance company developing products spanning confectionary, coated cereals, flavored yogurt, granola bars, ice cream, baked goods, and over-the-counter medications.

* * *

Outpaced student peers by securing a sought-after internship supporting three senior scientists in the sweet-development laboratory. Utilizing a range of natural and synthetic flavor enhancers, produced sample ranges that met each client's brief for exceeding customers' taste preferences.

- Met the pressures of devising creative, fresh ideas for clients in this highly competitive industry. Researched existing markets and extended ideas that ensured new products were bold and unique.

- Prioritized own workflows, juggling a diversity of special projects daily for client-tasting or consumer panel evaluations.

- Transitioned from "fresh" recruit to a seasoned performer, working autonomously without scrutiny. Recognized during performance appraisals for attention to detail and distinctively creative approach.

- Contributed to pyramid testing of three product samples via computerized consumer testing.

ACADEMIC SHOWCASE

Examples of academic projects, challenges, and team work that support career goals

Research Project: *"How Diets Correlate Body Image in Teenagers"*
Personal Contribution: *Research and Class Presentation*
Partnered with peers in a team of three to produce a research paper within stringent time constraints. Overcame conflicting schedules threatening the deadline by collaboratively setting strategic and realistic goals for work completion and exploiting Internet-messaging technologies for progressive communications. Successfully delivered project on time.

Research Project: *Human Ecology*
Personal Contribution: *PowerPoint presentations, research, class address*
Key participant in team of three assigned to research and identify the major changes to human ecology over the past 50 years. Conflicting team dynamics and a diversity of personal views were united through diplomatic communications and re-clarification of primary issues. Personally produced all PowerPoint presentations supporting research findings and contributed to the class address.

Education Project: *Nutrition Education Techniques*
Personal Contribution: *Group training/education, self-evaluation, learning aids*
Solo project presenting nutritional information to a "real-life" group of adult learners. Adapted presentation techniques to encompass sensory learning by introducing fresh fruit to the classroom experience, launching Wordsearch interactive activities, and designing colorful posters that reinforced benefits of effective nutrition. Surveyed responses demonstrated that despite group's skepticism members absorbed information presented.

OTHER EXPERIENCE

POWER PLACEMENTS, London, UK   2/2000–5/2000
Temporary Contractor

Rapidly acquired reputation as a competent, adaptable contractor, flexible to the needs of diverse workplaces and personalities. Offered superior administrative and computer services to prominent London-based legal, accounting, and investment firms.

ADVANCED BARCODE SOLUTIONS, Melbourne, Australia   10/1999–12/1999
Technical Support /Trainer (contract)

Short-term contract role offering expert telephone and on-site technical support and end-user training. Configured computer hardware and software and presented informal one-on-one and group training sessions to lessen each client's dependence on first-level support mechanisms.

DEPARTMENT OF HUMAN SERVICES, Melbourne, Australia   6/1999–10/1999
Technical Support /NT Support

Mobile technical support specialist. Installed and troubleshot hardware and software issues on-site, and provided new user education and desktop support for networks, Windows platforms, and Lotus Notes.

AUSTRALIA POST, Melbourne, Australia   12/1998–6/1999
IT Helpdesk

High-pressure role assuring continuity of computer operations by resolving end-user hardware and software issues via remote dialup, telephone/on-site support, and advanced technical training.

PERSONAL

Enjoy creative writing, cooking, yoga, walking, travel, reading, and family activities.

HOUSTON MCLEAN

8433 Rattlesnake Drive
Seattle, Washington 98911
Phone 204.667.8112

CANDIDATE: MARKETING / PUBLIC RELATIONS SPECIALIST

An established record of effectiveness in media and public relations, coupled with leadership and supervisory responsibilities in high-precision environments. Accomplished in generating national media exposure, coordinating and managing events, and guiding public opinion through focus groups and committees. Analytical, energetic, disciplined, and proactive.

Bachelor of Arts – Public Relations / Psychology - Cum Laude (2004)
UNIVERSITY OF WASHINGTON – Seattle, Washington
Major areas of coursework: Principles of Public Relations ~ Public Relations Campaigns
Public Relations Writing ~ Print and Digital Media Writing ~ Strategic Issues Management

PROFESSIONAL EXPERIENCE

Simmons Nutrition – Seattle, Washington
(February to November – 2003)
Distributors of sports and nutritional supplements; $20 million in annual revenues.
Intern / Project Administrator – Get Lean Seattle Campaign

Quickly assigned daily tactical responsibility for Jerry Simmons (Mr. Universe 1994) *Get Lean Seattle* public relations campaign, an integral leg of the marketing department's three-fold initiative to reposition Simmons-branded nutritional products and techniques -- previously an exclusive offering to power weight lifters and professional body builders -- for more mainstream consumption.

Championed the *Get Lean* message, assuming accountability for campaign effectiveness commencing with the campaign's launch – a press conference with Mayor Jerry Brown appointing Jerry Simmons as Fitness Czar in the wake of Seattle's being named Fattest City in the nation.

Daily Responsibilities
- Spearheaded message of "getting lean," acting as the *Get Lean Seattle* Ambassador to a wide variety of corporate, charitable, and civic organizations. Successfully countered initial media skepticism of the program as a partisan commercial venture.
- Authored numerous deadline-conscious press releases, feature articles, biographies, and testimonials for use on the company's website, as marketing collaterals, and for publication in the mainstream print media.
- Tactical responsibility for executing numerous events including press conferences, body-building and fitness tournaments, VIP parties (catering, venues) and sponsor relations.
- Created media kits and interacted with media representatives providing background information on developments and strategies.
- Conducted ongoing research into story placements and media "hits" for press releases and feature placements. Conducted deep background investigations on nine biographies destined for publication in 2005 by a major A-list publisher.

Successful Contributions
- Generated extensive national media interest and publicity as Burger King officially co-sponsored the *Get Lean* campaign and introduced their "Salads and More" lean menu. Achieved 2.7 million TV impressions, 800,000 cable impressions, and significant Internet exposure on sites including Excite.com, CNN.com, and Forbes.com.
- Consistently placed stories, or earned coverage based on submissions, from the Associated Press, Reuters, and local print media (including the Spanish press).
- Personally orchestrated three major press conferences for Seattle Mayor Jerry Brown, including the launch of the city-wide "Fat Drive" urging citizens to "donate" pounds.

Inland Empire Engineering – Richland, Washington
(1998-2000)
Purchased by GE Medical Systems – 2000
Engineering Technician – Team Lead, Surface Mount Technology

Directed the robotic manufacture of electronic circuitry used in cardiac diagnostics and treatment equipment used by major hospitals nationwide. Accountable for establishing the manufacturing pace and tempo for 30 subsequent assembly functions. Coordinated the surface mount placement for nearly 1,000 parts per motherboard and a daily volume in excess of 50 boards.

- Authored the departmental process documentation during the company's ISO 9000 certification initiative encompassing procedures ranging for solder viscosity to high-temperature oven operations.
- Approved daily equipment programming, including specialized research and development instructions for emerging technology prototypes.
- Produced an ongoing record of only minor technical quality control issues, a result of disciplined equipment maintenance and personal abilities to perform Tier One troubleshooting or repairs.
- Oversaw schedule optimization as well as parts and inventory management.

Pacific-Tech – Pasco, Washington
(1997 – 1998)
Team Lead – Surface Mount Technology

Recruited to direct the daily effort of a 15-person assembly team manufacturing a variety of electronic components (motherboards, video / sound cards) for mobile phones. Oversaw staff scheduling and annual performance reviews, provided Tier One technical support, and assured manufacturing standards were achieved.

Charles Hadley
5715 North Drive, Apartment 13
San Diego, California 92101
☎ [619] 555.1129 chchch@bellsouth.net

WHAT I CAN OFFER **BELK** AS YOUR NEWEST **EXECUTIVE TRAINEE**...

Proven success in cross-cultural communications   Documented experience in guiding employee involvement teams   Practiced in job task analysis and design   Experienced in leveraging employees' needs to increase productivity

EXAMPLES OF PROBLEMS SOLVED RECENTLY...

AS PART OF MY COLLEGE COURSE WORK...

Analyzed every aspect of a complex sexual harassment complaint in an industry in which I had never worked. Beat the six-month deadline for comprehensive written recommendations by more than five months. *Outcomes:* **My plan approved without change**. Awarded highest possible grade.

Balanced the unique needs of an employee returning to the workplace with corporate requirements by industry. *Outcomes:* **Seasoned HR professional endorsed my logic with top marks.**

ON THE JOB...

○ *Part-time promoted from a pool of 18 eligibles to full-time* Security Technician (Asset Control), California Army National Guard, San Ysidro, California   Nov 03 — Present

○ Automotive Consultant, City Chrysler—Jeep, La Jolla, California   Feb 01 — Nov 03

Played an important role during a difficult takeover. Guided senior decision makers' planning when the productivity gains they wanted failed to materialize. *Outcomes:* **Sales rose and stayed high. Morale improved** across the board.

○ Store Detective *selected from 50 eligibles to enter the* **Management Internship Program** *later promoted to* Lead Cashier, Target, Grand Forks, North Dakota   Jun 99 — Jan 01

Worked with a team that proposed using old resources in new ways to stop costly shrinkage. Persuaded management to move away from "conventional wisdom." *Outcomes:* Yearlong **problem stopped cold in a few days**. Investments protected. **Liability lessened.**

Stepped in to work under a manager whose cultural background had limited his success. Patiently built his trust; then encouraged him to try new techniques. *Outcomes:* Workplace **stress reduced**. Customers got much better service.

Solved a classic problem: how could we deliver quality to the customer without enough trained employees and no prospect of recruiting new people? My cross-training idea carried the day. *Outcomes:* **Customer complaints fell away.** Coverage in other areas virtually unchanged. **Employees responded well.**

O Security Specialist, United States Air Force, Grand Forks Air Force Base, North Dakota
Jan 95 — Jan 99

Helped management and employees resolve a chronic scheduling problem. Overcame initial resistance to change at every level. *Outcomes:* Twelve-hour shifts became a thing of the past. Morale rose. **Productivity increased** as employees learned each others' jobs well.

Replaced long-standing vacation assignment program that was too easy to "game." *Outcomes:* **Employees saw my** "lottery" **system** as **fair and equitable.**

EDUCATION AND TRAINING...

O B.S., **Resource Management**, Coller University, Center City, California
Expect graduation in May 05
Working 32 hours a week to pay for my education. Dean's List every quarter since I enrolled.

O College course work, **Business Management**, Park College, Grand Forks, North Dakota
97 — 98

Worked nights and weekends while attending classes.

O "Combating Substance Abuse and Violence in the Workplace," California Army National Guard, total of one day   04
O "Managing Time to Boost Productivity," Sonic Automotive Corp., two days   01
O "Providing Quality Customer Service," "Balancing Inventory to Maximize Profits," and "Assets Protection," Target Corporation, a total of seven training days   98

COMPUTER SKILLS...

O Expert in a proprietary inventory control and product management software suite.

O Proficient in Word, Quicken, and Internet query methods.

O Familiar with Excel, PowerPoint, and Outlook.

PROFESSIONAL AFFILIATIONS...

O Student member, Society for Human Resource Management   Since 97

Appendix A

List of Contributors

Following is a detailed listing of all 46 of the professional resume writers who have contributed their work and knowledge to this book. Each has earned at least one, if not several, notable certifications or credentials for their expertise in resume writing and design. (See end of Chapter 1 for details about each of the certifications.)

What's more, each of these writers is a member in good standing of the Career Masters Institute (www.cminstitute.com), a prestigious professional association supporting the top resume writers, career coaches, career counselors, outplacement consultants, and other career professionals in the U.S., Canada, and abroad. Feel free to visit their websites to learn more or contact them directly to discuss your resume project. You'll be delighted with the professionalism, expertise, and caring attitude of each and every one of these professionals. I guarantee it!

Janet Beckstrom, CPRW
Word Crafter
1717 Montclair Avenue
Flint, MI 48503
Phone: 800-351-9818
Email: wordcrafter@voyager.net

Arnold G. Boldt, CPRW, JCTC
Arnold-Smith Associates
625 Panorama Trail, Bldg. One, Ste. 120C
Rochester, NY 14625
Phone: 585-383-0350
Email: Arnie@ResumeSOS.com
Website: www.ResumeSOS.com

Carolyn Braden, CPRW
Braden Resume Solutions
108 La Plaza Drive
Hendersonville, TN 37075
Phone: 615-822-3317
Email: bradenresume@comcast.net

Martin P. Buckland, MRW, CPRW, JCTC, CJST, CEIP
Elite Resumes
1428 Stationmaster Lane
Oakville, Ontario, Canada L6M 3A7
Phone: 905-825-0490
Email: martin@aneliteresume.com
Website: www.AnEliteResume.com

Freddie Cheek, M.S. Ed., CPRW, CRW, CWDP, CCM
Cheek & Cristantello Career Connections
406 Maynard Drive
Amherst, NY 14226
Phone: 716-839-3635
Email: fscheek@adelphia.net
Website: www.CheekandCristantello.com

Annemarie Cross, CEIP, CPRW, CRW, CCM, CECC
Advanced Employment Concepts/AEC Office Services
PO Box 91
Hallam, Victoria, Australia 3803
Email: success@aresumewriter.net
Website: www.aresumewriter.net

Norine T. Dagliano, CPRW, BA
ekm Inspirations
616 Highland Way
Hagerstown, MD 21740
Phone: 301-766-2032
Email: norine@ekminspirations.com
Website: www.ekminspirations.com

Darlene Dassy, BBA, CRW
Dynamic Resume Solutions
602 Monroe Drive
Harleysville, PA 19438
Phone: 215-368-2316
Email: darlene@attractiveresumes.com
Website: www.attractiveresumes.com

Christy Donner, ACCC, CPRW
Innovative Strategies Coaching
1205 NW Sawgrass Dr.
Grain Valley, MO 64029
Phone: 816-847-8057
Email: christy@innovativestrategies4life.com
Website: www.innovativestrategies4life.com

Dayna Feist, CPRW, JCTC, CEIP
Gatehouse Business Services
265 Charlotte Street
Asheville, NC 28801
Phone: 828-254-7893
Email: gatehous@aol.com
Website: www.BestJobEver.com

Louise Fletcher, CPRW
Blue Sky Resumes
15 Merriam Avenue
Bronxville, NY 10708
Phone: 914-337-5742
Email: lfletcher@blueskyresumes.com
Website: www.blueskyresumes.com

Gail Frank, NCRW, CPRW, JCTC, CEIP, MA
Frankly Speaking
10409 Greendale Drive
Tampa, FL 33626
Phone: 813-926-1353
Email: gailfrank@post.harvard.edu
Website: www.callfranklyspeaking.com

Louise Garver, MA, CPRW, JCTC, CMP, CEIP, MCDP
Career Directions, LLC
115 Elm Street Suite 203
Enfield, CT 06082
Phone: 860-623-9476
Email: TheCareerPro@aol.com
Website: www.resumeimpact.com

Susan Guarneri, CPRW, NCCC, LPC, CCMC, CEIP, MS, CCM
Susan Guarneri Associates
1905 Fern Lane
Wausau, WI 54401
Phone: 866-881-4055

Email: Resumagic@aol.com
Website: www.resume-magic.com

Beate Hait, CPRW, NCRW
Resumes Plus
80 Wingate Road
Holliston, MA 01746-1261
Phone: 508-429-1813
Email: beateh1@aol.com
Website: www.resumesplus.net

Alice Hanson, CPRW
Aim Resumes
PO Box 75054
Seattle, WA 98175
Phone: 206-527-3100
Email: alice@aimresumes.com
Website: www.aimresume.com

Beverly Harvey, CPRW, JCTC, CCM, CCMC
Beverly Harvey Resume & Career Services
P.O. Box 750
Pierson, FL 32180
Phone: 386-749-3111 or 1-888-775-0916
Email: beverly@harveycareers.com
Website: www.harveycareers.com

Gayle Howard, CCM, CPRW, CERW, CRW
Top Margin
PO Box 74
Chirnside Park, Melbourne, Australia 3116
Email: getinterviews@topmargin.com
Website: www.topmargin.com

Marcy Johnson, NCRW, CPRW, CEIP
First Impression Resume & Job Readiness
11805 US Hwy. 69
Story City, IA 50248
Phone: 515-733-4998 or 1-877-215-6009
Email: success@resume-job-readiness.com
Website: www.resume-job-readiness.com

Bill Kinser, MRW, CCM, CPRW, CEIP, JCTC
To The Point Resumes
P.O. Box 135
Fairfax, VA 22038-0135
Phone: 703-352-8969 or 1-866-RESUME-1
Email: bkinser@tothepointresumes.com
Website: www.tothepointresumes.com

Myriam-Rose Kohn, CPRW, CEIP, JCTC, CCM, CCMC
JEDA Enterprises
27201 Tourney Road, Suite 201M
Valencia, CA 91355-1857
Phone: 661-253-0801
Email: myriam-rose@jedaenterprises.com
Website: www.jedaenterprises.com

Cindy Kraft, CCMC, CCM, CPRW, JCTC
Executive Essentials
PO Box 336
Valrico, FL 33595
Phone: 813-655-0658
Email: cindy@career-management-coach.com
Website: www.career-management-coach.com

Louise Kursmark, MRW, CPRW, JCTC, CEIP, CCM
Best Impression Career Services, Inc.
9847 Catalpa Woods Court
Cincinnati, OH 45242
Phone: 513-792-0030 or 1-888-792-0030
Email: LK@yourbestimpression.com
Website: www.yourbestimpression.com

Lorie Lebert, CPRW, IJCTC, CCMC
The LORIEL GROUP/Resumes For Results
PO Box 267
Novi, MI 48376
Phone: 248-380-6100 or 1-800-870-9059
Email: Lorie@DoMyResume.com
Website: www.CoachingROI.com

Marilyn McAdams, CPRW
Ms. Secretary
1214 Murfreesboro Rd., Suite 102
Franklin, TN 37064

Phone: 615-794-3223
Email: mssec101@yahoo.com

Sharon McCormick, MS, NCC, NCCC, CPRW
Sharon McCormick Career & Vocational Consulting Services
1061 85th Terrace North #D
St. Petersburg, FL 33702
Phone: 727-824-7805
Email: career1@ij.net
Website: www.careersolutions.net

Jan Melnik, MRW, CCM, CPRW
Absolute Advantage
PO Box 718
Durham, CT 06422
Phone: 860-349-0256
Email: CompSPJan@aol.com
Website: www.janmelnik.com

Nicole Miller, IJCTC, CCM, CRW, CECC
Mil-Roy Consultants
145 Moreuilwood Boulevard
Petawawa, Ontario, Canada K8H 1A7
Phone: 613-687-2708
Email: resumes@milroyconsultants.com
Website: www.milroyconsultants.com

Eva Mullen, CPRW
A+ Resumes/A+ Business Services
3000 Pearl St., Ste. 111
Boulder, Colorado 80301
Phone: 303-444-3438
Email: eva@aplusres.com
Website: www.aplusres.com

William G. Murdock, CPRW
The Employment Coach
7770 Meadow Road, Suite 109
Dallas, TX 75230
Phone: 214-750-4781
Email: bmurdock@swbell.net
Website: www.resumesinaction.com

John O'Connor, MFA, CRW, CPRW, CECC, CCM
CareerPro Resumes & Career Advancement

3301 Womans Club Dr. #125
Raleigh, NC 27612-4812
Phone: 919-787-2400 or 1-866-717-2400
Email: john@careerproresumes.com
Website: www.careerproresumes.com

Debra O'Reilly, CPRW, CEIP, JCTC
A First Impression Resume Service / ResumeWriter.com
16 Terryville Avenue
Bristol, CT 06010
Phone: 860-583-7500
Email: debra@resumewriter.com
Website: www.resumewriter.com

Don Orlando, MBA, CPRW, JCTC, CCM, CCMC
The McLean Group
640 South McDonough Street
Montgomery, AL 36104
Phone: 334-264-2020
Email: yourcareercoach@aol.com

Ross Primack, CPRW, CEIP, GCDF
Connecticut Department of Labor
200 Folly Brook Boulevard
Wethersfield, CT 06109
Phone: 860-263-6041
Email: rossprimackcmi@yahoo.com

MeLisa Rogers, CPRW, MSHRD
Ultimate Career
270 Live Oak Lane
Victoria, TX 77905
Phone: 361-575-6100 or 1-866-573-7863
Email: success@ultimatecareer.biz
Website: www.ultimatecareer.biz

Teena Rose, CPRW, CEIP, CCM
Resume to Referral
1824 Rebert Pike
Springfield, OH 45506
Phone: 937-325-2149
Email: teena@resumetoreferral.com
Website: www.resumebycprw.com

Jennifer Rushton, CRW
Keraijen
Level 14, 309 Kent Street
Sydney NSW, Australia 2000
Email: info@keraijen.com.au
Website: www.keraijen.com.au

Barbara Safani. MA, CPRW
Career Solvers
980 Madison Avenue
New York, NY 10021
Phone: 866-333-1800
Email: info@careersolvers.com
Website: www.careersolvers.com

Janice Shepherd, CPRW, JCTC, CEIP
Write On Career Keys
2628 East Crestline Drive
Bellingham, WA 98226-4260
Phone: 360-738-7958
Email: janice@writeoncareerkeys.com
Website: www.writeoncareerkeys.com

Igor Shpudejko, MBA, CPRW, JCTC
Career Focus
23 Parsons Court
Mahwah, NJ 07430
Phone: 201-825-2865
Email: ishpudejko@aol.com
Website: www.CareerInFocus.com

Patricia Traina-Duckers, CPRW, CRW, CFRWC, CEIP
The Resume Writer
P.O. Box 595
Edison, NJ 08818-0595
Phone: 732- 239-8533 or 1-877-260-1333
Email: sales@theresumewriter.com
Website: www.theresumewriter.com

Vivian VanLier, CPRW, JCTC, CEIP, CCMC
Advantage Resume & Career Services
6701 Murietta Ave.
Los Angeles (Valley Glen), CA 91405
Phone: 818-994-6655

Email: Vivian@CuttingEdgeResumes.com
Website: www.CuttingEdgeResumes.com

Ellie Vargo, CPRW, CFRWC
Noteworthy Resume Services
11906 Manchester Road #112
St. Louis, MO 63131
Phone: 314-965-9362
Email: noteworthyservices@sbcglobal.net

Julie Walraven, CPRW
Design Resumes
1202 Elm Street
Wausau, WI 54401
Phone: 715-845-5664 or 1-888-435-7131
Email: design@dwave.net
Website: www.designresumes.com

Joellyn Wittenstein-Schwerdlin, CPRW, JCTC
A-1 Quality Résumés & Career Services
1819 Oriole Drive
Elk Grove Village, Illinois 60007
Phone: 847-285-1145
Email: joellyn@interaccess.com
Website: www.prwra.com/a-1resumes/
Website: www.a-1qualityresumes.com

Janice Worthington, MA, CPRW, JCTC, CEIP
Worthington Career Services
6636 Belleshire Street
Columbus, Oh 43229
Phone: 614-890-1645 or 1-877- 973-7863
Email: janice@worthingtonresumes.com
Website: www.worthingtonresumes.com

Appendix B

Your Writing Toolkit

Following are three word lists that are critical when writing your resume and cover letters – Action Verbs, High-Impact Phrases, and Personality Descriptors. Review the lists carefully, select the words and phrases that accurately reflect you and your skills and experience, and then strategically integrate them into the text of your resume, cover letters, thank-you letters, and all of your other job search communication.

Action Verbs

- ❑ Accelerate
- ❑ Accomplish
- ❑ Achieve
- ❑ Acquire
- ❑ Adapt
- ❑ Address
- ❑ Advance
- ❑ Advise
- ❑ Advocate
- ❑ Analyze
- ❑ Apply
- ❑ Appoint
- ❑ Arbitrate
- ❑ Architect
- ❑ Arrange
- ❑ Ascertain
- ❑ Assemble
- ❑ Assess
- ❑ Assist
- ❑ Author
- ❑ Authorize
- ❑ Brief
- ❑ Budget
- ❑ Build
- ❑ Calculate

- ❑ Capture
- ❑ Catalog
- ❑ Champion
- ❑ Chart
- ❑ Clarify
- ❑ Classify
- ❑ Close
- ❑ Coach
- ❑ Collect
- ❑ Command
- ❑ Communicate
- ❑ Compare
- ❑ Compel
- ❑ Compile
- ❑ Complete
- ❑ Compute
- ❑ Conceive
- ❑ Conclude
- ❑ Conduct
- ❑ Conserve
- ❑ Consolidate
- ❑ Construct
- ❑ Consult
- ❑ Continue
- ❑ Contract

- ❏ Convert
- ❏ Coordinate
- ❏ Correct
- ❏ Counsel
- ❏ Craft
- ❏ Create
- ❏ Critique
- ❏ Decrease
- ❏ Define
- ❏ Delegate
- ❏ Deliver
- ❏ Demonstrate
- ❏ Deploy
- ❏ Design
- ❏ Detail
- ❏ Detect
- ❏ Determine
- ❏ Develop
- ❏ Devise
- ❏ Direct
- ❏ Discover
- ❏ Dispense
- ❏ Display
- ❏ Distribute
- ❏ Diversify
- ❏ Divert
- ❏ Document
- ❏ Double
- ❏ Draft
- ❏ Drive
- ❏ Earn
- ❏ Edit
- ❏ Educate
- ❏ Effect
- ❏ Elect
- ❏ Eliminate
- ❏ Emphasize
- ❏ Enact
- ❏ Encourage
- ❏ Endure
- ❏ Energize
- ❏ Enforce
- ❏ Engineer
- ❏ Enhance
- ❏ Enlist
- ❏ Ensure
- ❏ Establish
- ❏ Estimate
- ❏ Evaluate
- ❏ Examine
- ❏ Exceed
- ❏ Execute
- ❏ Exhibit
- ❏ Expand
- ❏ Expedite
- ❏ Experiment
- ❏ Export
- ❏ Facilitate
- ❏ Finalize
- ❏ Finance
- ❏ Forge
- ❏ Form
- ❏ Formalize
- ❏ Formulate
- ❏ Found
- ❏ Generate
- ❏ Govern
- ❏ Graduate
- ❏ Guide
- ❏ Halt
- ❏ Head
- ❏ Hire
- ❏ Honor
- ❏ Hypothesize
- ❏ Identify
- ❏ Illustrate
- ❏ Imagine
- ❏ Implement
- ❏ Import
- ❏ Improve
- ❏ Improvise
- ❏ Increase
- ❏ Influence
- ❏ Inform
- ❏ Initiate
- ❏ Innovate
- ❏ Inspect
- ❏ Inspire
- ❏ Install
- ❏ Institute

- ❏ Instruct
- ❏ Integrate
- ❏ Intensify
- ❏ Interpret
- ❏ Interview
- ❏ Introduce
- ❏ Invent
- ❏ Inventory
- ❏ Investigate
- ❏ Judge
- ❏ Justify
- ❏ Launch
- ❏ Lead
- ❏ Lecture
- ❏ License
- ❏ Listen
- ❏ Locate
- ❏ Maintain
- ❏ Manage
- ❏ Manipulate
- ❏ Manufacture
- ❏ Map
- ❏ Market
- ❏ Mastermind
- ❏ Measure
- ❏ Mediate
- ❏ Mentor
- ❏ Model
- ❏ Modify
- ❏ Monitor
- ❏ Motivate
- ❏ Navigate
- ❏ Negotiate
- ❏ Nominate
- ❏ Normalize
- ❏ Observe
- ❏ Obtain
- ❏ Offer
- ❏ Officiate
- ❏ Operate
- ❏ Orchestrate
- ❏ Organize
- ❏ Orient
- ❏ Originate
- ❏ Outsource
- ❏ Overcome
- ❏ Oversee
- ❏ Participate
- ❏ Perceive
- ❏ Perfect
- ❏ Perform
- ❏ Persuade
- ❏ Pilot
- ❏ Pinpoint
- ❏ Pioneer
- ❏ Plan
- ❏ Position
- ❏ Predict
- ❏ Prepare
- ❏ Prescribe
- ❏ Present
- ❏ Preside
- ❏ Process
- ❏ Procure
- ❏ Program
- ❏ Progress
- ❏ Project
- ❏ Project manage
- ❏ Promote
- ❏ Propose
- ❏ Prospect
- ❏ Provide
- ❏ Publicize
- ❏ Purchase
- ❏ Qualify
- ❏ Question
- ❏ Rate
- ❏ Realign
- ❏ Rebuild
- ❏ Recapture
- ❏ Receive
- ❏ Recognize
- ❏ Recommend
- ❏ Reconcile
- ❏ Record
- ❏ Recruit
- ❏ Redesign
- ❏ Reduce
- ❏ Reengineer
- ❏ Regain

- ❑ Regulate
- ❑ Rehabilitate
- ❑ Reinforce
- ❑ Rejuvenate
- ❑ Render
- ❑ Renegotiate
- ❑ Reorganize
- ❑ Report
- ❑ Reposition
- ❑ Represent
- ❑ Research
- ❑ Resolve
- ❑ Respond
- ❑ Restore
- ❑ Restructure
- ❑ Retrieve
- ❑ Review
- ❑ Revise
- ❑ Revitalize
- ❑ Satisfy
- ❑ Schedule
- ❑ Secure
- ❑ Select
- ❑ Separate
- ❑ Serve
- ❑ Simplify
- ❑ Sold
- ❑ Solidify
- ❑ Solve
- ❑ Speak
- ❑ Specify
- ❑ Standardize
- ❑ Stimulate
- ❑ Streamline
- ❑ Structure
- ❑ Succeed
- ❑ Suggest
- ❑ Summarize
- ❑ Supervise
- ❑ Supply
- ❑ Support
- ❑ Surpass
- ❑ Synthesize
- ❑ Systematize
- ❑ Tabulate
- ❑ Target
- ❑ Teach
- ❑ Terminate
- ❑ Test
- ❑ Thwart
- ❑ Train
- ❑ Transcribe
- ❑ Transfer
- ❑ Transform
- ❑ Transition
- ❑ Translate
- ❑ Troubleshoot
- ❑ Unify
- ❑ Unite
- ❑ Update
- ❑ Upgrade
- ❑ Use
- ❑ Utilize
- ❑ Verbalize
- ❑ Verify
- ❑ Win
- ❑ Write

High-Impact Phrases

(NOTE: Some of these phrases are not appropriate for the traditional college graduate with limited work experience. However, there are more experienced graduates reading this book as well; therefore, all the high-impact phrases have been included.)

- ❑ Accelerated Career Track
- ❑ Accelerating Revenue Growth
- ❑ Aggressive Turnaround Leadership
- ❑ Benchmarking
- ❑ Best In Class
- ❑ Business Process Redesign
- ❑ Business Process Reengineering
- ❑ Capturing Cost Reductions
- ❑ Catalyst for Change
- ❑ Change Agent
- ❑ Change Management
- ❑ Competitive Market Positioning
- ❑ Competitive Wins
- ❑ Competitively Positioning Products and Technologies
- ❑ Contemporary Management Style
- ❑ Core Competencies
- ❑ Creative Business Leader
- ❑ Creative Problem-Solver
- ❑ Cross-Culturally Sensitive
- ❑ Cross-Functional Expertise
- ❑ Cross-Functional Team Leadership
- ❑ Decisive Management Style
- ❑ Delivering Strong and Sustainable Gains
- ❑ Direct and Decisive Organizational Leadership
- ❑ Distinguished Performance
- ❑ Driving Customer Loyalty Initiatives
- ❑ Driving Innovation
- ❑ Driving Performance Improvement
- ❑ Driving Productivity Gains
- ❑ Emerging Business Ventures
- ❑ Emerging International Markets
- ❑ Entrepreneurial Drive
- ❑ Entrepreneurial Leadership
- ❑ Entrepreneurial Vision
- ❑ Executive Leadership
- ❑ Executive Liaison
- ❑ Fast-Track Promotion

- ❏ Global Market Dominance
- ❏ High-Caliber
- ❏ High-Growth
- ❏ High-Impact
- ❏ High-Performance
- ❏ High-Quality
- ❏ Matrix Management
- ❏ Multi-Discipline Industry Expertise
- ❏ Organizational Driver
- ❏ Organizational Leader
- ❏ Outperforming Global Competition
- ❏ Outperforming Market Competition
- ❏ PC Proficient
- ❏ Peak Performer
- ❏ Performance Improvement
- ❏ Performance Management
- ❏ Performance Reengineering
- ❏ Pioneering Technologies
- ❏ Proactive Business Leader
- ❏ Proactive Manager
- ❏ Process Redesign
- ❏ Process Reengineering
- ❏ Productivity Improvement
- ❏ Self-Starter
- ❏ Start-Up, Turnaround, and High-Growth Organizations
- ❏ Strategic and Tactical Operations
- ❏ Strong and Sustainable Financial Gains
- ❏ Strong and Sustainable Performance Gains
- ❏ Strong and Sustainable Productivity Gains
- ❏ Strong and Sustainable Profit Gains
- ❏ Strong and Sustainable Quality Gains
- ❏ Strong and Sustainable Technology Gains
- ❏ Team Building
- ❏ Team Leadership
- ❏ Technologically Advanced Organization
- ❏ Technologically Sophisticated Operations
- ❏ Top Flight Leadership Competencies
- ❏ Top Tier Executive
- ❏ Visionary Leadership
- ❏ World Class Leadership
- ❏ World Class Operations
- ❏ World Class Organization

Personality Descriptors

- ❑ Abstract
- ❑ Accurate
- ❑ Action-Driven
- ❑ Adaptable
- ❑ Adventures
- ❑ Aggressive
- ❑ Amenable
- ❑ Analytical
- ❑ Artful
- ❑ Assertive
- ❑ Believable
- ❑ Bilingual
- ❑ Bold
- ❑ Brave
- ❑ Communicative
- ❑ Competent
- ❑ Competitive
- ❑ Conceptual
- ❑ Confident
- ❑ Conscientious
- ❑ Conservative
- ❑ Cooperative
- ❑ Courageous
- ❑ Creative
- ❑ Credible
- ❑ Cross-Cultural
- ❑ Culturally Sensitive
- ❑ Customer-Driven
- ❑ Dauntless
- ❑ Decisive
- ❑ Dedicated
- ❑ Dependable
- ❑ Determined
- ❑ Devoted
- ❑ Diligent
- ❑ Diplomatic
- ❑ Direct
- ❑ Dramatic
- ❑ Driven
- ❑ Dynamic
- ❑ Eager

- ❑ Earnest
- ❑ Effective
- ❑ Efficient
- ❑ Eloquent
- ❑ Employee-Driven
- ❑ Empowered
- ❑ Encouraging
- ❑ Energetic
- ❑ Energized
- ❑ Enterprising
- ❑ Enthusiastic
- ❑ Entrepreneurial
- ❑ Ethical
- ❑ Experienced
- ❑ Expert
- ❑ Expressive
- ❑ Forward-Thinking
- ❑ Global
- ❑ Hard-working
- ❑ Healthy
- ❑ Helpful
- ❑ Heroic
- ❑ High-Impact
- ❑ High-Potential
- ❑ Honest
- ❑ Honorable
- ❑ Humanistic
- ❑ Humanitarian
- ❑ Humorous
- ❑ Immediate
- ❑ Impactful
- ❑ Important
- ❑ Impressive
- ❑ Incomparable
- ❑ Independent
- ❑ Individualistic
- ❑ Industrious
- ❑ Ingenious
- ❑ Innovative
- ❑ Insightful
- ❑ Intelligent
- ❑ Intense

- ❏ Intuitive
- ❏ Judicious
- ❏ Keen
- ❏ Leader
- ❏ Loyal
- ❏ Managerial
- ❏ Market-Driven
- ❏ Masterful
- ❏ Mature
- ❏ Mechanical
- ❏ Methodical
- ❏ Modern
- ❏ Moral
- ❏ Motivated
- ❏ Motivational
- ❏ Multilingual
- ❏ Notable
- ❏ Noteworthy
- ❏ Objective
- ❏ Observant
- ❏ Opportunistic
- ❏ Oratorical
- ❏ Orderly
- ❏ Organized
- ❏ Outstanding
- ❏ Participative
- ❏ Participatory
- ❏ Peerless
- ❏ Perfectionist
- ❏ Performance-Driven
- ❏ Persevering
- ❏ Persistent
- ❏ Personable
- ❏ Persuasive
- ❏ Philosophical
- ❏ Photogenic
- ❏ Pioneering
- ❏ Poised
- ❏ Polished
- ❏ Popular
- ❏ Positive
- ❏ Practical
- ❏ Pragmatic
- ❏ Precise
- ❏ Preeminent

- ❏ Prepared
- ❏ Proactive
- ❏ Problem-Solver
- ❏ Productive
- ❏ Professional
- ❏ Proficient
- ❏ Progressive
- ❏ Prominent
- ❏ Prudent
- ❏ Punctual
- ❏ Quality-Driven
- ❏ Reactive
- ❏ Reliable
- ❏ Reputable
- ❏ Resilient
- ❏ Resourceful
- ❏ Results-Driven
- ❏ Results-Oriented
- ❏ Savvy
- ❏ Sensitive
- ❏ Sharp
- ❏ Skilled
- ❏ Skillful
- ❏ Sophisticated
- ❏ Spirited
- ❏ Strategic
- ❏ Strong
- ❏ Subjective
- ❏ Successful
- ❏ Tactful
- ❏ Talented
- ❏ Teacher
- ❏ Team Builder
- ❏ Team Leader
- ❏ Team Player
- ❏ Technical
- ❏ Tenacious
- ❏ Thorough
- ❏ Tolerant
- ❏ Top Performer
- ❏ Top Producer
- ❏ Traditional
- ❏ Trainer
- ❏ Trilingual
- ❏ Troubleshooter

❏ Trustworthy
❏ Truthful
❏ Understanding
❏ Unrelenting
❏ Upbeat
❏ Valiant
❏ Valuable
❏ Venturesome
❏ Veracious
❏ Verbal
❏ Victorious
❏ Vigorous
❏ Virtuous
❏ Visionary
❏ Vital
❏ Vivacious
❏ Well-Balanced
❏ Well-Versed
❏ Winning
❏ Wise
❏ Worldly
❏ Youthful
❏ Zealous
❏ Zestful

Career Resources

The following career resources are available directly from Impact Publications. Full descriptions of each title as well as nine downloadable catalogs, videos, and software can be found on our website: www.impactpublications.com. Complete the following form or list the titles, include shipping (see formula at the end), enclose payment, and send your order to:

IMPACT PUBLICATIONS
9104 Manassas Drive, Suite N
Manassas Park, VA 20111-5211 USA
1-800-361-1055 (orders only)
Tel. 703-361-7300 or Fax 703-335-9486
Email address: info@impactpublications.com
Quick & easy online ordering: www.impactpublications.com

Orders from individuals must be prepaid by check, money order, or major credit card. We accept telephone, fax, and email orders.

Qty.	TITLES	Price	TOTAL
	Books By Wendy S. Enelow		
____	101 Ways to Recession-Proof Your Career	14.95	_____
____	The $100,000+ Job Interview	19.95	_____
____	Best KeyWords for Resumes, Cover Letters, and Interviews	14.95	_____
____	Best Cover Letters for $100,000+ Jobs	24.95	_____
____	Best Resumes and CVs for International Jobs	24.95	_____
____	Best Resumes for $100,000+ Jobs	24.95	_____
____	Best Resumes for People Without a Four-Year Degree	19.95	_____
____	College Grad Resumes to Land $75,000+ Jobs	24.95	_____
____	Cover Letter Magic	16.95	_____
____	Expert Resumes for Computer and Web Jobs	16.95	_____
____	Expert Resumes for Managers and Executives	16.95	_____
____	Expert Resumes for Manufacturing Careers	16.95	_____
____	Expert Resumes for People Returning to Work	16.95	_____
____	Expert Resumes for Teachers and Educators	16.95	_____
____	Insider's Guide to Finding a Job	12.95	_____
____	KeyWords to Nail Your Job Interview	17.95	_____

Attitude and Motivation
____ 100 Ways to Motivate Yourself   18.99 _____
____ Change Your Attitude   15.99 _____
____ Reinventing Yourself   18.99 _____

Inspiration and Empowerment
____ The 8th Habit   26.00 _____
____ 101 Secrets of Highly Effective Speakers   15.95 _____
____ Do What You Love for the Rest of Your Life   24.95 _____
____ Dream It Do It   16.95 _____
____ How to Create Your Own Good Luck   24.95 _____
____ Life Strategies   13.95 _____
____ Power of Purpose   20.00 _____
____ Practical Dreamer's Handbook   13.95 _____
____ The Purpose-Driven Life   19.99 _____
____ Self Matters   13.95 _____
____ Seven Habits of Highly Effective People   15.00 _____
____ Who Moved My Cheese?   19.95 _____

Testing and Assessment
____ Career Tests   12.95 _____
____ Discover the Best Jobs for You   15.95 _____
____ Discover What You're Best At   14.00 _____
____ Do What You Are   18.95 _____
____ Finding Your Perfect Work   16.95 _____
____ I Could Do Anything If Only I Knew What It Was   13.95 _____
____ I Want to Do Something Else, But I'm Not Sure What It Is   15.95 _____
____ Now, Discover Your Strengths   27.00 _____
____ Pathfinder   14.00 _____
____ Quit Your Job and Grow Some Hair   15.95 _____
____ What Should I Do With My Life?   14.95 _____
____ What Type Am I?   14.95 _____
____ What's Your Type of Career?   17.95 _____

Career Exploration and Job Strategies
____ 5 Patterns of Extraordinary Careers   17.95 _____
____ 25 Jobs That Have It All   14.95 _____
____ 50 Cutting Edge Jobs   15.95 _____
____ 95 Mistakes Job Seekers Make and How to Avoid Them   13.95 _____
____ 100 Great Jobs and How to Get Them   17.95 _____
____ 101 Ways to Recession-Proof Your Career   14.95 _____
____ America's Top 100 Jobs for People Without a Four-Year Degree   19.95 _____
____ Best Jobs for the 21st Century   19.95 _____
____ Career Change   14.95 _____
____ Career Intelligence   15.95 _____
____ Change Your Job, Change Your Life (9th Edition)   21.95 _____
____ Cool Careers for Dummies   19.99 _____
____ Directory of Executive Recruiters   49.95 _____
____ Five Secrets to Finding a Job   12.95 _____
____ High-Tech Careers for Low-Tech People   14.95 _____

____	How to Get a Job and Keep It	16.95 _____
____	How to Succeed Without a Career Path	13.95 _____
____	Knock 'Em Dead	14.95 _____
____	Me, Myself, and I, Inc.	17.95 _____
____	Monster Careers	18.00 _____
____	Occupational Outlook Handbook	16.90 _____
____	O*NET Dictionary of Occupational Titles	39.95 _____
____	Rites of Passage at $100,000 to $1 Million+	29.95 _____
____	What Color Is Your Parachute?	17.95 _____
____	Working Identify	26.95 _____

Internet Job Search

____	100 Top Internet Job Sites	12.95 _____
____	America's Top Internet Job Sites	19.95 _____
____	Career Exploration On the Internet	24.95 _____
____	Cyberspace Job Search Kit	18.95 _____
____	Directory of Websites for International Jobs	19.95 _____
____	Guide to Internet Job Searching	14.95 _____
____	Haldane's Best Employment Websites for Professionals	15.95 _____
____	Job Search Online for Dummies (with CD-ROM)	24.99 _____

Resumes and Letters

____	101 Great Tips for a Dynamite Resume	13.95 _____
____	175 Best Cover Letters	14.95 _____
____	201 Dynamite Job Search Letters	19.95 _____
____	America's Top Resumes for America's Top Jobs	19.95 _____
____	Best KeyWords for Resumes, Cover Letters, & Interviews	17.95 _____
____	Best Resumes and CVs for International Jobs	24.95 _____
____	Best Resumes for $100,000+ Jobs	24.95 _____
____	Best Resumes for People Without a Four-Year Degree	19.95 _____
____	Best Cover Letters for $100,000+ Jobs	24.95 _____
____	Cover Letters for Dummies	16.99 _____
____	Cover Letters That Knock 'Em Dead	12.95 _____
____	Cyberspace Resume Kit	18.95 _____
____	e-Resumes	14.95 _____
____	Gallery of Best Cover Letters	18.95 _____
____	Gallery of Best Resumes	18.95 _____
____	Haldane's Best Cover Letters for Professionals	15.95 _____
____	Haldane's Best Resumes for Professionals	15.95 _____
____	High Impact Resumes and Letters	19.95 _____
____	Military Resumes and Cover Letters	21.95 _____
____	Nail the Cover Letter	17.95 _____
____	Nail the Resume	17.95 _____
____	Resume Shortcuts	14.95 _____
____	Resumes for Dummies	16.99 _____
____	Resumes for the Health Care Professional	14.95 _____
____	Resumes in Cyberspace	14.95 _____
____	Resumes That Knock 'Em Dead	12.95 _____
____	The Savvy Resume Writer	12.95 _____

Networking

____	Dynamite Telesearch	12.95	_____
____	A Foot in the Door	14.95	_____
____	Golden Rule of Schmoozing	12.95	_____
____	Great Connections	11.95	_____
____	How to Work a Room	14.00	_____
____	Masters of Networking	16.95	_____
____	Networking for Job Search and Career Success	16.95	_____
____	Power Networking	14.95	_____
____	The Savvy Networker	13.95	_____

Dress, Image, and Etiquette

____	Dressing Smart for Men	16.95	_____
____	Dressing Smart for the New Millennium	15.95	_____
____	Dressing Smart for Women	16.95	_____
____	Power Etiquette	14.95	_____
____	Professional Impressions	14.95	_____

Interviews

____	101 Dynamite Questions to Ask At Your Job Interview	13.95	_____
____	Haldane's Best Answers to Tough Interview Questions	15.95	_____
____	Interview for Success	15.95	_____
____	Job Interview Tips for People With Not-So-Hot Backgrounds	14.95	_____
____	Job Interviews for Dummies	16.99	_____
____	KeyWords to Nail Your Job Interview	17.95	_____
____	Nail the Job Interview!	13.95	_____
____	The Savvy Interviewer: The Nonverbal Advantage	12.95	_____

Salary Negotiations

____	Better Than Money	18.95	_____
____	Dynamite Salary Negotiations	15.95	_____
____	Get a Raise in 7 Days	14.95	_____
____	Haldane's Best Salary Tips for Professionals	15.95	_____

Military in Transition

____	Jobs and the Military Spouse	17.95	_____
____	Military Resumes and Cover Letters	21.95	_____

Ex-Offenders in Transition

____	9 to 5 Beats Ten to Life	15.00	_____
____	99 Days and a Get Up	9.95	_____
____	Ex-Offender's Job Hunting Guide	14.95	_____
____	Man, I Need a Job	7.95	_____
____	Putting the Bars Behind You (6 books)	57.95	_____

Government and Nonprofit Jobs

____	Complete Guide to Public Employment	19.95	_____
____	Federal Applications That Get Results	23.95	_____
____	FBI Careers	18.95	_____
____	Find a Federal Job Fast!	15.95	_____
____	Ten Steps to a Federal Job	39.95	_____

International and Travel Jobs

___	Back Door Guide to Short-Term Job Adventures	21.95 ___
___	Big Guide to Living and Working Overseas	49.95 ___
___	Inside Secrets to Finding a Career in Travel	14.95 ___
___	International Jobs	19.00 ___
___	International Job Finder	19.95 ___
___	Jobs for Travel Lovers	17.95 ___
___	Teaching English Abroad	15.95 ___
___	Work Your Way Around the World	17.95 ___

Changing Addictive and Not-So-Hot Behaviors

___	Angry Men	14.95 ___
___	Angry Women	14.95 ___
___	Denial Is Not a River in Egypt	11.95 ___
___	If Life Is a Game, These Are the Rules	15.00 ___
___	No One Is Unemployable	29.95 ___
___	No One Will Hire Me!	13.95 ___
___	Passages Through Recovery	14.00 ___
___	Sex, Drugs, Gambling and Chocolate	15.95 ___
___	Stop the Chaos	12.95 ___
___	The Truth About Addiction and Recovery	14.00 ___
___	Understanding the Twelve Steps	12.00 ___
___	You Can Heal Your Life	17.95 ___

VIDEOS

Video Series

___	50 Best Jobs for the 21st Century	545.00 ___
___	60- Minute Self-Renewal Video Series	1999.95 ___
___	Job Finding for People With Disabilities Video Series	199.95 ___
___	Job Search Skills Video Series	799.00 ___
___	Job Success Without a College Degree Series	560.00 ___
___	Managing Your Personal Finances Series	499.00 ___
___	One Stop Career Center Video Series	599.00 ___
___	Portfolio Resumes Series	150.00 ___
___	Quick Job Search Video Series	545.00 ___
___	Road to Re-Employment Video Series	219.95 ___
___	Welfare-to-Work Video Series	545.00 ___
___	Work Maturity Skills Video Series	799.00 ___

Individual Videos

Interview, Networking, and Salary Videos

___	Build a Network for Work and Life	99.00 ___
___	Common Mistakes People Make in Interviews	79.95 ___
___	Exceptional Interviewing Tips	79.00 ___
___	Extraordinary Answers to Interview Questions	79.95 ___
___	Extreme Interview	69.00 ___
___	Make a First Good Impression	129.00 ___

____ Mastering the Interview   98.00 _____
____ Seizing the Job Interview   79.00 _____
____ Quick Interview Video   129.00 _____
____ Quick Salary Negotiations Video   129.00 _____
____ Why Should I Hire You?   99.00 _____

Dress and Image Videos
____ Looking Sharp: Dressing for Success   99.00 _____
____ Looking Sharp: Grooming for Success   99.00 _____
____ Tips and Techniques to Improve Your Total Image   98.00 _____

Resumes, Applications, and Cover Letter Videos
____ The Complete Job Application   99.00 _____
____ Effective Resumes   79.95 _____
____ Ideal Resume   79.95 _____
____ Quick Cover Letter Video   29.00 _____
____ Quick Resume Video   129.00 _____
____ Resumes, Cover Letters, and Portfolios   98.00 _____
____ Ten Commandments of Resumes   79.95 _____
____ Your Resume   99.00 _____

Assessment and Goal Setting Videos
____ Career Path Interest Inventory   149.00 _____
____ Career S.E.L.F. Assessment   89.00 _____
____ Skills Identification   129.00 _____
____ You DO Have Experience   149.00 _____

Attitude, Motivation, and Empowerment Videos
____ Down But Not Out   129.00 _____
____ Gumby Attitude   69.00 _____
____ Know Yourself   109.95 _____
____ Positive Feet   129.00 _____
____ Take This Job and Love It   79.95 _____

Career Exploration Videos
____ Career Exploration and Planning   98.00 _____
____ Great Jobs Without a College Degree   98.00 _____

Job Search Strategies Videos
____ Tough Times Job Strategies   89.95 _____
____ Very Quick Job Search Video   129.00 _____

SOFTWARE
____ Interview Skills for the Future   199.00 _____
____ Job Browser Pro 1.4   359.00 _____
____ Job Search Skills for the 21st Century   199.00 _____
____ Multimedia Career Center   385.00 _____
____ Multimedia Career Pathway   199.00 _____

_____ Multimedia Occupational GOE Assessment Program   449.00 _____

_____ Multimedia Personal Development CD-ROM Series   450.00 _____

_____ OOH Career Center   349.95 _____

_____ School-to-Work Career Center   385.95 _____

SUBTOTAL _____

Virginia residents add 5% sales tax _____

POSTAGE/HANDLING ($5 for first
product and 8% of SUBTOTAL) _____

8% of SUBTOTAL – – – – – – – – – – – – – – – – – – [_____]

TOTAL ENCLOSED – – – – – – – – – – – – – [_____]

SHIP TO:

NAME _____

ADDRESS _____

_____

_____

PAYMENT METHOD:

❏ I enclose check/money order for $ _____ made payable to   IMPACT PUBLICATIONS.

❏ Please charge $ _____ to my credit card:

❏ Visa   ❏ MasterCard   ❏ American Express   ❏ Discover

Card # _____ Expiration date: _____/_____

Signature _____

Keep in Touch . . .
On the Web!

www.impactpublications.com
www.ishoparoundtheworld.com
www.travel-smarter.com
www.contentfortravel.com
www.winningthejob.com
www.veteransworld.com
www.contentforcareers.com